Body Piercing and Identity Construction

Body Piercing and Identity Construction: A Comparative Perspective—New York, New Orleans, Wrocław

Lisiunia A. Romanienko

palgrave
macmillan

First published in 2011 by
PALGRAVE MACMILLAN®
in the United States—a division of St. Martin's Press LLC,
175 Fifth Avenue, New York, NY 10010.

Where this book is distributed in the UK, Europe and the rest of the world,
this is by Palgrave Macmillan, a division of Macmillan Publishers Limited,
registered in England, company number 785998, of Houndmills,
Basingstoke, Hampshire RG21 6XS.

Palgrave Macmillan is the global academic imprint of the above companies
and has companies and representatives throughout the world.

Palgrave® and Macmillan® are registered trademarks in the United States,
the United Kingdom, Europe and other countries.

ISBN: 978–0–230–11032–8

Library of Congress Cataloging-in-Publication Data

A catalog record for this book is available from the Library of Congress.

Design by Newgen Imaging Systems (P) Ltd., Chennai, India.

First edition: February 2011

10 9 8 7 6 5 4 3 2 1

Printed in the United States of America.

To all the exiled, pierced or unpierced, that I've met in New York's Rikers Island Correctional Facility, the shooting galleries of the South Bronx, the flea markets of Amsterdam, the Fruits and Vegetables squat of Berlin, the underground of Bucharest, the spulinkas of Kiev, the Orthodox church basements of Minsk, the bombed-out buildings of Sarajevo, the goat-filled dumpsters of Suez, the back allies of Shanghai, and the French Quarter cesspools of New Orleans:

In appreciation for teaching me the resilience of the human spirit, I dedicate this book to you.

Contents

Images, Figures, and Tables

Images

Figures

Tables

Preface

For fifteen years, I found myself immersed among defiant trans-Atlantic communities who engage in body modification. By coincidence, chance, and circumstance, I have never had to exert myself to find these magical people. They were always simply there. Many situational antecedents enabled me to live among, and gather data from, these unique individuals. Initially, this phenomenon occurred with chance regularity due to economic hardships that I experienced living in New York, New Orleans, and Poland. Poverty served as a filtering mechanism that enabled us to reside side by side in the most undesirable but fashionable of neighborhoods struggling for survival.

Street credentials notwithstanding, my membership in a particular age cohort also facilitated longitudinal research of these unique individuals. Socialized during the disco era and acculturated on the expressed class struggles that elevated the entire genre of punk to its deserved historical status, we later grew up as isolated individuals wedged precariously among the more popular social phenomena of extreme conservatism, conspicuous consumption, and ruthless capitalism of the 1980s. Aside from the influence of competing social movements and my political preferences toward remaining outside of the dominant ideologies of the day, my personal tastes in music most certainly facilitated the collection of the data. Of lesser importance, but influential all the same, was my role as a woman. This gender status, particularly in the Deep South of the United States, enabled my subjects to view me as essentially harmless and reduced suspicion regarding my curiosity substantially. Also, as a vintage motorcycle enthusiast, I was ascribed a particular status that enabled me to see a view of the body-modification movement that I otherwise would not have caught a glimpse of without the benefit of two wheels. Though my relentless drive to acquire the truth did not necessarily result in any particular lack of objectivity, it may have indeed colored my perception to the extent that I have, at times, suddenly found myself in very compromising and hazardously illegal situations. I made certain judicious choices in the process of gathering data for this book, which would by some be interpreted as a violation of my ethical standards as a social scientist. In retrospect, I do not regret any decisions regarding my personal involvement with the individuals portrayed in the pages that follow. Many of these intimate affairs, intrigues, and interactions cannot even be chronicled in the public pages of such a scholarly investigation, but suffice to say that I did attempt, where feasible, to paint as vivid, truthful, and intimate a portrait as possible. Many of my expectations of what these saboteurs would have accomplished by now in terms of social, economic, and political change have proven delusional and brutally disappointing, but I have, nevertheless, learned much from them over the decades that I have spent enthralled in their stories, and trust our readers will too. I am especially grateful to my father Peter Romanienko (posthumously), the Kosciuszko Foundation, Alliance Française Elzbieta Wozniakowa Wrocław, John C. Leggett, Judy Aulette, Laila Valli, Jerzy Przystawa, and Danuta Zalewska for believing in me even when I did not believe in myself.

Lisiunia A. Romanienko
Wrocław, Poland 2010
Salutations to Ganesh

Nonverbal Communication

Every symbol is subject to the criteria of ideological evaluation. The domain of ideology coincides with the domain of symbol. They equate with one another. Wherever a symbol is present, ideology is present, too. Everything ideological possesses semiotic value.

Valentin Nikolaevich Voloshinov

Background

There is an increasingly popular phenomenon in modern, contemporary, Western societies known as body modification. Body modification includes permanent transformations of the flesh through the practices of tattooing, piercing, branding, cutting, stretching, and scarification. These practices have their historic origins in non-Western societies, but have recently been emulated by large numbers of individuals in the Western world. One of the most common forms of body modification found since civilization began is body piercing. In the practice of piercing, the flesh is impaled and the hole is adorned with a decorative object. The most common place of body piercing has historically been through the earlobe. Contemporary body piercing has, however, expanded this practice to include puncturing other parts of the ear, parts of the lips, the tongue, the brow, the nasal septum, the nostrils, the nipples, the belly button, and various parts of the genitals. The object of adornment impaled through the flesh has similarly been expanded to include metal rings, hoops, plugs, pins, staples, weights, and even nails. In order to interpret what, if anything, the individuals who engage in these practices are communicating in contemporary industrialized society, an analysis of body piercing within the theoretical framework of symbolic interaction can be a particularly fortuitous departure.

Construction of the Self

Symbolic interaction has contributed extensively to the concept of the *self* (Blumer, 1969). Dissatisfied with psychological constructs of theories involving personality, symbolic interactionists argue that the self is a much more consciously constructed identity than psychologists believe. The self is intentionally constructed by the individual through a variety of mechanisms for a variety of purposes. Our language, our statements, our dress, our mannerisms, our impressions are all seen as highly manipulated in order for us to display the proper expression of the self that we desire to be and become, that we desire the world to believe we already are. Our daily interactions are developed as a perpetual performance so that the world will take seriously our intentional construction of the self. To that end, we express our intended self through verbal and nonverbal expressions that support our constructions, through meanings that are consistent with the genuine image toward which we aspire. We strive for accurate interpretations, and avoid misrepresentations at all cost. There are agreed-upon meanings, rules, and boundaries within which we perform in an unusual spectacle of identity construction that is understood by all participants. Those who accurately interpret our images of self engage in a process of duplicity and collusion that reinforces our concepts of self, clarifies meanings, solidifies commonalities, facilitates impression management, motivates accurate communication, and strengthens the forum by which we are able to continue to attend to the construction of the self (Goffman, 1959).

Use of Symbols

These complex, integrated, intentional self-construction processes lead to the comprehensive fulfillment of our identities. The conceptualization, actualization, and completion of the self is developed further through the use of symbols (Hewitt, 1976, 1989). Symbols are used to expedite the process of self-actualization, and are crucial in the exchange of meaning in self-construction. They are the signifiers and images that are used to connect the individual with the social world. The meanings of symbols are shared among others in a system of common belief, understanding, and mutually reinforcing reciprocal communication. Our symbolic capacity helps us to communicate verbally and nonverbally, and enables us to strive toward the full development of our identity. Without symbols, the construction of the self would be difficult and problematic, if not entirely unlikely.

Symbolic construction of the self begins at birth with our name, and continues throughout our lives. The name we are assigned at our birth is a signifier of culture, ethnic background, and gender, considered by many to be the first symbol distinguishing our being, the identifying label of language that sets us apart from others, separates us as unique individuals, and begins the process of defining who we are. In our earlier stages of development, the world influences our self-construction substantially. Gradually we gain more control in the defining of the self that we present to the world. The self is not something we discover, but rather is a conscious, malleable, authentic creation (Mead, 1934).

The development of the self becomes more complex as the self becomes more refined. Symbols used in support of that development similarly become more complex and take on a variety of specialized functions. Symbols can express meaning regarding our identities through our appearance, our gestures, our actions, our expressions, our language, and our associates. There are many symbols that are available for use to support our self-constructions that convey meaning within a common framework of shared understanding. These meaningful symbols are viewed as an important function of the constructed self. According to symbolic self-completion theory (Wicklund and Gollwitzer, 1982), the individual strives to present to the world the most comprehensive, highly developed, and credible self possible, in order to maximize the legitimacy and authenticity of the constructed self. Individuals strive emphatically toward their identity goals, which often requires the use of symbols to most comprehensively construct the intended self one aspires to present. We employ numerous profound, intense, effective communicative symbols to express the intended constructed self. In addition to legitimating the authentic self, symbols have also been observed to have a variety of other functions. For example, symbols are useful in communicating meaning (Mead, 1934), facilitating the identification of like-minded others (Shibutani, 1994), promoting in-group communication (Berger and Luckman, 1967), reinforcing group norms (Hewitt, 1989), and alienating those outside of group networks (Hechter, 1987).

The Public and Private Self

Clearly, the self is not a simple construct. Many theorists have argued, in fact, that there are many *selves* that we develop, which emerge given the appropriate situational cues. Each self can further be expected to develop specialized action involving role-making and role-taking depending on the needs of a particular situation. One of the ways in which the diverse variety of selves can be distinguished is through the development of the model of *public and private self*. The public self is the self manifested in the presence of others, formed when other people attribute traits and qualities to that individual (Baumeister, 1986). The private self, on the other hand, is the way we intimately self-disclose to limited groups of close others (Tedeschi, 1985). Through the dichotomization of public–private self, symbolic self-completion theory, and other paradigms found within the symbolic interaction perspective, we might effectively launch our body-modification inquiry within a uniquely suited theoretical framework for analysis, in order to identify shared meanings of the complex symbols involved in body piercing. Body modification through piercing is characteristic, therefore, of that which defines the private self, and that which defines the public self. The development of the self is a fundamental process in symbolic interaction that enables the individual to define, identify, and evolve his or her own identity (Callero, 1985). The process of identity construction occurs both through the private, reflective, intimate display of piercings, and through the public, expressive, defiant display of piercings. Distinguishing these two types of divergent identity construction patterns in greater detail will be useful in examining their relevance to the contemporary body-piercing phenomenon.

Private Symbols

In the private realm of body-piercing, modification practices tend to take on a highly utilitarian form, with the symbol intended for more intimate interaction at a variety of levels. Here, clothing must be removed for effective communication to take place. Intimate placement of the piercing is positively correlated with the level of intimacy required to view the piercing. The nipples, for example, cannot be viewed widely by the public, but instead must presumably be observed in a forum of a more intimate nature in the context of the industrialized West. Similarly, piercings of the genitalia must presumably be viewed within the most intimate of interactions between individuals. The meaning derived behind the private symbol is typically one of subservience to the sexual gratification of another person, or empowerment and dominance based on the placement of the piercing to enhance the sexual gratification of the self. The primary message inherent in private body piercing is to indicate an authentic orientation of sexual pleasure sought through intimacy, in light of pain inflicted. In other words, the essential meaning of the nonverbal communication inherent in the private symbolism that body piercing expresses is the extent to which the individual has demonstrated a willingness to endure intentional and purposeful infliction of substantial levels of pain, in order to communicate commitment to the sexual pleasure of the self or others. The commitment of pleasure as communicated in the meaning of symbols of the modification of the private self serves to help the individual identify like-minded others, promote in-group communication, and alienate those outside of pleasure-seeking, sensual, alternative, libertine group networks.

These private self-symbolizers have historically been composed of individuals with involvement in alternative sexualities such as prostitutes, sadomasochists, gay-lesbian-transgendered people, and swingers (Myers, 1992). But those ranks have expanded of late to include members of motorcycles gangs (Ferrell and Sanders, 1995), producers and consumers of music within the genre of hard-core, thrash, heavy metal, punk (Levine and Stumpf, 1983), and other artistic, communicative, avant-garde communities. These alternative subcultures have used private body piercing as an effective method of nonverbal communication to symbolically express sensual identity construction processes by formally instrumentalizing the salience of sexual pleasure of the self or others. Private body piercing has been so effective in advancing sexual identity construction processes that modification of the private intimate self has now become extremely popular among more conventional social groups, at all socioeconomic levels, and of all ages. Piercing and other forms of modification involving the private embodied self have, in fact, become so widespread that even conventional, heterosexual, monogamous couples adhering to the sexual conventions are now seeking piercing and other forms of modification in intimate places of the body such as the nipples and genitalia. In examining legislation regarding these practices, content analysis of subcultural literature, and data gathered through interviews conducted with pierced individuals for over a decade on two continents, contemporary strategic private self-symbolizers who seek body-piercing services on the most intimate places of the private body express, through efficient symbolic devices, a profound commitment to sensual, often narcissistic, coitus-facilitating identity construction processes.

Public Self-Symbolizers

The second category of piercing modification comes from the public self-symbolizing domain. Here, individuals engage in body piercing with the primary intent of communicating readily demonstrable public displays of defiance. Because the face is the primary gesticulative source of most verbal and nonverbal communication, the face is employed to exhibit these unique symbols, for the most effective display of intended symbolic communicative messages. The message content has different implications than private symbolic construction, however. Public symbolic identity construction through body piercing is motivated by rebellion and defiance, serving as a mechanism of cultural, social, economic, and political dissent that communicates rejection of conformity and conventionality, rejection of conventional rigors of beauty and fashion, rejection of the blind obedience now necessary to participate in the neoliberal labor market economy, and willingness to endure substantial levels of pain in order to genuinely express the salience of a strategic symbolic defiant self. Public piercings are extremely effective in symbolically communicating defiance of conventional power and authority, facilitating the identification of like-minded others, and perhaps most expeditiously, alienating conventional members of society benefiting from existing socioeconomic arrangements beyond these defiance networks. Conventionally submissive individuals outside authentically defiant body-modification enclaves who observe these symbols, particularly when adorned with objects such as nails or pins that are observable around the face, are so typically repulsed by the meanings communicated, that acute and instantaneous fear often permeates interactions among piercers and non-piercers. These interactions are effective in widening social distances between conventional elites and those exhibiting these public self-symbolizing defiant displays. Multiple public piercings in frightening but strategic locations on the brow, septum, nostrils, and lips contribute to alienation of conventional others and subvert existing power arrangements in society by expeditiously communicating nonverbal defiance through the symbolic mechanism of public piercing, even if only for a fleeting moment.

Socioeconomic Communication

One motivating characteristic associated with private as well as public symbolic self-construction is the desire to influence the quality, methods, and participants in one's own future life events. As the individual moves through the life cycle and discovers increased autonomy, independence, and self-determination in identity construction, the ability to expedite the identification of like-minded others as well as the filtration of those with differing ideological, political, occupational, and sexual worldviews is increasingly desired. With the autonomous construction of the self, there is also a shared sentiment to influence the outcome of future interactions. Because so many of the individuals who engage in piercing and other forms of modification are in developing phases of identity construction taking place throughout late adolescence and early adulthood, the sense of powerlessness over exogenous socioeconomic and political conditions and the desire to gain control over the direction and quality of future social interactions becomes highly influential in determining placement and type of piercing sought. These individuals are faced with greater uncertainty brought on by deteriorating cultural and economic conditions than any other demographic youth cohort in history. This uncertainty occurs as a result of tenuous family structures due to unprecedented rates of divorce, weakened support systems among friends and families (Elkind, 1994), reduced occupational opportunities due to the increased educational and technological demands placed on the working classes (Schement and Lievrouw, 1987), and unstable residential patterns (Heimer and Matsueda, 1994).

To further exacerbate the challenges facing individuals who engage in body piercing as a form of identity construction, evidence suggests that they have access to a broader array of psychotropic designer drugs (Knutagard, 1996), experience more physical and sexual abuse in and out of the home (Thrane, et al., 2006), attend failing educational school systems that increasingly produce students with dwindling scholastic abilities (Smith, 2003), and have earlier exposure to violence within intimate relationships as well as in peer groups (Steffensmeier et al., 2005). Increasingly, excessive servitude and obedience necessary for survival under normative conditions presented by savage capitalism characterized by deindustrialization and neoliberal market economics, coupled with a lack of consistent institutional and interpersonal coping mechanisms for support via family, friends, trade unions, or political parties, facilitate dissention and resistance among unconventional subcultural youth factions in an atmosphere of pervasive uncertainty and mass societal downward economic mobility. The sense of dissention advanced through symbolic public piercings and other body-modification practices momentarily subverts existing power relations while functioning to advance empowerment and self-determination through non-institutional, nonmaterial, interactive public cultural contexts.

Those who use body piercing for symbolic public identity construction are capable not only of advancing defiance and resistance, but also of alleviating many of the obstacles facing them by establishing their own set of utilitarian goals, developing specialized measures of alternative achievement, and engaging in complex cultural production in markets and arenas beyond the grasp of conventional normative social controls. These activities of cultural production drive an alternative economy that includes production, sales, marketing, and distribution of music, clothing, piercing accoutrements, alternative dance and other musical and theatrical performance venues, apprenticeships in skilled vocational trades such as tattooing or piercing, computer programming for alternative video games or culturally relevant internet sites, and other services catering to the needs of members of body-piercing alternative subcultural communities. These alternative status objectives, once reached, are extremely effective in enhancing self-esteem. Legitimacy is obtainable and status is determined by the level of salience exhibited in this alternative social and economic network. The more commitment one expresses through multiple public piercings, the more prestige one will acquire within the company of similarly symbolizing like-minded others. Because legitimacy through conventional avenues is perceived to be highly problematic under contemporary socioeconomic circumstances, the alternative avenue of legitimacy through public body modification enables the constructed self to exercise significant levels of autonomous identity control. Self-esteem is achieved through these strategic symbols, as the individual identifies nontraditional support networks, attains prestige through public piercing modification practices, alienates those who represent inaccessible opportunity structures, and thus strives toward identity self-completion with fewer perceived impediments.

These are just a few of the motivating factors behind public body piercings. The participation in self-symbolizing through public piercing is an innovative and functional mechanism for individuals to create and sustain an alternative economic, social, and cultural network, to ameliorate the extreme obstacles brought about through the complexities of exploitative neoliberal markets composing capitalist society, and to provide a way to reduce environmental uncertainty through swift and informal identification of other individuals participating in this powerful alternative subcultural network.

Intended Audiences

As crucial as symbols are to the process of identity construction, so too are audiences. Identity goals have legitimacy only when recognized by an intended audience, whose perception has substantial impact on the intensity of the effort made and the choice of symbols deployed. Audiences motivating an individual's use of symbols may be real, as in reference groups, or imaginary, as in perceived groups (Schlenker, 1985, 1986; Shibutani, 1994). Audiences can involve the self, close intimates, extended social networks, even acquaintances. As is the case with body piercing, the audience can be extended widely so as to include even the most remote strangers casting judgmental glances upon the unconventional body in public places. Regardless of the size of the audience defined, when identity goals are successfully achieved through effective use of symbols to the audiences for whom they are intended, self-esteem is enhanced, the legitimacy of performance is satisfied, and authentic identity construction is in full progress.

Private Piercing Audiences

In the private domain, people usually have a perceived, imaginary audience of the most intimate nature in mind when obtaining piercings that will enhance sexual gratification of the self or others. The primary function of private piercing is to expedite future sexual interactions. Through private modification, a commitment to future sexual pleasure is symbolically expressed. The precursory interaction composing contemporary courtship rituals often involves dialogue regarding commitment to the type of sexual gratification that is sought through the piercing obtained. The crucial element in these courtship rituals is modification disclosure, which can be described as the culminating moment when the revelation of body-modification membership takes place. In the process of disclosure, audience reaction is solicited to expedite the potential for imminent sexual contact, and likely to serve as an effective filtering mechanism in the pursuit of ideologically compatible, sensually libertine partners for potentially intimate relations.

For example, when the sexual gratification of the self motivates the type of modification obtained, the primary audience intended may be those with an orientation to encourage sensual narcissism. Here, tendencies toward exhibitionism sometimes emerge, and audience reaction to the commitment of self-gratification is solicited to reinforce the actualization of the narcissistic self. Used among feminist female heterosexuals, the reaction of the male to the commitment of the female to her own sexual gratification serves as a filtering mechanism to identify a potentially compatible sex partner who subscribes to egalitarian relationship ideologies. Even when the modification communicates the commitment to the sexual gratification of the self, self-gratification is rarely the exclusive impetus for private modification. Reaction from an imaginary, perceived, or real audience is consistently the underlying motivation driving exchanges of narcissistic sensual pleasures communicated through the acquisition of specialized genital piercings that expedite one's own sexual pleasure.

Similarly, when the sexual gratification of others is expressed in the type of modification obtained, there is a perceived, imaginary, reciprocal interaction that is anticipated with an imaginary, perceived, or real intended audience. Apparent among male homosexuals, the expressed commitment to the sexual gratification of others is communicated in private piercings, is recognized by like-minded others, and is rewarded through intimate contact. Through genital body piercing that exclusively fosters male stimulation, commitment to the reciprocal pleasure of anticipated imaginary others serves to reinforce interactions exclusively among other gay males, serves as a mechanism of cohesion within the gay community, facilitates the identification of audiences who reflect similar sexual reciprocating sentiments, and results in mutually gratifying anatomically focused sexual exchanges within a forum of shared beliefs and common world views surrounding male pleasure cultures.

Among libertines and other sensual audiences who are committed to sexual experimentation with power involving sexual dominance and submissiveness, the piercing of the tongue is another common expression of the commitment to the strategic sexual gratification of women by both heterosexual males and lesbians. On the other hand, the commitment to oral stimulation of men by heterosexual women and homosexual men can also be observed by strategically distinct piercings of the tongue. The private modification on the tongue is perhaps the most unique of all, in its ability to become quickly expressed in the most public of circumstances, even disclosing partner gender preferences. But beyond the tongue, there are other submissive-dominant power orientations explored through private piercings, which are emphasized in a variety of locations on the body, with a variety of intended audiences, requiring the implementation of a variety of restrictive rings, weights, and other devices, using a variety of metallic and/or decorative accoutrements for adornment and/or site-specific stimulation, for a variety of spectacularized sadomasochistic and/or alternatively dramatic interactive physiological explorations (Brame and Brame, 1996). For example, strategic piercing of the penis not only facilitates gender of potential future sex partners through either prostate gland or G-spot stimulation, but is also indicative of the position of stimulation desired (i.e., face-to-face or rear penetration) as well as dominant or submissive role preferences sought. Private piercings therefore represent a complex discursive mechanism of authentic sensual identity construction used to symbolically express power hierarchies and related roles anticipated in potential sexual opportunities that may arise as a result of private modification disclosure to relevant heterosexual, homosexual, or bisexual audiences.

In other circumstances, the intended audience may be not be imagined future sex partners, but rather those engaged in exclusive, long-term, monogamous relationships. Under these conditions, the individual who is willing to endure pain for the sexual gratification of the partner expresses commitment to the union through body modification as an alternative to the ritual of marriage. Here, sacrificial pain is a symbolic communicative alternative to the societally recognized, conventional institution of marriage. Due to legal restrictions on participants able to benefit from state-sanctioned marriage, committed homosexual couples often engage in piercing and other body-modification rituals in order to solidify their union through this less-regulated alternative ceremony. These private piercings symbolically express that the pierced partner is willing to endure significant levels of pain in oftentimes irreversible procedures on the genitals, in order to communicate commitment to the sexual gratification of the partner. Clearly, these expressions hold substantial significance to those within the union. These piercing customs between committed heterosexual and homosexual intimates are perceived as personalized, specialized, and accommodating the particular sexual practices of their private, personal, long-term union. As in traditional heterosexual institutions of marriage and other conventional social customs surrounding romance, the modern piercing ritual often expresses emotions of the participants and symbolizes the permanence of the union to the exclusion of others. To recapitulate, whether a monogamous heterosexual dyad, an open lesbian relationship, or an unattached highly active dominant gay male, audiences are of paramount importance in determining the type of private piercing, the placement of the private piercing, the meaning of the private piercing, and the object adorned in the private piercing. Perceived or real intimates inspiring the acquisition of private body piercing in the most intimate places has, therefore, profound significance for those engaging in body modification to advance the construction of private, libertine, unconventional, interactive sensual identities.

Audiences of Public Self-Symbolizers

Where public piercings are concerned, audiences take on even greater importance. Here the expressed political and ideological meanings inherent in the symbolic modifications are intended for a broad audience, primarily for the purpose of alienating those who are representative of conventional society and related authority. Instilling fear in audiences is a crucial element in the acquisition of multiple public facial piercings, which functions to empower the individual. This process occurs by meeting intended objectives in the creation of the defiant self, which enhances self-esteem, thus transforming perceptions of an unjust world into a new, more egalitarian forum. Often motivated by social, cultural, and economic obstacles experienced, the interaction in the public domain and the audience reaction of fear enables the actualization of the defiantly symbolic self to become empowered by challenging the status quo. By removing the institutional arena that solidifies existing power arrangements in society under conditions of neoliberal deindustrialization, and focusing on instilling fear in public through individual-level interactions at interpersonal levels; the meaning inherent in the symbols of the process of self-completion becomes realized, perceived hegemony is momentarily weakened, and authentically defiant identity construction processes are fully under way.

In addition to alienating conventional elites, another function motivating the acquisition of public piercings of defiance is the identification of like-minded others. The swift camaraderie apparent among those who display public piercings and the inherent support system that modification networks provide makes body-modification practices a highly rational, utilitarian method of symbolic communication for identifying in-group audiences under transient conditions of modernity. Dress, appearance, mannerisms, and obstacles experienced are shared among those in this unique publicly pierced community, whose members are easily identifiable through the proud, defiant facial displays exhibited through multiple public piercings adorning the face. Legitimacy is obtained within the group through endogenous audience evaluations, and prestige is sought and acquired through a variety of objective measures. These include the accumulation of piercings, the expressive placement of the piercings, the relevant decorative adornment exhibited, as well as the amount of pain willingly endured to display defiance messages. Status enhancement through public piercing and other forms of body modification is therefore not an unregulated spontaneous anarchistic devil-worshipping ritual as some on the religious right have ludicrously suggested, but rather represents a thoroughly formalized, highly regulated, excessively premeditated ritual involving standardized impalement practices based on complex biological and sexual utilitarian factors that attract and repel specified audiences to facilitate desired sexual and/or political interactions within a complex, entrenched alternative prestige structure.

2

Verbal Communication

Ain't no such thing as no fuckin' gutter punk. And there ain't no fucking gutters around here. Where do you see a gutter in New Orleans?

Scooby

Sometimes you've got to get out of the house that you're livin' in just cause there's so much shit going on. If your parents are raping you and like beating you up and shit, it's better on the street.

Dogboy (both quotes from the New Orleans documentary Gutterpunks)

Introduction

The previous chapter attempted to elucidate some of the changing, multifaceted dimensions of symbolic *nonverbal* communication used to advance defiant and/or sensual identities constructed by members of body-modification communities. The communication method used to advance identity construction processes are not, however, limited to nonverbal symbolism in the visual domain. Discursive mechanisms such as those surrounding *verbal* communication can also be helpful in understanding the social forces driving these authenticating modified bodily displays. The social scientific tool of discourse analysis can be particularly insightful in demystifying verbal exchanges and related meanings that permeate interactions among the more unique members of this innovative community living on the street. Given the expansive ideological nature of individuals seeking body-piercing services longitudinally, discourse can be particularly fortuitous in exemplifying the underlying motivations for piercing and other forms of modification sought by lowest-status members. As body piercing becomes more popular, and with it the neutralization of some of the original underlying meanings associated with its roots, it is important for our analysis to chronicle discourse among some of the more genuine members of modification enclaves living on the streets, known as *gutterpunks*. By focusing on these highly authentic individuals whose salient identities embody some of the more profound aspects of body piercing, the analysis will further demystify modification identity construction through this discursive component of inquiry. Before proceeding further, it may be useful to describe the relevance of verbal communication among individuals engaged in piercing and other forms of embodied defiance.

Significance of Discourse

Both reality and the identities that operate within it are believed to be socially constructed (Berger and Luckman, 1967). If audiences are fundamental for identity construction processes to take place, do these processes operate beyond symbols at individual levels? Prior research suggests that audiences validate identities through communal interaction, enabling self-construction to take place at the individual and group levels simultaneously. The mechanism that assures that both individual and group identity is constructed, reinforced, and even contested is verbal discourse using language.

> Language participates in a central way in the formation of our conception of reality. Language is centrally an area of interaction between people. [It] is an inseparable part of existence…function[ing] in all areas and levels of communal life. [L]anguage has an active role in the formation of meanings: it sets its own restrictions to meanings, determines human life through its own way of sorting out what can be said of reality.[1]

Verbal discourse is believed to be crucial in accepting, contesting, or rejecting identities that individuals or groups attempt to advance. As a normative process of negotiating identities, group discourse involving highly regulatory verbal communication has been demonstrated as focusing on status measures within groups (Watt, 2006), relationships with individuals outside groups (Yanay, 1996), and effective in perpetuating the desired traits and behaviors defining parameters of group membership (Leander, 2002; Li, 2006). The articulation of complex normative elements of social control advancing identity construction processes are further complicated by contextual setting, usually distinguished by institutional and noninstitutional identities (Drew and Heritage, 1992).

> [I]nteraction is institutional insofar as participants' institutional or professional identities are somehow made relevant to the work activities in which they are engaged. [T]here are special and particular constraints on what one or both participants will treat as allowable. [When] institutional and professional identities are made relevant in interaction, then this is a member accomplishment.[2]

In institutional and noninstitutional settings, verbal discourse is considered to be a powerful tool used in the process of formulating individual and group identities that often vary given the needs of a particular context. This is especially true in constructing ideological identities that form oppositional resistance communities.

> [L]anguage is also a terrain of resistance. In addition to external signs—gesticulation, ways of dressing, behavior, and so on—resistance is often manifested in the breaking of linguistic norms.[3]

Language can therefore be considered an active medium that provides opportunities for the transmission of conventional ideological and cultural ideas, as well as language reflecting contestational opposition to those ideals (Lehtonen, 2000). The discursive medium known as *active language* can also provide tremendous insight into the perpetuation and resistance of status and other stratification nuances driven by ideological, socioeconomic, and cultural ideals and beliefs (Briggs and Bauman, 1992). The determinants of both in-group and out-group inequality and other forms of social control that emerge in the process of group dialogue can capture ascribed or achieved power related to such factors as gender, race, ethnicity, class, region of origin (Bourdieu, 1991), as well as the extent to which members can articulate relevant cultural capital to demonstrate status competencies (Besnier, 1989). Social stratification and related inequality is therefore a prime determinant of active linguistic mechanisms of communication, group status, shared histories, mechanisms of resistance, and clarification of authenticating capital needed to determine inclusion and rank (Bourdieu, 1984). Resistance groups often share discursive, intersecting, historical vignettes of oppression that are known as conflict narratives (Briggs, 1996). Conflict narratives are often expressed to identify, through active language, the common environmental conditions of degradation leading to the emergence of resistance identities.

> In the case of conflict narratives, narrators focus on conflictual events, the circumstances that purportedly gave rise to them, past attempts at mediation and the like, while linking them to the narrative process. [Conflict] narratives do not simply describe ready-made events; rather, they provide central means by which we create notions as to what took place, how the action unfolded, what prompted it, and the social effects of the events.[4]

Nowhere is the significance of historical biographical discourse as a determinant of resistance identities and related cultural capital more dramatically demonstrated than among the homeless gutterpunks of New Orleans. Gutterpunks are low-status, publicly pierced communities of defiant young people who poetically and metaphorically equate themselves with the least desirable element of the street that captures discarded refuse, the gutter.

> [These youth] are part of a growing underclass of the dispossessed, a secret society of despair hidden in plain sight. They have no homes and no future, as

they thumb rides and hop freight trains. They move because of the weather, the law or because they just feel like it. Many hide abusive pasts, just as many hide track marks. Though no one officially keeps track of the gutterpunk populace, estimates [are] in the low seven figures. New Orleans is just one stop in the circuit of street kids, gutterpunks, anarchists, train hoppers and hitchhikers that extend city by city across the United States. The streets of New Orleans are alive with punks. The city's storied past as a sopped drinker's haven and a teeming hive of anarchy have made it a prime destination for gutterpunks for decades.[5]

Gutterpunks, often possessing extremely high levels of *resistance capital* exemplified through dress, mannerisms, and familiarity with the musical genre known as punk, can be characterized as poor, homeless, defiant, communal, and highly geographically mobile. Due to their low status, transient nature, and highly restrictive network, this group of pierced individuals tends to be extremely elusive but, nevertheless, is critical to our understanding of piercing and other forms of body modification (Skelton and Valentine, 1997). Based on their deeply salient oppositional identities, gutterpunks circulating through New Orleans have remained the most consistently authentic substrata of the entire community of punk body modification in the United States. To achieve the highest status among gutterpunks of America, publicly body-modified members are expected to have, at some point in their development, a requisite street internship to accumulate participatory culinary, musical, festival, and interracial alternative cultural capital through immersion within the gutters of New Orleans. Given the persistence of these alternative arrangements in such cultural enclaves, it is surprising that social scientists have ignored the gutterpunk phenomonen for so long, and neglected to study any aspect of their unique subcultural identity construction processes underway. Even after my own decade of immersion among these homeless transient youth concentrated around the historic French Quarter of New Orleans, gutterpunks are, and will likely remain, one of the most mysterious, enigmatic, and geographically elusive of all the bohemian resistance communities staking their claim in squats and gutters around the world.[6] The gutterpunks of New Orleans are not only an enigmatic population not amenable to systemic study, they also engage in highly exclusionary customs and specialized rituals that have been evolving for decades.

> To develop our understanding of these [resistance communities], it is necessary to consider again the range of culturally available stereotypes about the categories of punks. As punks and punk rock emerged in the mid-70's, tabloid press coverage focused on and glorified the more extreme characteristics of their lifestyle and the music: rejection of societal convention, self-mutilation as personal decoration, violence, uncleanliness, [and] rebellion. The sometimes violent exploits of bands like the Sex Pistols and some of their followers ensured that the punk subculture was ideally suited to be the subject of a media-initiated moral panic.[7]

Originally of British ancestral origins, classic punk, as well as its modern downwardly mobile and abused American stepchild, gutterpunk, now reflects an evolving subculture indicative of a half century of powerful, entrenched, identity construction surrounding youth outrage over deteriorating class structures.

> Thus we have seen a proliferation of a number of urban subcultures of resistance, transgression, and inversion. Identities of resistance, as disdain of dominant culture, publicly repudiate the norms, values, and life styles of the larger society, often seek [to] set the person apart in terms of cultural tastes expressed in fashion, adornment, and self-presentation. [T]he decoration of the body that has itself become a template upon which aesthetic sensibilities are inscribed and through which selfhood is articulated. [A]n increasing part of [contemporary subculture] is devoted to the transgressive. Mardi Gras of New Orleans features various street displays of breasts, genitals and even an occasional sex act.[8]

New Orleans gutterpunk culture is one unique and highly authentic community of resistance that can advance our analysis of body-modification enclaves. Because gutterpunk culture is highly impenetrable and unpredictable due to its insular and transient nature, because the lifestyle is constantly under attack by local law enforcement agencies, and because one of the most stable squats on the parameters of the French Quarter suffered significant fire damage in the course of this study, it became increasingly problematic to conduct interviews with these individuals with any regularity.

> Increased destruction of marginal space led to enclosure which denied squatting punks a valuable resource for their subculture. As the quality and availability of marginal space deteriorated, punks increasingly had to fight for [its] use form[ing] gangs to protect themselves against other street subcultures. The subculture went through three generations according to local lore—the first, most outspokenly political, the second oriented the musical and symbolic aspects of the subculture and the third, dominated largely by lower class kids—more demonstrably violent. Nevertheless, the loss of 'prime' marginal space, in the form of squats, forced some changes in punk survival strategies, with a rise in panhandling, and a tendency [to engage in] survival sex—that is the exchange of sex for food, money, or shelter. To fully appreciate these activities as acts of resistance which contain within them a potential for societal transformation, we need to focus more upon their relationship to a wider social and spatial setting.[9]

After years of collecting fragmented data, systematic orderly discourse analysis was finally made possible due to the interviews captured in the documentary Gutterpunks.[10] The discourse analysis presented here is based on these informal interviews conducted on the streets of New Orleans, as well as more formal interviews recorded in controlled institutional and noninstitutional settings captured during filming.

Relevant Paradigmatic Approaches

In addition to the demystification of resistance identities formulating gutterpunk culture, the current analysis represents an attempt to contribute to the historical debate on the controversial relationship between identity and action. Discourse theorists have argued that the relationship between identity and action is causal (Hollway, 1989), that the relationship is mutually reinforcing (Shotter, 1993), or that the relationship does not exist at all (Wylie, 1979). Recent work has even suggested that the two are so intertwined as to render them virtually indistinguishable (Widdicombe and Wooffitt, 1995). In all these approaches, cognitive processes take precedence over other situational antecedents. The perspective advanced in the current treatment moves beyond social psychological explanations at the individual level, and argues instead that social structure is the prime influence in determining both action and identity construction among communicative individuals and their groups. The context of discourse and the different structures of interaction sequences that manifest as a result of social, cultural, and economic contexts have been greatly downplayed in both institutional and noninstitutional discourse analysis. The intention of the current treatment is to speak to this weakness of the contemporary state of knowledge surrounding discourse analysis. The relative lack of sociological interest in examining societal discourse has contributed, to some extent, to the prevalence of cognitive functions over structural determinants in popular discursive literature. The current discourse analysis surrounding French Quarter gutterpunks will not only demystify the unique content of discourse circulating throughout this elusive community, but will dismantle this paradigmatic vacuum by demonstrating the profound influence that social structure has in body-modification identity construction processes, particular at the group level. By exploring the inherent differences found in institutional identity construction processes (derived from drop-in center interviews) and noninstitutional identity construction processes (derived from street interviews), the analysis will provide compelling evidence that identity construction and related activities are highly authentic and do not fluctuate according to cognitive or contextual attributes.

Functions of Discourse

Discourse analysis, called the linguistic turn of the social sciences (Kuipers, 1989), has had a long history of distinguishing between talk in formal and informal settings. Though identity and related discursive action remains socially constructed, access to knowledge and its linguistic manipulations is thought to fluctuate based on differential settings. By exploring the elements of identity construction processes in both institutional and noninstitutional settings, our gutterpunk analysis will provide compelling evidence that identity construction using body piercing and other forms of modification is formulated in response to perceived conflict and environmental threats felt among group members. Individuals who perceive their environment as presenting impediments that hinder their own social, cultural, and economic development will often articulate tremendous hostility toward out-group members, and express this defiance through both nonverbal and verbal discursive mechanisms. The perception of profound environmental hostility manifests as a primary impetus for what gutterpunk members perceive to be defensive identity construction, particularly among transient members of the body-piercing community. Body piercing is therefore a mechanism of verbal communication used to advance protective identities to combat a political environment perceived as extremely threatening to the self. Nowhere is this phenomenon more apparent than in the French Quarter community of transient homeless gutterpunks, who routinely use piercing and other forms of body modification as expressions of defiance against adversarial forces developed through antagonistic identity construction.[11] Before examining the actual texts of discourse documented on the street and in institutional settings, it may be useful to describe the influence of social structure and its importance in discursive identity construction processes in greater detail.

Language and other forms of subversive communication have been widely established as a crucial factor in the construction of resistance identities (Howarth, Norval, and Stravrakakis, 2000). Membership in subordinate power groups produces feelings of alienation that lead to innovative reactionary responses commonly involving discrete communicative resistance (Jackman, 1996). These oppositional identities can be demonstrated through the overt breaking of linguistic norms in differing social contexts (Hall, 1975), the contestation of gender hegemony in music subcultures through provocative lyrics (Leblanc, 1999), the maintenance of distinct regional accents in certain areas of the United States (Dixon et al., 2002), the exclusionary urban street dialogue among people of color (Rampton, 1999), the development of language hybrids (Sangari, 1987), language extinction and other adaptations (Landweer, 2000), or through noninclusive technical discourse used among experts intended to alienate those outside specialist networks (Erickson and Rittenberg, 1987). These nonconforming, often iconoclastic linguistic tendencies formulate a site of social, economic, and political resistance, as well as form a communicative vehicle for in-group solidification and empowerment. Furthermore, the extent to which these unifying mechanisms are demonstrated is often determined by the audiences in attendance as well as the cultural context specified. Norm-breaking language is therefore used to alienate out-group members, while its exclusionary severity tends to be invoked relative to audience needs produced by a given setting. The extent to which norm-breaking language is invoked to advance resistance identities will be shown in the analysis to be associated with the levels of antagonism produced by audiences within a given environmental context. Like any other community, gutterpunks' norm-breaking language will be demonstrated to be an effective filtering mechanism designating group membership, a tool used to express unifying beliefs, and perhaps more importantly, a status measure to evaluate potential members' proficiency toward relevant cultural knowledge. As a social determinant of group inclusion, norm-breaking discourse will be shown to function as a powerful tool to designate membership parameters and advance confrontational communicative processes needed for identity construction simultaneously at the individual and group level.

The current treatment is not the first attempt to provide evidence of the primacy of social structure surrounding low-status discursive group identity construction processes. Discourse analysts have examined power inherent in dialogue surrounding doctor–patient interactions, (Schegloff, 1980), radio media (Hutchby, 1996), on debate strategies (Sacks, 1992), and in courtroom proceedings (Drew and Heritage, 1992). Conflict narratives advancing oppositional identity construction processes among adversarial groups are often solidified through asymmetrical discourse and related interaction, resulting in negotiated polemics that articulate the need to develop forms of unity to combat mutual victimization against a threatening exogenous other. In this way, verbal dialogue among low- and high-status groups known as *unequal power speech exchange systems* (Markee, 2000) use ethnic, racial, gender, religious, or class measures of identity to explore narratives of unity and narratives of opposition. Language serves as a crucial mechanism to enable members to identify commonalities among group members, as well as to express sentiments that alienate the traits, customs, and rituals defining adversarial others. Inequality in group identity construction process therefore involves complex narratives of unity and narratives of opposition that empower and unify individuals on the basis of identity while simultaneously repudiating and resisting others. By observing verbal communication among those with membership in low-status groups who perceive themselves to be antagonized by more powerful adversaries, discourse analysis highlighting experienced conflict can demonstrate how social structure rather then cognitive processes plays a key role in both individual and group identity construction processes. Our analysis will show that the perception of antagonistic relationships is particularly acute when groups are in competition over scarce resources, such as access to diminishing public spaces offered by the streets of New Orleans.

Relevant Variables

To extract the necessary discursive elements needed to advance such an analysis, a suitable sample of dialogue in institutional and noninstitutional settings was required (Denzin and Lincoln, 1998). Using discourse among groups of gutterpunks, texts were first categorized through the coding of transcripts in drop-in center interviews.[12] Utterances here would be expected to be orderly, structured by turn-taking, and otherwise highly controlled by relevant institutional constituents such as social workers, physicians, psychologists, disease prevention counselors, and other health professionals (McHoul and Rapley, 2001). The second type of extraction involved coding data from street-level interviews. These were expected to be less orderly, relatively unstructured, and not socially controlled. Coding of the discourse derived from these two distinct environments using N-Vivo software (Gibbs, 2002) required the identification of structures of interaction sequences, which were expected to differ depending on the environmental context within which the identity construction processes were taking place. By distinguishing between the context in which identity negotiation and related conversation is embedded (Li, 2006), the analysis is expected to show that identity construction processes differ based on context.

Because the current analysis asserts that social structure rather than cognition is the primary influence in identity construction among pierced gutterpunks, it may be useful to operationalize this argument by formalizing variable relationships. Within the structured sequences that present themselves in a given discursive context, institutional drop-in center interactions and noninstitutional street interactions should be approached comparatively to assert that contextual cues influence the extent to which antagonistic group identity construction manifests. The discursive features that derive from these distinct settings should illustrate how these contextual environments, as our independent variable, influence the ways in which a noninstitutional identity for the street, or institutional identity for the service center, are constructed.

> The most important point to be aware of here is that categories should emerge from the text, rather than being imposed upon it. [S]imilar instances of talk must be identified and grouped together. The first [analytical tool] is the search for systematic patterns in the data. The second is the search for functional effects and consequences. [Researchers have] identified variation as the single most important principle in guiding [discourse] analysis.[13]

Our dependent variable is thus found in the variations in discourse that formulate different identities that emerge given differing contexts. Systemic patterns in the text were identified, and dialogue was grouped according to the following thematic variations: (1) subjects' lack of status, (2) their profoundly transient nature, (3) their perception of oppositional forces in their lives, and (4) the importance of group membership in combatting the problems associated with low-status, transient lifestyles, and oppositional forces. These discourse patterns and sequences were prevalent throughout gutterpunk interviews in both institutional and noninstitutional contexts. Utterances were aggregated in terms of frequency and levels of intensity in both settings (Lepper, 2000). This approach enabled the exploration of contextual cues that influence distinct observable patterns of verbal communication indicating defensive identity construction processes to protect against antagonistic adversaries perceived in the environment. The evidence supported the view that situational antecedents found within the social structure (i.e., status, transient lifestyles, opposition, and group member-ship), as opposed to cognitive elements at the individual level, take prece-dence in formulating gutterpunk speech patterns. It is expected that the analysis will demonstrate that gutterpunks "do" their low-status opposi-tional identities differently on the street, than, say, in the sanctity of a social service program designed to attend to their emotional and physiological needs. Thus action and related language will be shown to be predicated or contingent on structural elements in their environment. Distinguishing the ways in which the dependent variables surrounding "gutterpunk" identity construction are influenced by independent variables inherent in institu-tional and noninstitutional settings, is the intended goal of the analysis. To recapitulate, gutterpunk identity and related linguistic action is expressed through interactive discourse surrounding status, transience, opposition, and membership. Furthermore, the analysis will demonstrate that the artic-ulation of these identity constructs fluctuates significantly by contextual setting.

To the extent that the analysis will provide a model that will opera-tionalize *what* is said, it is also crucial that it simultaneously elaborates *how* it is said. Discourse analysis provides many interesting processual tools to demonstrate, for example, power relations embodied in content and processes of group talk. There are three commonly used discursive devices that can be useful to explore the group relations under examina-tion. The first is *embedded repetition*, which defines structures of talk that recur around common themes. Because interactions can be characterized as extended discourse sequences reflecting longer, more extended stories (Schenkein, 1977), it may be useful to examine the frequency of embedded repetition in interviews, or story-telling that refers to historic biographi-cal vignettes derived from discourse that has already taken place. Thus it is necessary to extract how often repetitive discourse explicitly refers back to historical accounts. In prior research, utterance structures often attempt to extract just enough historical story-telling so as to bolster iden-tities. This linguistic tactic may be used by subjects to elaborate episodes of oppositional forces.

The second process structure to be used is known as *organization of repair*. This is a talk tool used among group members to "fix" what they perceive to be errors in speech among other (often lower-status) group members, particularly prevalent in the presence of out-group audiences (Markee, 2000). In the current treatment we are particularly interested in exploring the ways in which organization of repair in speech constructs or maintains power inequalities within or between groups and may be used to foster authoritarian identities.

Finally, the analysis will explore the *power of summary*. There is signifi-cant power available to those who have the privilege to define or reiterate sets of questioning or to paraphrase answers within groups. Asymmetrical power relationships and related identities are commonly reinforced through this tactic of summarizing conversation. Summarizing discourse can involve power-taking by high-status members through the privilege of defining, summarizing, paraphrasing, and highlighting. Summarizing can solidify existing status relations within groups through reinforcement of elite identity via summary articulation, or it can lead to disagreement and conflict in summary re-negotiation and related status (Drew and Heritage, 1992). Here we are interested in examining any contextual distinctions in witnessing the power of summary on the street and in the center. The negotiated features of talk that empower speakers are of particular interest. Do setting types (institutional or noninstitutional) present different levels of restrictive options that limit the latitude for paraphrasing, agenda setting, and summary? Does repair of speech benefit group identity? Does the relative transient nature of gutterpunk life influence the prevalence of repetitive vignettes? Using embedded repetition, repair, and summary, the current analysis will attempt to build a linguistic collection seeking discourse patterns of power reflected in gutterpunk interactions. By examining four dependent thematic variables composing identity construction among homeless gutterpunks (their complete lack of status, their profoundly transient nature, their perception of oppositional forces in their lives, and the importance of group membership to combat these problems) and by measuring these in light of authoritative linguistic structural features known as repetition, summary, and repair, the analysis will demystify how discourses of resistance among homeless pierced youth are used to advance identity construction, how discourse is used to establish status and power within the group, how status within gutterpunk communities is used to drive strategies in formalizing resistance group identities, and finally, the ways that differing contextual factors provide environmental cues influencing the extent to which antagonistic identity construction processes are needed in defense of threats embedded in the environment.

In the model illustrated in Figure 1, we hypothesize that as a result of situational antecedents such as intimate and other family violence, gutterpunks perceive their social structure as an extremely hostile one. Discourse occurring in a variety of contexts greatly influences the construction of responsive identities on the basis of status, transient lifestyles, oppositional forces, and importance of group membership. Hierarchical processes surrounding discourse repetition, summary, and repair is believed to further solidify group identity, leading to linguistic innovation in defensive tactics to combat adversarial forces. Adversarial elements of hostile social structures might be described in relationships to intimates, the family, and other systemic authoritarian regimes. The actions to combat adversarial relationships are hypothesized to include discussion surrounding the acquisition of defiant public piercings, alternative dress, other forms of unconventional adornment, and the accumulation of relevant racial, ethnic, musical, visual, culinary, and other aesthetic forms of cultural capital. These oppositional actions are expected to bolster adversarial identities, which in turn reinforce perceptions of conventional social structure as hostile to gutterpunk existence.

HOSTILE SOCIAL STRUCTURE
Family, intimates, other systematic authoritarian
regimes (local, national, and international)
reinforce perceptions

ACTION
Tactics to combat
adversarial forces

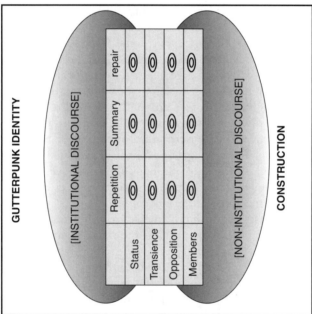

GUTTERPUNK IDENTITY

[INSTITUTIONAL DISCOURSE]

	Repetition	Summary	repair
Status	◎	◎	◎
Transience	◎	◎	◎
Opposition	◎	◎	◎
Members	◎	◎	◎

[NON-INSTITUTIONAL DISCOURSE]

CONSTRUCTION

Situational
Antecedents

HOSTILE SOCIAL STRUCTURE PERCEIVED

Figure 1 Oppositional Social Structural and Action in Relation to Gutterpunk; Identity Construction by Discourse Elements, Processes, and Contexts

Methodology and Results

Passages were extracted from two hours of dialogue provided through film transcripts. N-Vivo software was used to extract patterns of speech. Filtering revealed 181 relevant passages as consequential, and the remaining "small talk" texts surrounding banal, mundane interactions pertaining to topics such as the weather were eliminated. Of the chunks of words composing the 181 passages, common themes were aggregated and textual subjects were coded according to the following emerging categories: subjects' lack of status, their profoundly transient nature, their perception of oppositional forces in their lives, and the articulation of the importance of group membership to combat problems. Hours of dialogue with hundreds of French Quarter gutterpunks over the course of a year indicated that most of the discourse was spent discussing overwhelming oppositional forces in their lives, followed by importance of group membership and barriers to transient lifestyles. Frequencies and percentages by contextual setting are presented in the table.

The theme surrounding perceptions of oppositional forces in gutterpunk lives overwhelmed talk in both institutional and noninstitutional settings, and constituted 68 lengthy passages of dialogue or nearly 40 percent of recorded discourse. There were no significant distinctions between conversations that took place in institutional or noninstitutional settings, but gutterpunk talk on the subject of adversaries did tend to be slightly more intense in noninstitutional settings, where it disclosed more intimate details of the sources of opposition, and where more pejorative language was used to describe antagonistic elements of society. Much of the noninstitutional, street-level discourse revolved around family and intimate opposition, and often centered on sexual and other forms of violence personally

Table 1   Variation in Themes of Gutterpunk Discourse by Frequencies and Institutional Context

	Institutional Service Center Interviews	Non-institutional Street Interviews	Both Institutional and Non-institutional Settings
Perception of oppositional forces	57.35 (39)	42.65 (29)	37.57 (68)
Importance of group membership	33.33 (11)	66.67 (22)	18.23 (33)
Challenges to transient lifestyles	37.50 (12)	62.50 (20)	17.68 (32)
Lack of social status	47.83 (11)	52.17 (12)	12.71 (23)
Other	64.00 (16)	36.00 (09)	13.81 (25)
TOTALS	49.17 (89)	50.83 (92)	100.00 (181)

Data: 181 cases (frequencies in parentheses).
Source: Interview data collected in New Orleans, Louisiana, 2003

experienced. Both male and female gutterpunks articulated regular victimization of sexual and other forms of violence in the family and on the
street. Sexual violence talk was not limited to scripts involving personal
historical biographies, but was also disclosed as a tactic voluntarily used
as a survival mechanism. Many gutterpunks disclosed that they were routinely driven to engage in (sometimes sadomasochistic) sex in exchange for
food, hot showers, money, alcohol, or other drugs. Such disclosure was
especially prevalent in talk among male-only groups in noninstitutional
settings. Thus oppositional forces such as sexual and other forms of violence in historical and contemporary biographies constituted much of the
gutterpunk discourse on the theme of oppositional forces in their lives, and
this occurred in both institutional and noninstitutional settings.

The second most prevalent discourse revealed gutterpunks' preoccupation with the importance of group membership. The camaraderie that is
offered by group membership was the theme of nearly 20 percent of all dialogue. The importance of group membership was generally disclosed during street interviews, and was not articulated much at the drop-in center
serving their individual health needs. Of almost equal importance were the
perceived structural challenges to transient lifestyles (17.68 percent of all
institutional and noninstitutional dialogue). Of primary interest were local
authorities and their increasingly hostile policies that persistently resulted in
seasonal arrests of gutterpunks during street festivals such as Mardi Gras,
Jazzfest, the French Quarter Fest, and Southern Decadence. In the institutional setting examined, perceptions of transient lifestyle challenges tended
to be focused on violent victimization brought on by local, national, and
international government activities. The discourse occurring at the drop-in
center tended to revolve around authoritarian regimes that they perceived
to be in opposition to their existence. Here gutterpunks were more likely to
articulate barriers to their economic production through capitalist forces,
cynicism about the future of local and national government, and strategies
to combat harassment by local law enforcement. They did not consider these
challenges by law enforcement as rooted in their specific identity as punks,
but rather saw these attacks as part of a greater resistance effort against
individuality, creativity, and uniqueness that gutterpunks shared with other
non-gutterpunk transient groups found on the streets of New Orleans, such
as musicians, prostitutes, magicians, tarot card readers, fortune tellers, and
other street performers. This perception of entrenched, systemic, authoritarian opposition to gutterpunks and other alternative communities composing
local street culture was articulated by historical biographical vignettes surrounding confrontation with law enforcement. These vignettes were often
advanced through norm-breaking linguistic devices such as use of profanity,
pejoratives, and paradoxical humor.

The category of "other" discourse sometimes involved the fragmented
articulation of tangential resistance strategies. One resistance strategy
optimistically articulated by gutterpunks involved political organizing
to reverse the policies of the environment they were in, and many were

sporadically active in a local anti-poverty campaign. Another strategy articulated resignation and hopelessness, focused on possibilities for relocating to another environment more hospitable to their presence (awareness of the existence of such a tolerant community, however, did not exist). The resistance strategy most frequently articulated in the "other" category was momentary escapism as a solution to counteract oppositional forces in their lives. Discourse surrounding escapism tended to revolve around the three spheres: alcohol, drugs, and the desire to find and maintain short- or long-term intimate partnerships with the opposite sex. Males frequently boasted about how pervasive their recent activities surrounding sex, alcohol, and drug acquisitions were, whereas female gutterpunks seemed to adhere to traditional sanctioning of female deviance by downplaying their unconventional behavioral patterns. Females were more willing to discuss the limitations and futility of alcohol and other drug use as an escapist strategy to transcend the strong oppositional forces in their lives, whereas males maintained that these were highly satisfactory objective-fulfilling activities.

Despite the prevalence of private piercings symbolizing adherence to the sexual narcissistic self, female gutterpunks adhered to more or less traditional sexual power conventions. When pressed, they attributed their sexual activities to the seductive efforts and successful sexual prowess of attractive gutterpunk males, who they described as highly assertive in terms of articulating frequent and demonstrable sexual desire for the women they found attractive within gutterpunk communities. By articulating gutterpunk sensuality within an atmosphere of profound egalitarian respect, high levels of sexual satisfaction and in-group amorous sexual empowerment were reported among gutterpunk men and women. There were also no gender differences in ubiquitous articulation of exasperation and powerlessness over both national and local authoritarian law enforcement regimes, which they considered operating in opposition to gutterpunk existence. Interestingly, only male gutterpunks admitted to engaging in prostitution activities through cash transactions in order to survive on the street. Both male and female gutterpunks admitted to engaging in nonmonetary sexual transactions, receiving food, hot showers, or housing in exchange for (sometimes violent) sexual activities with tourists or local residents. Vacationing males visiting from places outside the New Orleans community tend to offer male and female gutterpunks cash for sex, whereas male and female residents with permanent homes in the New Orleans area offer nonmonetary resources such as food, alcohol, clean clothing, hot showers, and other gifts in exchange for sexual favors. Both male and female gutterpunks reported that they never had to directly solicit themselves through prostitution but rather, despite the defiant displays of multiple facial piercings, there appeared to be little social distance thwarting sexual interactions among unconventional hedonistic tourists and locals. Gutterpunks' alternative cultural capital symbolically displayed as sensual and political defiance appears to facilitate sexual interactions with certain unconventional people outside gutterpunk networks.

As far as the structures of dialogue are concerned, two of the three standard discourse analysis dialogic structures for status measures in speech among groups—power of summary and organization of repair—were not supported in the analysis. Recalling that power of summary refers to speech tactics by which high-status members assert power over lower members by defining, summarizing, or paraphrasing group interests, and that organization of repair refers to speech tactics of intervention to fix identity portrayals deemed erroneous by higher-ranking group members, neither structure was supported at all in the analysis. Though both summary and repair are discourse structures that have been observed in mixed-gender groups as tactics of control and degradation for high-status males to assert power over low-status females, or similarly in hierarchical bureaucratic organizations as tactics to assert managerial status over non-managers, neither summary nor repair were ever observed in dialogue among mixed gender or mixed status groups of gutterpunks. In previous research focusing on dialogue among more conventional members of society, summary and repair tactics usually involve interruptions, elaborations, paraphrasals, or other interventions of speech as a form of personal aggrandizement. In the current analysis, at no time did any member of the gutterpunk community under examination ever attempt to assert themselves in any authority over other group members, male or female. No summarizing or repairing of speech took place in any setting. Discourse among gutterpunks in both institutional and noninstitutional settings was therefore observed to be unusually egalitarian, and so the absence of structures reflecting repair or summary was a driving force to advance narratives of unity. Members exercise tremendous patience and restraint in allowing others to express themselves fully and without reservation, and no demonstrable attempts were made to "fix," "summarize," or otherwise alter members' speech at any time and in any given context. Embedded repetition, on the other hand, was a primary driving force to advance narratives of opposition. Talk was repeatedly structured around historical biographies invoked to find shared commonalities. Biographical stories involving abuse, neglect, and suffering were frequently embedded in discourse to articulate underlying motivations for protective and defensive identity construction.

Discussion

These findings provide evidence of extraordinary identity construction processes underway. Because dialogue advancing identity construction demonstrates negligible variability with regard to institutional and noninstitutional settings, the analysis suggests that unique discourse patterns among gutterpunks are observable. Although our analysis did originally hypothesize that gutterpunk identity construction processes, like other conventional identity construction processes, are primarily influenced by environmental conditions prevalent in the immediate social structure, findings suggest that discourse is distinguishable neither by street nor service center settings. Gutterpunks therefore appear to exhibit tremendous authenticity regardless of sociocultural contextual settings. Evidence suggesting that identity construction discourse remained unchanged regardless of location does not indicate that our initial hypothesis of the primacy of structural factors influencing discourse was erroneous. On the contrary, the lack of variability in patterns and themes found in both institutional and noninstitutional interviews suggests that gutterpunk perception of hostility in their environment is such a salient part of discourse surrounding their identity, that the articulation of defensive authenticity strategies and related community-building for survival is a perpetual element in their daily struggle for existence, regardless of setting.

> An authentic identity requires a strong identification with one's own interests and values. A person's interests and values…are constitutive of a person's identity, components of a 'true self'. To neglect these values is ultimately to endanger the integrity of this self and its connection with genuine processes of formation. Individuals who, in this way, are persuaded to abandon the essential link with their interests, the substantial identity, which is at the heart of the process of formation, weaken their access to the further processes in which authenticity interests can be 'discovered and formed'. [The] West…provides many examples of [those] who have 'sold out' for the sake of ambition.[14]

The lack of fluctuation surrounding identity construction processes exhibited by gutterpunks in both institutional and noninstitutional settings is not, incidentally, unprecedented. The tendency for identity and related discourse to remain unaffected or otherwise detached from a particular social or cultural context is known as *decontextualization* or the "…active social process of extracting discourse from setting,"[15] which is a discursive tactic frequently employed to contest authoritarian settings among members of resistance communities.

> Decontextualization describes the ideological, linguistic, and interactional processes by which a given piece of discourse comes to be gradually detached (decentered) from its immediate conversational and contextual surround, thus removed from the hazards of interruption, face-threatening negotiations, and challenges to its very existence. [This] corresponds broadly to that transcendent semiotic modality [intended to reduce] uncertainty and disorder. Accordingly, most of the ethnographic research to date…emphasizes a political view in which [decontextualization] is seen as working to confound and resist authoritative collective orders. [W]hat is proposed here is a holistic view of the relation between situated conversation and decontextualized discourse as an…interactionally accomplished process. This gradual objectification and decontextualization of discourse from its immediate situation of utterances exercises power.[16]

Thus, gutterpunk discourse surrounding defiant identity construction processes is rendered highly authentic due to decontextualization. The language of resistance that gutterpunks demonstrate in both institutional and non-institutional settings indicates that defiance in opposition to an antagonistic social structure is such a highly salient part of member identity that these construction processes, so pervasive as to infiltrate speech patterns, result in both norm-breaking language and highly egalitarian relationship-building among gutterpunk group membership regardless of setting.

Popular theoretical frameworks driving discourse analysis have asserted that cognitive processes are primarily responsible for linking identity and action. The current treatment has demonstrated that social structure, particularly that found in antagonistic situational antecedents, is the primary influence in determining active language and related identity construction among communities of individuals known as gutterpunks, who engage in body piercing. Like more conventional groups, language among gutterpunks is a crucial vehicle by which norms are broken, identities are expressed, and opportunities are provided for the transmission of cultural ideas. Prevalent also in other oppositional groups whose discourse reflects unequal power exchange systems advanced by conflict narratives, social structures perceived as highly antagonistic are extremely influential in constructing identities and action taken to defend against persistent environmental hostilities found in social structural actors and circumstances. Though variation based on institutional and noninstitutional settings was deemed to be negligible, it was demonstrated that gutterpunk discourse was largely dichotomized by narratives of unity and narratives of opposition regardless of setting. Narratives of unity invoke language used to advance shared endogenous identities constructed through the articulation of common biographies, experiences, and rituals. Narratives of opposition invoke language used to advance forms of exclusionary action needed to protect group interests in defense of attacks by higher status exogenous adversaries. Narratives of unity and narratives of opposition are both types of highly regulatory discourse that define group parameters and generate expectations regarding actions, practices, and perceptions of in-group members and out-group observers. Because narratives of unity and narratives of opposition did not fluctuate at all by institutional context, dialogue surrounding gutterpunks' identity construction processes indicated relationship-building based on trust and understanding resulting in a high degree of nonhierarchical anarchistic authenticity in interactions with all members of gutterpunk society. Authenticity regarding gutterpunk identity construction has therefore been shown to be decontextualized, wherein dialogue neglects any setting contingencies. Although prior research has demonstrated that decontextualization is common among groups engaged in political resistance against authoritarian others, no study to date has made the link from decontextualized talk to salience of anarchy and its importance in the discursive construction of punk authenticity. The current analysis has therefore provided preliminary evidence that gutterpunks' decontextualized talk not only reflects detachment from a social structure perceived to be perpetually hostile to their existence, but also serves to bolster supportive relationships through defiant community identity construction and related trust among highly authentic members of body-piercing communities regardless of context.

In addition to high levels of authenticity demonstrated in gutterpunk discourse under decontextualized conditions, the analysis also provided evidence of unique harmonious democratic group relations demonstrated in dialogue. Gutterpunks under examination expressed highly egalitarian mechanisms of discourse, rarely interrupting member speech and never repairing any of their discourse. This was especially evident in mixed-gender groups, where speech among conventional non-gutterpunk communities is often used as a mechanism to assert patriarchal privilege of men over women. Mixed-gender group talk among members of conventional society has often been found to be highly regulatory in order to diminish the frequency, status, and duration of discursive contributions made by women, even among the highest status women in institutional settings (Drew, 1990; Palmer, 2002). Gutterpunk communities, on the other hand, have systemically disavowed patriarchal privileges exemplified by conventional dialogic speech structures that diminish the strength, depth, or other amplitude of female contributions to discourse. The discourse prevalent among gutterpunk communities observed in the analysis indicates that males are highly unlikely to employ conventional speech mechanisms that assert male domination over women, or any other forms of authority among members. Gutterpunk females were given full opportunities to express themselves at all times, and thus freely engage in dialogue that was never publicly repaired or summarized by fellow male (or other female) group members. It is important to note that this interesting finding was not a mere anomalous convention attributable to etiquette patterns of grace found in the Deep South. On the contrary, the finding of egalitarian speech structures wase ubiquitous and not limited to exchanges between men and women. All gutterpunk males were also treated in the same highly egalitarian fashion by both males and females, thus demonstrating that language is universally used by migrating gutterpunks as an iconoclastic force to dismantle traditional status hierarchies in advancing the creation of an alternative egalitarian discursive community.

Because gutterpunks have experienced so much opposition in their personal and public lives, much of their group identity tends to adhere to anarchist ideologies that reject all forms of domination, and this philosophy tends to permeate discursive interactions among all group members, in all public cultural contexts, and in all institutional and noninstitutional settings. Both males and females, however, do engage in significant levels of story-telling and historical referencing known as the device of repetition. This may indicate a preoccupation toward the past, with no particular orientation or optimism for the future. More research surrounding gutterpunk discourse is needed to determine with greater specificity what these devices represent. The current analysis was nevertheless able to demonstrate that through discursive patterns, themes, contexts, and settings, gutterpunk discourse is ubiquitously oppositional to outsiders by employing norm-breaking language to advance powerful hegemony-resistant adversarial identities through narratives of opposition, while simultaneously connecting endogenous group members through utopian community-building articulated in unusually egalitarian narratives of unity.

3

Bohemian Network

Having passed in review the Bohemia of well nigh all sections of America, he loves it all; but if a choice had to be made in favour of any one corner of it, [Alson Skinner] Clark would be inclined to select the Bohemia of New Orleans as the most appealing. "It is so remote that it is distinct," he offers in explanation. "The Bohemia of practically all other cities is more or less the same, but in New Orleans there is a more resigned attitude, less striving and less energy…which in other places sometimes lifts Bohemia out of its' normal self."

Louis Bourg, 1911, in Grana and Grana

Introduction

The previous examination of group dynamics surrounding pierced individuals focused on verbal and nonverbal discursive factors distinguishing in-group members from those outside body-modification networks. From the viewpoint of piercing, conventional networks of society are composed of individuals typically thought to represent inaccessible economic, social, and cultural opportunity structures. In prior approaches, I suggest that one fundamental utilitarian purpose for public piercing is to serve as a defiant mechanism of symbolic communication intended to momentarily scare, provoke, or otherwise intimidate those elusive but privileged individuals benefiting from existing socioeconomic and political arrangements. To extend the analysis further, it might be useful to explore meaningful network-level features that these community practices have upon individuals aspiring for membership among these unique body-modification enclaves in New Orleans and other urban environments around the world.

Expediting Ties

Social network analysis involves the systematic study of relationships among entities organized within society, and is often described by examining emotional or other connections among individuals in a specific network of interest whose connectedness is referred to as *network ties*. These ties, often of an affective type, can be explored by examining relationships among network members with positive sentiments toward others within the group. Affective ties are often reciprocal, but not always necessarily so. Research has shown that, over time, the potential for positive sentiment increases with subsequent interaction, thus strengthening ties and in effect unity of the entire network (Fischer, 1982). Body modification is no exception. When examining networks whose members possess salient body-modification identities, discourses, and practices, evidence suggests that positive sentiments also exist among members, developing and strengthening over time. There is one feature however, that is unique to the peculiar network under examination. In various body-piercing networks closely observed for decades, new actors seeking membership have an unprecedented ability to use body piercing and other communicative symbols inherent in modification cultures as a functional strategy to *rapidly expedite* the construction of affective ties. In these innovative networks, there appears to be relatively swift acceleration of relations among piercers, often with no prior interaction whatsoever. Long-standing body-modification members appear rather willing to construct ties to new but appropriately adorned individuals seeking network attachments, and develop affective sentiments swiftly based on commitment cues displayed during preliminary introductions. This distinct feature of *accelerated camaraderie* repudiates prior social network analysis, which argues that network memberships typically require a long process of reciprocal exchanges of emotional and other resources flowing among new and old members through frequent and stable trust-building interactions over time. Yet the swift relationships constructed among members of body-piercing networks appear to fluctuate as an anomalous exception to conventional network society. If members of body-piercing networks are under constant variability and demonstrate a relative unrestrictiveness to new member, as observations in the current analysis indicate, what factors associated with these alternative social network arrangements might contribute to the accelerated camaraderie and other unprecedented forms of rapid connectivity that make genuinely affective relations under extraordinarily inhibiting transient conditions possible?

The data to be presented here suggest that rapid construction of ties and the development of affective relations among body piercers under transient conditions of modernity are expedited through one intervening factor. There is evidence that financial *transactions* flowing throughout the network at specific foci of activity facilitate affective tie construction and influence the development of positive sentiments. By examining transactional exchanges concentrated around particular body-modification action, the analysis intends to explore linkage creation through the acquisition of body piercing and related alternative subcultural services within a bounded network of body modifiers located in New Orleans. By examining the flow of revenue toward body-modification businesses owned by high-status members, the analysis intends to identify the resource exchange mechanisms that facilitate linkages in the direction of newly introduced actors within existing networks, in the absence of time investments and other ecological impediments inherent in transient lifestyles. To that end, integration of the foci of activity paradigm (Feld, 1981), differential association (Festinger, Schacter, and Back, 1950), and resource exchange theory (Grannovetter, 1973) can together identify network costs and benefits that are in operation influencing an individual to seek body-piercing services as a mechanism to accelerate camaraderie within these preferred networks. The acquisition of body piercing and other forms of modification will be shown to be a primary determinant enabling the new network actor to immerse him- or herself in these high-status reciprocal alternative networks, as well as to participate in crucial resource exchanges that take place within this supportive culture. The purpose of the current analysis, then, is to elucidate patterns of actor introduction to the network, extrapolate the financial and social control obligations that are understood and accepted by these new members, identify the activity patterns around which these financial flows come about, and despite significant ecological impediments, highlight a few of the macro-socioeconomic survival tactics supporting and reinforcing migratory defiant and/or sensual identity construction processes at the community level.

Relevant Features of Networks

Every social network, even those espousing anarchistic ideologies, has certain rules of engagement as well as sets of obligations and privileges associated with membership. No matter how unconventional, non-hierarchical, or egalitarian the community, network theorists have demonstrated that relationships among members may reflect profound normative mechanisms of social control that operate in subtle ways using formal and informal sanctions to dictate many complex aspects of group identity construction, such as preferred discourse (Greve and Salaff, 2005), appearance and style (Allahar, 2001), capital competencies and other forms of status and rank (White, 1992) in exchange for membership benefits. Studies of social networks have also found evidence of their utility in efficiently delivering various types of emotional and/or material resources that have been traditionally derived through linkages to family.

Networks can determine the extent to which individuals are free to deviate from group norms, a freedom that fluctuates exponentially based on ties to members. (Festinger, Schacter, and Back, 1950). The more ties one has to a given network, the higher the potential for other members to exert social control on the individual. The socialization process within networks is highly influential as a source of pressure for individuals to conform to network expectations, and is known as *differential association* theory (Sutherland, 1974). Research suggests that, given a desire to be accepted in a particular network of interest, members will enthusiastically adopt dominant traits and attributes desired by high-ranking network associates in exchange for access to network resources. Under conditions of differential association, there is a tendency to exert pressure toward new network members to produce conformity to group norms, especially true of concentrated dense networks. The higher the density, the more ties apparent within social networks. The more ties apparent within networks, the more opportunities for social contact among members. The more social contact among a given network's members, the more effective the pressures for members to conform toward desired behaviors. The more effective the pressures to produce specific behaviors, the more success that network exerts in influencing normative behaviors that homogenize and legitimate network identities. Having dense ties to members of a particular network enables individuals to obtain accurate and relevant information swiftly as a highly valued form of cultural capital. Density and the resources that accompany this privileged embedded position has been shown to be accumulated over time based on the number of ties an individual has within a given network (Granovetter, 1973), reciprocal sentiments and direction of ties (Coleman, 1961), as well as the individuals' centrality within a given network. Migratory transient body-piercing networks operating under extreme transient cnditions often pose challenges to these generally accepted conditions of network organizing, yet seem to thrive nevertheless. Do these conditions weaken or otherwise dilute modification networks? If not, what are the distinguishing features contributing to the strength of these alternative networks?

Networks and Social Control

A cursory examination into the gutterpunk network of New Orleans suggests an anomalous web of affective ties created under transient conditions that flies in the face of conventional canons of social network analysis. Here, pierced individuals, particularly those espousing anarchist and/or libertine ideologies, participate in a very dense alternative network structure that, though defying conventional societal networks, still produces conforming behavior to the alternative oppositional community. Data to be presented suggest that, though body-modification groups are unique, normative social controls are, nevertheless, in operation to influence those seeking membership to conform to the status-enhancing, self-aggrandizing practices and customs popular among their networks. This includes the acquisition of multiple piercings sought through preferential professionals, the accumulation of cultural capital surrounding specific genres of music such as punk and gothic, drug and alcohol consumption, and adherence to an alternative aesthetic and cultural worldview consistent with locally conceptualized interpretations of body-modification culture. New membership within body-piercing networks is not only contingent on displays of punk, gothic, and other alternative fashion and accoutrements, but is also determined by new member participation in group activities revolving around certain aesthetic, cultural, recreation, and sensual foci of activity that may be consistent with global trends albeit with local distinction and particularized for home audiences. Piercing network participation, no matter how unique its members are in a given urban environment, still entails some form of obligatory financial support. Acceptance within body-piercing networks is most often (but not exclusively) contingent upon members' support of commercial alternative business enterprises in the form of revenue redistribution. As one of the most important forces driving the relative openness within which new members are preliminarily welcomed, financing of commercial activity that legitimates alternative body-modification culture is required to access genuine benefits associated with membership. This financing takes the form of consumption and production of preferential body-piercing and tattooing services, relevant live local music, and alcohol and other sensual escapist activities within network-authorized alternative establishments owned or operated by high-ranking network members. As primary gatekeepers within body-piercing networks, these high-status, nontransient alternative cultural entrepreneurs with roots in local defiant communities tend to have significant financial and cultural capital at stake invested in local body-modification enterprises and hence, in the long-term perpetuation of embodied, politically contestational, alternative modification cultures in society at large.

In addition to financial redistribution of scarce resources, new members seeking admittance into high-status localized body-piercing networks are compelled to exhibit an alternative aesthetic, to articulate a general similarity of sentiments of marginality with regard to worldviews, and to exhibit network loyalty through aversion to simultaneous membership in other more conventional networks. This criteria naturally fluctuates from city to city. In New York, for example, competencies surrounding political worldviews and familiarity with related literature has more value among body-piercing network members, whereas in New Orleans competencies surrounding sensual and hedonistic escapist activities tend to be more fortuitous in expediting new member acceptance in local networks. Despite the prevalence of some universality of defiant identity construction throughout body-modification subcultures around the world, local networks such as that of New Orleans, in actuality, exert tremendous influence on new members to reflect and embrace distinctive particularized defiance identities in order to advance privileged standing for new recruits in a given community setting. According to Bennett (2000), "the process of localization...may rely on local affinities...at the level of the experiential and which, in turn, demands a more abstract form of analytical engagement with the situated properties of local environments."[1] Local network influence exerted on members is therefore the primary authenticating mechanism of legitimacy that simultaneously refines the defiant global and reinforces particularized rituals and customs defined at the alternative local level.

Critics might suggest that the process by which new members access crucial knowledge regarding local network preferences through immersion in alternative enterprises inadvertently commodifies body-piercing cultures, and this may indeed be true. Yet these high-ranking, what we might call *discursive body entrepreneurs*, are in the process of using their cultural, aesthetic, political, and financial capital in formalizing and institutionalizing this subculture through their integrative economic activities, indicating the entrenchment of defiant lifestyles in a given urban environment. This formalization and institutionalization is made possible only through network membership, in which new recruits are needed to participate in elaborate capital-accumulating transactions involving financial transfers in exchange for access to the information and accoutrements surrounding the subcultural capital necessary for member inclusion. These arrangements lead to the general stability and harmony of both enterprises and networks within a given local environment. Although highly complex and time-consuming for all involved, they are solidified through a variety of commercial and non-commercial beneficial rituals and customs reflecting shared beliefs and attitudes needed to drive this alternative network.

Given the significant expectations regarding dress, fashion, piercings, music, sexuality, and the articulation of certain worldviews, why would an individual adhere to these somewhat excessive obligations in light of the transient nature and defiant tendencies of pierced individuals considering immersion in a given body-piercing network? In addition to defining physical aesthetic attributes and adornment expectations consistent with body-modification cultures, there are enormous benefits in community-building that can be derived from such associations, even if network participation is fleeting or otherwise temporary. Ten years of observation of body-modification networks in New Orleans suggests that members genuinely need the emotional and material resources that are locally offered through authentic network immersion. An examination of the emotional and material resources being sought by new members can be particularly fortuitous in demystifying the factors that lead an individual to acquire multiple body piercings as well as make other financial or aesthetic investments in these unique alternative networks throughout the Western world. With these elaborate transaction costs and benefits in mind, let us now explore these functional aspects of social network membership in greater detail.

Information Dissemination

Many network theorists have explored benefits associated with social networks, and have found that efficient *dissemination of information* is among the most important benefits of network membership available. Having ties to particular networks enables individuals to access types of information they otherwise would not have. Obtaining accurate and relevant information within a swift period of time is a highly valued form of cultural capital and is facilitated by, and correlated with, the number of ties an individual has within a given network (Granovetter, 1973), reciprocal sentiments and direction of ties, as well as the individual's centrality within a given

network. In addition to information resources, personal networks also provide material, social, and emotional benefits. Access to emotional support
systems, mutual aid in terms of empathetic understanding, the articulation
of similar reinforcing worldviews, and shared understanding of economic
struggle under contemporary deindustrialized conditions together expedites ties within the network.

Structural Influences of Modernity

Network benefits are not, however, limited to affective sentiments associated with resources exchange. Urbanization and modernity can be seen as
having tremendous influence over the construction of network ties. Body-
piercing networks are highly influenced by the deleterious consequences of
modernity, where family structures are eroded or weakened and personal
network structures increasingly take on non-kin characteristics (Fischer,
1982). Those who seek memberships in piercing networks are often migrating young people who find themselves pushed to urban areas in order to
find environments of political resistance, sensuality, and other forms of
tolerance necessary to allow their highly symbolic identity expressions on
the body to accumulate with relatively few social sanctions. With increased
tolerance in the city comes heightened anonymity, which necessitates more
strategic efforts at finding similar-minded others. Under transient conditions associated with deindustrialization and related occupational displacement, piercing facilitates the construction of networks among those with
highly migratory lifestyles seeking acceptance in host communities with a
history of attracting young bohemians in exile with alternative lifestyles.
Increased alienation experienced as a result of eroded ties to community
of origin, decreased barriers to geographic mobility, and the decomposing
occupational opportunities overwhelmingly affecting young people have
together contributed to the emergence of this unique method of affiliation
to fluid embodied networks.

Foci of Activity

These networks may indeed be instrumental in providing new migratory
members with a variety of material and nonmaterial resources in their
new, albeit temporary host community. But once preliminary network
entrance has been established, what factors contribute to the ongoing
commitment to membership? Here it may be useful to approach the analysis not merely in terms of randomly developed connectivities to high-
ranking network members, but rather according to ties that are made
by people focusing on, or concentrated around, specific activity contexts
called *foci*, "defined as a social, psychological, legal, or physical entity
around which joint activities are organized" (Feld, 1981). Ties can revolve
around current foci, or can be maintained based on past foci of activity.
The analysis should not stop at the connecting network activity tie per se,

but continue on to more structural matters where network connections among members are viewed as embedded in a contextual environment and organized around particular sets of activities. This framing upon activity foci indicates how clustering comes about among members within *active social networks* and is highly applicable for the community under examination.

Like other more conventional action networks, body-piercing networks that proliferate in bohemian urban communities under decomposing labor market conditions are generated by members who are very active in alternative cultural interests. Because networks are considered to reflect the larger social structure, body-modification networks would similarly be expected to reflect the interests of members and related activities. Thus, like conventional networks, body-piercing networks should be expected to organize around particular foci of activity based on clustered member interests. Given the findings disseminated thus far surrounding verbal and nonverbal discourse and related identity construction, activities foci are expected to include escapist strategies such as the acquisition and consumption of alcohol and other drugs, body-modification and tattoo services, as well as the need to express affective sensual relations through the identification of potential sex partners. These findings, if evident in the analysis, would indicate that new members seeking acceptance in body-modification networks organize themselves around different body-modification activity foci that, though unconventional and defiantly oppositional, paradoxically perpetuate the commodified capitalist economic arrangements that some more politically oriented body modification members claim they oppose.

The working hypothesis then would suggest that, despite significant levels of normative social controls exerted, membership into local networks is sought and acquired through formal enterprises institutionalized by body-modifying entrepreneurs for the purpose of material and non-material resources exchanges that include dissemination of information and other resources facilitated through affective tie construction. The likelihood of new recruits succeeding in establishing themselves within a given alternative bohemian community body-modification network is largely determined by the flow of revenue willingly invested into alternative enterprises owned by higher-ranking network members. Financial commitment to the network facilitates rapid connectivity as well as the development of affective relationships in the absence of a longstanding history of reciprocal exchanges. A financial investment in one or more of these foci of activities determines the speed of tie construction, the concentrated density of ties within the modification network, and expedites development of affective relationships and related support among members of body-modification networks. This analysis is expected to demonstrate that investment by new members on particularized foci of activity clustered around recreational, sensual, and cultural activities formalizes existing economic institutions as it enhances the status of modification entrepreneurs driving it.

Methodology

To support these hypotheses, the empirical strategy of *decomposition* was employed. As one of the earliest advances of quantitative social network analysis designed to support theoretical contributions with greater confidence, James Davis developed decomposition techniques that enable researchers to understand entire network structures by gathering information regarding certain subsets of members. This strategy focuses on a particular subgroup or *bounded network*, enabling generalizations to be made about the larger social structure in which networks are embedded. Decomposition applied in the current study was performed on a bounded network of New Orleans body modifiers in order to demystify the rapid construction of ties, the swift development of affective relations, type of activity clusters within networks, and the way that these activities solidify economic arrangements driving internal hierarchies. The strategy exploring status and other determinants of rank is considered the *positional approach*, enabling a bounded sample to be drawn from a relatively large network with various status characteristics. Using this approach with a sufficiently diverse subset of body piercers, status differentials were examined to elicit relationship development between new and old members as well as the strength of these emerging affective ties. The desire here is to determine the length of time needed for new members to gain network admittance, the emotions exhibited to facilitate tie construction, the resources exchanged, and finally, to explore the kinds of activity clusters that are supported by new members through financial investments.

A bounded network of body modifiers was then identified and examined. Without any significant deviation, preliminary observations indicated that network activities of the New Orleans body-piercing community were clustered around foci of activity surrounding consumption of body-piercing and tattooing services, drinking and drugging, and cultural pursuits such as music. The clusters were triangulated through a self-disclosure survey, in which participants were compelled to identify and rank the activities they felt were most strongly associated with important aspects of their public group identity, through forced-choice activity inventory. This measure was expected to be problematic when extracting data from new members seeking admission to the community. Surprisingly, even those who had been in the area for as little as a month could report with some certainty that they had at least a *loose* association and *some* formal acceptance into their network cluster of choice. As participants were interviewed to gather more detailed data regarding their concentrated centralities within a particular activity cluster, it became increasingly clear that those exhibiting the necessary cultural capital with no history of network immersion were

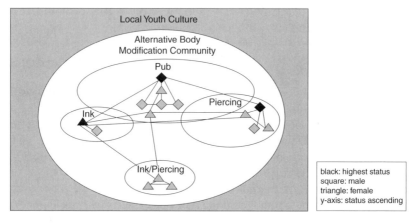

Figure 2   Body-Modified Social Network of New Orleans

capable of developing weak ties within their preferred activity clusters quite rapidly, whereas members with a longer history were capable of developing stronger and more affective ties among high-status members within their preferred network activity clusters. It is important to note that even among outsiders who were completely unknown to network members, affiliation within body-modification networks was granted with relative ease. Given the appropriate displays of body modification and articulated forms of cultural competencies, new members could gain access to these relatively open network clusters dedicated to three foci of activity, often simultaneously. To find empirical evidence of expedited tie construction paradigm facilitated through body modification among migrating young people traveling through New Orleans, I examined a series of complex interactions that occurred in the dense network surrounding a popular French Quarter pub where virtually all modification network associations [admittance and refusals] were determined. In addition, interactions among new entrants seeking network admission were also observable at the oldest body-piercing studio in the French Quarter, as well as on the street, where opportunities for articulation of music and other forms of cultural capital were provided.

Formal Linkages by Clusters

Although there were a few members, old and new, who reported simultaneous affiliations among all three clusters, nearly all members tended to report that the Pub was the primary or secondary network cluster with which individuals were associated. The deepest cleavage appeared to exist between tattooing and piercing, although a few members, primarily men, reported strong affiliations with both. Because so many network members reported a strong or weak association with the Pub, data were collected in this establishment in order to capture the greatest numbers of members in this community network of body modifiers. Although there are limitations to this approach based on obvious problems such as failure to capture those pierced individuals who do not consume alcohol or other drugs, who may be older, and who are employed during regular business hours, the data were nevertheless collected using this strategy, in order to demonstrate the typical clusters of activity most popular among both old and new members of one socially constructed, bounded, alternative body-modifying cultural network.

A sociogram was created [Figure 2] to display relationships found among associates involved in the body-modification community.[2] A sociogram is the visual aid configuratively representing social network relations within groups among different individuals. The plotted relationships presented in the sociogram along the x-axis show density within the network. The closer respondents fall toward 0, the more central their membership is within the network. Conversely, the more positive the respondent falls along the y-axis, the more status the individual has within the network. As evident in the sociogram and already elaborated on elsewhere in this chapter, the network can be seen as clustered primarily around three foci of activity. The most highly dense network, the Pub, had the greatest primacy of association reported.

Once respondents ranked the foci of activity, they were asked to report the strength of their association as measured by two factors: (1) number of months [0–24] having consistently interacted within the network, and (2) strength of affective ties based on empirically ranked quality of interactions [0–3]. The intensities of interactions were evaluated on a Likert Scale of 1 to 3 (with 3 rated as high degree of interaction) based on self-reported data indicating transactions involving benefits and obligations surrounding group membership. These included access to information or having simple interactions with network members for emotional support [1 point], requesting favors of, or doing favors for, members in the network [2 points], or unidirectional resources flowing from new to high-ranking entrepreneurial members by consuming body-modification services, alcohol in network-authorized establishments, or displays of sensual or musical cultural capital [3 points]. These empirically ranked interactions attempted to capture levels of obligation to the network, with the highest score ascribed to those who invested significant resources (such as time and money) in solidifying the ranking of high-status members via support of alternative bohemian enterprises or sex partnerships. The consumption of body-modification services and recreational drinking within network-authorized establishments expedited tie construction within local networks, and indicated the highest possible commitment to the network. In addition, new members lacking this level of commitment exemplified through financial investments were unable to force ties to the network cluster of their choice as rapidly as those making substantial financial contributions to local bohemian alternative economies. An attempt was made to quantify the intensity of these ties, and results are presented below.

Findings

Ten network members were careful observed and data was gathered using an activity inventory. Each member had an *affect index* calculated by multiplying the ranking of activity [column a] by benefits of association derived [column c]. This index was then compared with the length of association reported [column b] and analyzed by contrasting the observed affect [Table 3, column e] by the expected affect. The expected affect was

Table 2   Network Cluster Matrix

	a			b			c		
	Ranked Foci of Activity			Length of Association			Benefits of Association		
Subject	Pub	Tattoo	Piercing	Pub	Tattoo	Piercing	Pub	Tattoo	Piercing
A	2	1	3	24	24	24	3	3	3
B	3	0	0	8	0	0	3	0	0
C	0	2	3	0	18	24	0	0	1
D	3	0	2	24	0	24	3	1	2
E	3	0	0	4	0	0	1	0	0
F	2	3	0	16	16	0	3	3	0
G	3	2	0	6	6	0	1	1	0
H	2	3	0	14	9	0	1	1	0
I	1	2	3	3	3	3	1	1	1
J	1	3	2	2	2	2	2	3	1

Table 3   Expected and Observed Affect Indices

	a			d			$(a \times c) = e$		
	Ranked Foci of Activity			Recoded Length of Association			Observed Affect Index		
Subject	Pub	Tattoo	Piercing	Pub	Tattoo	Piercing	Pub	Tattoo	Piercing
A	2	1	3	1	1	1	6	3	9
B	3	0	0	3	0	0	9	0	0
C	0	2	3	0	1	1	0	0	3
D	3	0	2	1	0	1	9	0	4
E	3	0	0	3	0	0	3	0	0
F	2	3	0	1	1	0	6	9	0
G	3	2	0	3	3	0	3	2	0
H	2	3	0	2	2	0	2	3	0
I	1	2	3	3	3	3	1	2	3
J	1	3	2	3	3	3	2	9	2

calculated by collapsing the length of association reported into three categories (those who were members of modification networks for 1–8 months [3], 9–16 months [2], and 17–24 months [1]) and comparing results of the affect index mean for that group.

If a comparable affect index was found for those with a relatively short association within the network, this finding would indicate support for expedited affect as a result of the strategic symbolism inherent in body-modification networks. Affect index group means were then calculated for each category of network membership based on length of associations, and were contrasted.

By inputting the data into UCINET, and partitioning block means by columns, we can calculate the *group affect index mean* in each length of association category, and observe that those who had participated in networks for the longest period [17–24 months or >] had a mean group affect index of 5.4, those with a medium duration [9–16 months] had a mean of 3, and those with the least time invested in networks reported a mean of 3.6. This finding provides evidence of the strength of affective ties over time among those with the longest association in body-modification networks (which yielded the highest group affect index mean), but also gives evidence of the efficacy of body-modification networks to expedite affective sentiments even at the earlier stages of association. The initial effect may, however, decline over time as the individual begins to develop a relationship within the network (as shown among those who have been associated with their networks at the interim period of 9–16 months). This finding suggests that even in the earliest stages of body-modification network association, affective ties among body piercers are swiftly formed and solidified *despite* the absence of significant history or other pattern of obligatory exchanges, become slightly reduced later, and significantly solidify after a longer period of time. The apparent financial investment among new members who seek piercing and tattooing services pays off, and network members accept new entrants with relatively strong positive sentiments, as evident in the group affect means calculated.

To distinguish if patterns of expedited linkage construction are consistent across types of modification network associations sought, and to lend further support to the findings, observational analysis was conducted with another network subset to ascertain that expeditious tie construction among new entrants is not a unique feature of the particular bounded network culture captured in the current analysis.

Triangulation through Observational Analysis

The calculated affective tie indices, coupled with the relationship patterns graphed in the sociogram, enable us to distinguish several patterns based on length of association. To determine if the empirical findings are justified, the site was again visited and data were gathered from an expanded network subset to see if the character of interactions reflected in the data were reliable. It appeared that three fundamental interaction patterns were discernible, consistent with the data. The first type involved loose linkages among those who came to the Pub as newcomers and were required to display at least some form of body modification such as excessive thinness, tattooing, or piercing in order to be addressed by the bartender, who performed in the arena of "gatekeeping."[3] Typically, if some minimal form of modification or alternative aesthetic expression was not publicly apparent, and the entrant seeking network recognition was unknown to others of higher historical status, the bartender would simply not acknowledge the individual. Complete refusal to sell alcohol to a new patron not appropriately adorned was not an extraordinary event and occurred with some regularity, particularly during bustling hours or festivals. The conventional patron was simply ignored. Thus alcohol consumption in high-ranking, network-authorized venues was a highly restricted ritual, prohibited for convention elites not exhibiting the appropriate accoutrements of hedonism and/or defiance inherent in body piercing and other forms of modification. On the other hand, those who displayed some form of public modification tended to have more affective preliminary interactions and would often be approached by at least one high-status network associate in the course of network immersion attempts. New member contacts initiated by old high-status members were expedited through financial flows. Thus, once the new entrant seeking admission fulfilled general aesthetic criteria, affective immersion into the network (albeit at superficial levels) was offered in exchange for consumption of goods and services offered in these member-owned enterprises.

The second type of interaction involved those who had a longer history within the network, who displayed appropriate public body modifications, but who had few pathways to high-status members. These interactions appeared to be more arbitrary, with patterns varying widely depending on other exchange factors such as information pertaining to jobs, drugs, or potential sex partners. It appeared that these individuals with a shorter history were *in need of more benefits from the network than they were capable of giving*. As such, they needed to pledge to longer term network association through financial exchanges due to the obligation of the network to provide information, emotional support, and other resources. In this phase, the initial allure is over, and the transfer of network benefits commences once a pattern of obligatory financial exchanges has been established and remains consistent over time.

The third pattern of interaction involves those with a significant history of reciprocating exchanges, who have multiple pathways to several high-status members, who tend to have many symmetrical ties of substantial strength, and typically exhibit interactions of the highest affective sentiments possible. These members with dense network ties articulate the relevant cultural capital with ease, have an established track record of hedonistic and/or sensual libertine activities within the network, and produce or consume music within the relevant genres of punk, metal, or gothic. It is not surprising that these individuals with salient defiant identities tend to exhibit multiple public piercings and other more extreme forms of body modification such as scarification, stretching, branding, and cartilage implants. Typically geographically mobile with high status and appropriate degrees of alternative cultural capital, their faces and bodies exhibit a unique tapestry displaying their amazing life histories across a variety of international bohemian communities. Their ongoing immersion into local modification cultures is expedited through the acquisition of multiple public and private piercings and other forms of modification, regardless of relocation and local normatice social controls. In this way, constantly evolving network affiliation creates a symbolic aesthetic *body archive* chronicling the history of culture-accumulating alternative capital among high-ranking transient bohemian members.

It is interesting to note that over time, these three distinct patterns of interaction and related social controls were continually reassessed, with high-status members filtering potential new members via perpetual tests of loyalty throughout network activity in all recreational, cultural, and aesthetic clusters. Even the highest status members were required to reassert their status, by maintaining knowledge surrounding new music and articulating familiarity with other emerging forms of cultural capital surrounding piercing, such as suspension parties. These highest status network positions were perhaps the most challenging to maintain, particularly in light of the decline in deviance throughout the lifespan and the relative monogamy that eventually settles upon even the most radical anarchist-activists composing high-status body-modification networks. Once very advanced positions in dense networks were established, these individuals assisted with filtering of new recruits involving other rounds of cluster evaluations. Here individuals who did not, for example, portray any modification other than excessive thinness usually were not granted network membership, despite earlier successful but temporary attempts at inclusion. These evaluations often lead the individual to obtain the necessary modifications and adornments in order to be re-evaluated and more fully accepted by high-status individuals upon subsequent membership attempts. Hence, social control is constantly in effect, throughout the process of membership acquisition. It is only through continued financial investment in body-modification services, coupled with significant fiscal outlays for alcohol-food-music or other sensual hedonistic activities that new network members are able to enhance their low prestige within body-modification communities. Multiple piercing expedites this process, and new recuits seeking entrance will often acquire more and more body-modification services in order to obtain greater prestige and access to broader network benefits. This is especially true for migratory transients with no intention of investing significant time in local alternative bohemian networks, but who may require network benefits for a fleeting time nevertheless.

Gender Differences

Though these patterns of network membership were highly distinctive, there was evidence to suggest that gender distinctions were also apparent among body-modifying networks. In the case of males, many attempt to gain high-status ascription among more than one modification network cluster at a time (i.e., high-status males accepted among both piercing and tattooing clusters). This strategy appears to maximize affective ties through the strategy of developing dense clusters throughout the network. Achieving concurrent cluster membership enhances centrality in dense clusters, decreases social distances among members, and increases ties (and thus resources) toward the new member. The increased centrality among dense clusters substantially facilitates information flows providing access to emerging employment vacancies, potential sexual partners, drugs, music, and other necessary accouterments enhancing cultural capital among body-piercing network affiliates.

Women, on the other hand, who tend to adorn themselves with more discrete private piercings that are indicative of commitment to sensual libertine pleasures as opposed to substantial defiance, sometimes require legitimation by a sex partner who has intimate familiarity with impalements upon her nipples or genitals. This is a form of indiscreet network validation that can be easily circumvented if the woman obtains the private piercings directly from high-status entrepreneurial members who perform the piercings themselves at preferred network authorized enterprises. The financial investment by the woman in obtaining multiple piercing services without the testimony of male sex partner(s) is thus interpreted as an autonomous feminist act whereby high-status male and female members certify in the most professional of circumstances that she is entitled to network membership. Whatever strategy is chosen, network status for privately pierced women tends to be enhanced either through sexual contacts or professional partnerships.

Conclusion

Although this discussion may have extended far beyond the implications of the data collected, the technique used to determine network association based on reported strength of ties, affective sentiments, and intensities of resource exchanged can provide tremendous insight into the importance of network membership among individuals with body piercing. (Knoke and Kuklinski, 1982) This is particularly true in the bounded local body-modification network under examination, whose new members were successfully able to create linkages in the absence of time invested. Even in primary attempts at linkage construction, those displaying body modification tended to have expedited ties (albeit weaker affective sentiments) within clusters, which were solidified over time throughout the network.

Body modifications such as piercing, tattooing, and other forms of symbolic expression can therefore be considered functional strategies used by the alternative bohemian migrants to create linkages to existing urban body-modification networks under transient conditions exacerbated by deinstrialization. The flow of revenue from low-status recruits seeking admission to high-status enterprises facilitates the production of affective ties, provides support and legitimacy to the most authentic highest-status members in the network, signifies a commitment toward particularized group activities at the local level, and provides a foundation of intimacy necessary to strengthen these alternative modification communities. Members within modification networks therefore actively seek and acquire multiple body-modification services such as piercing, tattooing, and stretching with the specific intent of acceptance in social networks perceived as high status. Multiple modifications over time are not merely conformity to a new fashion aesthetic as some would suggest, but rather enable the body to become a symbolic archive indicative of multiple migratory bohemian network immersion episodes throughout the lifespan. Body piercing and other commodified exchange is an important impetus for constructing patterns of alternative supportive non-kin relations, as well as a strategy to enhance prestige in new local networks. Furthermore, without the migratory, transient lifestyles that modifying network actors embody, along with the economic necessity to provide financial support for high-status network members by new, low-status ones; it is unlikely that these malleable, evolving networks and related body-piercing practices would have ever enjoyed such widespread popularity in contemporary urban America.

Postscript

As a final caveat, post-Hurricane Katrina observations conducted by the author in New Orleans in 2006 and 2009 tragically supports these findings. Because the devastated community no longer benefits from the influx of large numbers of migrating anarchists and other transients, many of the body-piercing, tattooing, and pub enterprises that were previously clustered around particularized network foci of activity catering to the distinct material and nonmaterial needs of members have vanished. Thus, as indicated in the analysis, migrating transients had indeed been a crucial economic and cultural factor in the development and solidification of body-modification networks and related status among alternative bohemian residents and their businesses in New Orleans. Due to the absence of alternative cultural capital and the inability of migrating exiles with body piercing to return to the city with any regularity after Hurricane Katrina, bohemian culture has been temporarily extinguished in one of the most progressive cities in America. The failures of local, state, and national public- and private-sector organizations to mitigate hurricane damages through concerted governmental and philanthropic efforts has been highly efficacious in dislocating and fragmenting the politically-oppositional networks historically concentrated in and around the French Quarter. Many conspiracy-oriented commentators have suggested that this was the intentional consequence of the non-interventionalist policies of the state and non-state disaster agencies that failed to minimize the impact of the catastrophe. At this time it appears doubtful that bohemian Americans will ever be able to return to provide the levels of financial and cultural capital needed to drive this unique alternative network. Only time will tell if these bohemian networks will eventually reactivate their travels through New Orleans with any regularity.

4

Ideological Apparatus

The picture which emerges...is one of a constantly changing but ever-present elite group whose members are in declared opposition to many of the accepted and institutionalized values of their times. The artist speaks from an inner compulsion, hence his insistence upon freedom of speech and his refusal to undergo the discipline of party or doctrine. The poet cannot, without renouncing his essential function, come to rest in the bleak conventionalities of a political party.

Barbara Chartier, 1950, in Grana and Grana

Introduction

Althusser argued that ideology is eternal. Nowhere is this philosophy more supported than in the contemporary phenomenon of body piercing in the modern world. The timing of the popularity of body piercing is consequential, in that its widespread emergence coincides with the reduction of formal political organizing and the demise of any traditionally organized ideological apparatus. In this chapter, I argue that ideology is alive and well in the alienated generation of youth today, but that the dismantling of ideological apparatus has facilitated the fragmented expression of the radical left through an unprecedented mass movement of body politics through piercing and other forms of embodied dissent. Body piercing as mass social movement in both the private and public domains indicates an orientation toward radical political activism among contemporary youth unlike any ever dreamed of by Marx or Trotsky. The dismantling of traditional ideological apparatus has served as a facilitating impetus for the energetic resurgence of the left among body modifiers under conditions of neoliberal deindustrialization, through the occasional amalgamation of individuals possessing innovative mechanisms of political dissention on the body. Skin has now become the primary discursive vehicle that is used to convey socioeconomic struggles under transient conditions of migration within fragmented, isolated, mobile, oppositional resistance networks.

In this chapter, I will discuss the historical, cultural, and environmental antecedents that maintained the mainstream ideological apparatus, describe the structural elements that have facilitated the dismantling of conventional ideological apparatus under contemporary conditions of uncertainty, examine body modification as an ecological response to these ideological and political changes, and provide a brief synopsis of ideological projections of the political modification movement for the future.

Ideological Apparatus and Political Action

Research suggests that there are several necessary conditions for collective action to be formalized through social movement organizations. These include opportunity, organizational apparatus, and the collective processes that mediate the two (McAdam, McCarthy, and Zald, 1996). Political opportunity structures are described as situations in which individuals are embedded that facilitate or hinder the realization of political action plans. Organizational forms (or political apparatus) are described as informal and formal mobilizing entities that facilitate political action through the provision of institutional infrastructures that enable individuals to express political will. Framing processes are the necessary forces that connect the individual to the proper mobilizing institutional vehicle. Without these conditions, social mobilization is problematic at best, according to McAdam et al. While their classic framework has provided accurate historic accounts of conventional political mobilization efforts, it fails to capture the diversity and innovation of emerging strategies of embodied political expression that arises in the absence of these features for effective mobilization. Though their analysis thoroughly outlines the situational antecedents commonly found in institutionalized political mobilizing cross-culturally, they fail to incorporate alternative mechanisms of political expression and outrage communicated upon the body that is widely in use today.

> If the combination of political opportunities and mobilizing structures affords groups a certain structural potential for action, they remain, in the absence of other factors, insufficient to account for political action. Lacking either one or both of these perceptions, it is unlikely that people will mobilize even when afforded the opportunity to do so.[1]

I will argue vehemently to the contrary, that when conditions for conventional political action are lacking, alternative innovative mechanisms of noninstitutionalized political mobilization and expression have been developed and are expressed on the body. Though I agree that institutionalized ideological apparatus is an important vehicle by which political identity can be expressed, I suggest that it is not the only one. As political institutions and ideological apparatuses increasingly fail to produce intended political consequences, individuals become more independent and creative in developing their preferred individualized mechanisms of political resistance.

In the absence of an effective stable apparatus of mobilization capable of addressing the complex character of transnational social problems, ideology has become internalized and political will has become expressed (to some extent, with greater urgency) among politically active youth. These conditions have given rise to the *body politic*, where the expression of political outrage has abandoned the innocuous apparatus of the old left, in favor of personal political sentiments endogenously expressed upon the body for explicit, symbolic, provocative, continuous public display. Political analysis involving social movements of the future will have to incorporate body piercing and other forms of body modification as an alternative mechanism of political expression outside the ideological apparatus, which should be extended to include such alternative discursive strategies for collective expression and action. Before examining the political dialogue exemplified through body modification in greater detail, it is necessary to examine, with some specificity, the demise of the historically effective apparatus, which has led to the innovative phenomenon under examination. The dismantling of conventional structures of institutional mobilization will be demonstrated to have contributed significantly to the rise of alternative mechanisms of political expression such as body piercing used for the purpose of identification and amalgamation of like-minded others under transient conditions of modernity.

Ideological Labor Apparatus

Trotsky wrote extensively on the role of formal labor organizing to combat state authority and to facilitate redistribution of societal resources. He attributed both the successes and failures of the October Revolution to apparatus construction, escalation, and dealignment. According to Trotsky, success in political action was expected to be found in the ability of workers to mobilize labor through processes and mechanisms of unionization. Failures of the Russian Revolution were attributed to a weakened union apparatus, which became fractured through the withdrawal of fearful students, intelligensia, and labor leaders. In hindsight, the Proletkult (apparatus for the promotion of Proletariat Culture) would not endure, and despite tremendous effort, poverty, and loss of life during the Revolution, the workers' party would crumble and eventually give rise to the state-authorized nonlabor ideological apparatus of domination orchestrated by Lenin.

> Our task in Russia is complicated by the poverty of an entire cultural tradition and by material destruction brought on by the events of the last decade. After the conquest of power and after almost six years of struggle for its retention and consolidation, our proletariat is forced to turn all energies toward the creation of the most elementary conditions of material existence.[2]

Though the Russian Revolution represents one of the earliest and most successful anti-imperial political labor amalgamations in history, the proletariat was never able to realize its full potential. Many an ideological labor apparatus has come and gone since this time, providing little more then bureaucratic systems for processing of innocuous grievances filed by disgruntled workers against unionized low-level working-class managers. The inability of labor unions to address cruel working conditions brought on by the industrial revolution as well as their perpetual systemic disregard for the most vulnerable labor force participants, such as women, children, and people of color, have together contributed to the paralysis of labor, which has consistently failed to live up to socialist expectations as the idealized and glorified mechanism through which productive means of power distribution can and should take place. This blind faith in unions despite pervasive failure of labor to fulfill such excessive revolutionary demands has paralyzed oppositional redistributive political mobilization. Rather than acknowledge the limitations inherent in this bureaucratized apparatus and the demise of redistributive ideology in labor disputes, intellectuals until the very end of the twentieth century have idealistically adhered to hundred-year-old texts loosely attributed to Marx, and recoiled in astonishment at the absence of redistributive justice efforts through syndicalism. To further exacerbate the weaknesses of the ideological labor apparatus, third-world runaway shops leading to complete collapse of industrial production, union corruption and their subsequent dismantling, closed-door contract bargaining among labor and management elite, international subcontracting abroad, the labor exploiting potential of international trade agreements, monopolized transnational competition, and the continued exploitation of laborers of the developing world have together rendered organized labor essentially innocuous in its potential to serve as an ideological apparatus. Yet despite the demise of labor apparatus to combat developmental working class struggles around the world, the ideologies behind unions remain nonetheless alive and well in contemporary society, and most certainly among independent members of the body-modified, geographically fragmented, unemployed, oppositional left.

Ideological State Apparatus

In narrow readings of Althusser, the claim is made that he is especially fond of the state as ideological apparatus. Though the splitting of political, paradigmatic hairs in translated text is not our current goal, the state apparatus will, nonetheless, serve to further bolster the argument presented. The state as ideological apparatus has been gradually dismantled since late capitalism, through a variety of internal influential forces delivered by each administration on either side of the deepest political cleavage. It has been argued that the climactic height of the ideological state apparatus in the United States was evident during the Roosevelt era, when the demand for prosperity for all people mobilized an entire nation across cultural, economic, and political lines. Back then, it would have been incomprehensible to extricate the ideological functions from the state apparatus. Since that time, ideology has gradually withered away. Just as no particular administration or party can be identified with the rise of the ideological state apparatus, neither can any be necessarily accused of its demise.

How did the state apparatus change? The gradual dismantling of ideology from the apparatus has been due to corporatism and the increasing demands of competing interests imposed on the state. Influences from administrations, lobbying groups, and pressure from citizens have been imposed upon the state, systematically preventing any ideology from institutionalizing particular interests. This pressure renders the state apparatus an empty vessel, with responsive impulses oriented toward momentary public opinion rather than any temporal ideological orientation. The state apparatus has become preoccupied with the peaks and valleys of economic indicators, popularity polls, quarterly performance measures, and manipulated fiscal accountability indices. Perhaps through mounting pressure from the mass media, each administration has gradually, inadvertently weakened the ideological orientation of the state apparatus by superficializing efficiency, increasing short-term micromanagerial accountability, contributing to bureaucratic complexity, perpetuating false polarities among political opponents, and rendering opposing parties innocuous by creating obstacles to nearly all legislation. Postmodern political intricacies within and among embedded public networks paralyze the state apparatus and essentially prevent any ideological orientation from influencing public policies.

> The primary structure of social differentiation at present is connected with the distinction according to function systems. A political theory that does not adjust itself to the realities of functional differentiation will oscillate between overestimation and resignation concerning political possibilities and try to conduct politics with promises and disappointments—and the politics that does not admit that it is incapable of doing something is caught in this dilemma.[3]

The chaos of the summer of 1996, when the largest federal government bureaucracy in the world was completely incapacitated for three days due to budgetary squabbling, marked the death of ideology in the apparatus of the state. The extent to which opposing interests could cripple the state apparatus in the United States without any ideological cause had been, up to this point, underestimated. Those three days signified the end of the state ideology, which has since been weakened further through additional deleterious factors. The complete elimination of all cultural, literary, and artistic mechanisms of state apparatus support, for example, is a clear indication of the state's inability to sustain even a remote, bipartisan ideological function. The disintegration of the National Endowment for the Arts, elimination of literary, musical, and artistic resource allocations for public schools by the Department of Education, and failures of the Health and Human Services Department to provide the minimal basic sustaining elements of food, shelter, and healthcare needed for survival together signify the last spark of the state's ability to furnish citizens with an ideologically oriented apparatus. To respond to such criticism, economists, capitalists, and libertarians would suggest that these changes were necessary to streamline state efficiency, and that purely economic objectives are responsible for the unfortunate but necessarily transformative features of an evolving postmodern government.

> What we must realize then, is that the economic base never works alone; it always acts in combination with other elements: national character, national history, traditions, national events, and accidents of history. An event…is not the mechanical result of the basis but something involving various levels and instances of social formation.[4]

Under the paradoxical guise of quality, accountability, and transparency, ideology is no longer an even distant memory of the state apparatus under contemporary corporatist conditions. Political mobilization through framing processes or any other suggested tactic of political expression by political theorists is discounted by contemporary youth movements and evaluated as an unnecessarily complex and inefficient means by which to express political dissatisfaction to an apparatus no longer capable of ideological reaction to unfavorable conditions articulated by its people. To submit organized, well-structured, political appeals to an apparatus without an ideological "central nervous system" is regarded by youth, and particularly the energetic body modifiers along the left, as politically futile. The ideological apparatus of political mobilization, therefore, can no longer be considered the appropriate instrumentation for ideological expression and social change.

Ideological Party Apparatus

Formal participation through *political parties* has been another mechanism of collective action among politically active youth, and can be used to further justify the impotence of the postmodern ideological apparatus. The party apparatus in the United States is bifurcated into two groups along Republican and Democratic factions. There are divisions within the parties as well, based on competing interests. The last historical ideological expression, which extinguished for eternity the party as ideological apparatus, was evident under Pat Buchanan's leadership of the Republic National Convention during the 1992 U.S. presidential election. On a platform marketed as "family values," he articulated a conservative domestic social policy and attacked the formation of contemporary family structures (including extended, multi-generational families, lesbians, gays, and single-parent families). Despite the absurdity of his message and the unexpected expression of his radical orientation to the right, he did attempt to bring ideology back to party politics. Though the content of his ideology is associated with significant losses for Republicans in the years to follow, his strategy of using the party as an ideological apparatus also backfired immediately. The polity no longer is capable or prepared to absorb ideological messages from party politics. Though he will be remembered more for his flagrant underestimation of the intellectual capabilities of the voting citizen, coupled with his expressions of hatred toward a huge constituency of his own party (gay and lesbian), he should go down in history instead, for his explicit attempts to return the party apparatus to an ideological (albeit divisive) footing. To be sure, the flavor of Buchanan's ideology will inhibit any future attempts for ideological renewal in party politics, a phenomenon that is already widely apparent.

The party apparatus has not only amputated ideology, but is barely capable of absorbing issues along discernible cleavages. Of late, liberal Democrats sound more like conservative Republicans, and the left might be more accurately represented among liberal Republicans. Though many would argue that the ideological political party apparatus has not experienced a decline but has instead become *ideologically diluted*, politically active youth on the left who express themselves through body modification believe the domestic political party system to be permanently ideologically dismantled. And if there is still some evidence of fragmented ideological party apparatus left that has not yet extinguished its final spark, the continued attempts to purchase votes for autonomous presidential ascendancy by circumventing the political party apparatus (i.e., Ross Perot and Steve Forbes) further supports the absence of any ideological remains within the party apparatus. This is not to suggest that ideology will not continue to be the singularly most influential determinant in future political outcomes in the United States, but that ideology will remain extracted from the highly marketed and neutralized political structure and become a cognitive influence, articulated only among intimate groups and exercised secretly in the minds of the voting public. The impotent party apparatus will sustain its structure, perhaps even expand in complexity; but is unlikely to function as ideological apparatus any time soon. Opposition against a threatening other, rather than ideology in support for something or someone, will be the combustible material energizing future party activity. As such, and in light of politically oriented youth on the left, recognition of this political party apparatus devolution and the potential of political participation within these impotent structures is perceived to be futile. The focus now turns to another historically utilized institutional apparatus for capturing the political participatory energy of the left, the university as political ideological apparatus.

Ideological University Apparatus

The university has been under increasing scholarly, political, and fiscal scrutiny from a variety of authorities, resulting in the inevitable paralysis of ideology under severe managerial constraints. Research outcomes are scrutinized by politicians with no expertise to establish reasonable criteria for social utility of research activity, bringing intellectuals to their knees upon seeing their lifelong work used as political fodder to market politicians' otherwise vapid careers by attracting support among cabinet members and generating patronage among constituents. Sophisticated federal funding streams further determine the social, political, and cultural agenda of American scientific and social scientific research communities, while private, philanthropic foundations attempt but are unable to fully bridge the necessary supportive gap of socially relevant research. The potential of research to alleviate the suffering associated with poverty, to contribute to the elimination of diseases that do not afflict aging white males, and other university research activities that can significantly improve a broader cross-section of lives and facilitate technological and economic development globally have been co-opted by these powerful, destructive influences. University administrators exacerbate these problems due to passive managerial philosophies that involve professional career protection within scarce resource environments, where academic administrative appointments are distributed through nepotism with intense competition and scrutiny.

Faculty members have also facilitated the apparatus dismantling process. Increased competition and pressure for prolific careers has rendered academics impotent as leaders of university advocacy groups or in direct political action. The difficulties associated with obtaining tenure, primacy of personal aggrandizement, the tolerance of sexual conquests of students for bartered protectionism, the drive to acquire and maintain external grant funding, ideological neutralization to protect personal grant resource accumulation, positivism and related neutrality of disciplinary research agendas, and the perception of student teaching as chore rather than privilege have all contributed to the demise of the university as ideological apparatus.

Students' involvement in the historic demise of the university as political apparatus is perhaps the most egregious affront, but critical analysis is perhaps better left to those who lived it (see Aronowitz, 1996;). As far as youth who engage in contemporary body modification as social movement in the postmodern era are concerned, their abandonment of the university as apparatus for social change stems from spiraling costs, skyrocketing admission requirements, expensive and elaborate standardized admissions tests, the devaluation of associate degrees and professional certifications, the elimination of mentoring and apprenticeships, and the decreased status of colleges and universities without an ivy-league infrastructure. A simple cost-benefit analysis where the costs associated with attending the type of educational institution now accessible to most young people today are weighed against the benefits found through the accumulation of degrees from such institutions, results in a cohort of young people who simply cannot see the utility of attending an over-priced college to fulfill their destiny of occupying the least skilled, lowest paying jobs accessible to those without collegial networks of nepotism. The postmodern, body-modifying left, therefore, do not access the university as ideological apparatus, perceiving the academic institution as functioning to provide exorbitant levels of technological training for the most low-status jobs, rather than fulfilling any necessarily ideological pedagogical function. The reduced status associated with many of these degrees, coupled with reduced access to elite academic opportunity structures whose admission policies are increasingly determined by openly nepotistic networks of government officials, charitable contributors, and alumni to fill scarce vacancies, are perceived by body-modifying leftists to be nothing more than institutions that facilitate and reproduce social, cultural, and educational features of the existing class structure. Hence, the university is no longer capable of serving as ideological apparatus. Any political mobilizing effectiveness of the academy enjoyed in the past is now considered negligible and inconsequential by those struggling from lower, middle, and working-class origins. The sentiment is largely based on the inaccessible character of the privileges historically attached to the modern academy. The dismissal and attempts to discredit Professor Ward Churchill only serve to neutralize the ideological capacity of American universities further.

Informal Sector as Ideological Apparatus

The nonprofit apparatus presents the greatest analytic challenges based on the diverse political nature of this sector. Clearly, ideology lingers among these formal collectives to some degree, but the extent to which ideology is salient is determined by type, complexity, and objective of the organization. Informal structures such as ad hoc community groups are included here, as well as more formal apparatuses such as the charitable sector, and professional organizations. This may include registered organizations that occasionally participate in social movements that have many differing ideological orientations, but are all under increasing attack by government to restrain activities.

Is this the apparatus that the postmodern, body-modifying left will chose as the vehicle of choice for political mobility? Presumably not. Given the tremendous cynicism associated with apparatus as political mobilizing institution among those engaged in body politics, the postmodern body-modifying left has and probably will continue to avoid the informal sector as a vehicle for political action. Functional differentiation and associated complexity is slowly crippling the nonprofit sector, similar to the deleterious effects already exhibited in government operations. Without immediate intervention and an infusion of the left into this apparatus, ideology is bound to be domestically extinguished here, as well.

Unlike many new social movements in the United States and Europe, the non-elite [Third World] NGO's have a different attitude toward the state. Of course they are all located in relationship to various governments, but their political programs are not contained by their governments. Instead, organizations concentrate on [specialized] issues. You have no idea the degree of expertise that exists among near-illiterate rural workers in these collectives; it is amazing how thoroughly they recognize what is going on. This is why I am saying that the old models will not work. In this sense, their relationship to the state is robustly contradictory, [and as such] notions of culturalism and identity politics are not applicable to this kind of work. Instead their focus is on hard-core economic resistance.[5]

Government involvement is not the only source threatening the soundness of ideological nonprofit apparatus. Veterans of the nonprofit sector have watched in amazement as Wall Street baby boomers entered the charitable sector in waves during the corporate restructuring of the late eighties, absorbing expectorated managers discarded from capitalist corporate ranks. These executives were expeditiously integrated into this occupational sector by overworked leaders of the executive voluntary cadre, who were more comfortable with community organizing than solidifying the necessary financial ties to corporate foundations. Government subsidies and public support loomed precariously on the horizon, as the economy continued to get weaker despite continued rhetoric delivered poignantly by an Academy Award-winning president. The influx of managers imposed complexity and efficiency on simple but effective national networks of unbureaucratic grassroots charities, introduced greed and corruption under the guise of efficiency, and eliminated ethical qualities and dedicated professionalism from job descriptions across a strong occupational employment sector that, in the City of New York alone, employs one out of every eight workers.[6] The overabundance of investment brokers, bond analysts, and attorneys who claimed to have had an ethical catharsis inspiring them into absorption into the nonprofit sector coincided precisely with their compulsory exodus from bankrupt brokerage firms across America. They were suddenly infiltrating nonprofit board meetings across the nation, vocalizing a commitment to the professional leadership of publicly supported charities, claiming their exclusive, specialized, corporate experiences were the only way to foster necessary sectoral advances. These occupational transformations had tremendous influence on managerial leadership in the nonprofit sector, causing transitions at decision-making levels that are still reverberating through charitable organizations today, and are largely the impetus for the assault of federal revenue authorities on fledgling, poverty-oriented, community-based grassroots organizations. Rather than ideological programming of the apparatus for empowerment of the poor, managers of this apparatus are now required to be fluent in Generally Accepted Accounting Principles. Instead of advocating on behalf of the disenfranchised, social workers are studying HMO guidelines that ultimately determine the duration of client counseling. Rather than observing fundraising departments filled with dedicated development professionals who express their heartfelt appreciation for financial support that is indicative of personal sacrifices, specialized accountants posing as estate officers are celebrating over cocktails after playing 'hardball' to 'nail' yet another bequest. If progress in this direction continues, the final bastion of ideological apparatus will be, like others before it, similarly extinguished.

The body-modifying left, who are often in a position to directly solicit services of the charitable sector for their own survival, are already acutely aware of wide abuses of power, and openly articulate resentment for the excessive requirements attached to aid. Proponents of the nonprofit sector warn that if the current trend continues, charities, lobbying groups, and political action committees will become nothing more than vacant, ideologically empty vessels that avoid addressing the genuine needs of the poor, in favor of programming associated with artistic and cultural exposure for the upper classes. Though the importance of cultural pursuits will be established elsewhere, it remains ideologically threatening when fewer newly created nonprofit organizations seek incorporation for purposes associated with increasingly unpopular empowerment of the poor.[7] Perhaps tax codes will eventually be used to motivate these necessary changes, and distinguish organizations on the basis of urgent need through federal incentives. Meanwhile, governments continue to relinquish responsibility for the economically disenfranchised, public welfare benefits are systematically eroded away, and corporate support is increasingly diminished based on the reluctance of federal revenue authorities to provide fair alleviation of tax liability. If these trends continue, it is certain that the nonprofit sector as apparatus will diminish in its ideological effectiveness (Romanienko, 2009).

Body Politic Collectives as Political Expression

Socialists, anarchists, and other ideological groups oriented toward the left have historically mobilized political action through community organizing, special interest groups, political action committees, charitable work, participation in political parties, protest activities, and/or voting. Yet these historically effective mobilization techniques through conventional ideological apparatus are becoming increasingly blocked for new generations on the body-modified left. The inability to rely on these conventional institutional options has been further exacerbated by the severe economic downward mobility currently experienced. New innovative mechanisms of symbolic political expression have been developed in order to create action alternatives and display fomenting hostilities. The feasibility of formal organizing through any apparatus lacking an ideological foundation is regarded as ineffective and politically futile. The contemporary body-modifying left has, as a result, withdrawn from formal political participation, accepted poverty as their inevitable destiny, and, among the minority of extreme body-modifying anarchists, sometimes resorted to constructive violence as effective redistributive political mobilization for survival. To a greater extent, the majority of the postmodern leftists engage in lively political discourse with enthusiastic dreams of economic upheaval and social revolution. In reality, the body-modified left is overwhelmingly in favor of passive political expression of social and cultural dissatisfaction through symbolic body modification through piercing and other forms of defiant symbolic expression, as opposed to any formal institutional mobilization efforts to change the political infrastructure or the oppressive forces that drive the machinery. As political strategy, the choice instead is to remain expressively active through the body politic, but politically innocuous through structural disdain and indifference.

In the long run, the strategy is not an illogical one. The new new left patiently awaits the huge cohort preceding them to gradually leave the employment sector through death and retirement, thereby evacuating huge numbers of jobs and creating massive opportunity through employment vacancies. This inevitable transformation for the future will thus enable empowerment of the left through economic stability, and create possibilities for more tangible collective mobilizing strategies for the future. In the meantime, acceptance of their transitory fate and understanding of their ultimate destiny are expressed in discourse aimed against "yuppie scum," who ironically possess ideological and political beliefs often indistinguishable from their alienated, body-modifying offspring. Despite similar political intergenerational sentiments, baby boomers are perceived by body-modifying leftists to absorb an exorbitant share of our nations' occupational, cultural, and educational resources. Perhaps due largely to demographic features rather than necessarily ideological orientations or consumption patterns, baby boomers are blamed for exacerbating many of the social, political, and economic problems currently experienced by the postmodern left due to their hypocritical lifestyles, exorbitant material needs, and conspicuous consumption patterns. Furthermore, the baby boom cohort is identified by the body-modified left as overwhelmingly in control of an inequitable proportion of financial resources, economic opportunity, and the mass media. Given their historic affiliation with socialism, a significant realignment in the eighties toward conservatism, and an unpredictable direction for the future, these aging 'hippies' are considered by the more cynical factions of the body-modified left to be the singularly most hypocritical generational cohort in American political history. This perception further solidifies "apparatus apathy" and eliminates the shame of panhandling and petty theft among body modifiers who are often children of the old new left and upper-class origins. This sentiment is perhaps best expressed in the simple but unifying mantra among body-modifying left, *die yuppie scum*, eventually evolving into nihilistic *fuck shit up*. This rallying cry parsimoniously expresses the conditions by which political, social, economic, and cultural participation among the body-modifying left will be brought about. Upheaval is unlikely. Death and destruction is inevitable. As such, intergenerational cleavages are currently the deepest influence preventing the unification of the left in the United States. Ideology (and any possible collective based on ideology) has been relegated to reduced prominence as occupational features of the economy create severe conditions of economic deprivation among the new new left, leading to wide generational opposition. This enables the maintenance of defiant, alienated, insulated boundaries among new generations of body modifying leftists, expressed through multiple piercings displayed prominently upon the face. These institutional circumstances prevent social, economic, or political participation in a world that is perceived to be increasingly controlled by a generation of aging, hypocritical radicals who are more preoccupied with their own investment portfolios than politically acculturating a new generation.

Why, then, do these pierced activists of the new new left choose the particular expressive mechanisms of body modification to communicate their feelings of oppression and to signify a refusal to placate the hegemonic classes of both right and left political orientations? There are many ways to communicate political sentiments in the absence of ideological apparatus. It is reported that the shock and permanence of piercing, branding, stretching, and scarification is the distinguishing feature desirable in an environment of pervasive uncertainty and risk. These conditions have been brought on by technological transformations, which are the primary impetus for these particular mechanisms of postmodern political expression. After all, conservatives and capitalists have, for decades, accused the left of political agendas that are anti-industrial and anti-scientific.

> [T]he essence—the fundamental principles, the psychological motivation, the ultimate goal—of the leftist-liberals has not changed. The essence is hatred of reason. Hatred of reason leads to fear of reality. The activists of the New Left are closer to revealing the truth of their motives: they do not seek to take over industrial plants, they seek to destroy technology.[8]

After three decades of retrospection, these provocative accusations may actually help to demystify the current social movement examined in this chapter. If there is one unifying ideological theme among postmodern body modifiers, it is that of personal economic struggle in light of unfairly distributed resources based on technologically induced industrial transformations. In a society where substantial risk is substituted for economic prosperity, where network embeddedness is substituted for community, where impressions of global unity are traded for cultural understanding, where relationships are reduced to linkages, and where virtual interaction is the preferred alternative to actual human contact; the radical modifying left certainly express reservations about the role of technology in the destiny of the world they are to inherit. Concerns of risk and technological influence are intimately linked to severe relative economic deprivation, parsimoniously expressed through body politics, and clearly articulated through a ubiquitous return to symbols originating in pre-industrial, underdeveloped, 'primitive' civilizations.

Conclusion

To recapitulate, the postmodern modifying left accepts their destiny of downward social and occupational mobility from their families of origin as inevitable, due to transformations in employment opportunities based on industrial transformations (brought on by increased reliance on technology), the post–baby boom birth cohort effect (where opportunities are perceived to be territorially occupied by a swollen generation of skilled professionals), and a postmodern institutional sector devoid of ideological thrust in a constant state of uncertainty and flux (resulting from political paralysis). Furthermore, historic anti-industrial sentiments, according to arcane accusations originally intended to weaken the left, are proudly identified as the primary motivation of political expression among radical leftist postmodern youth. There is substantial evidence to suggest that body piercing, as cultural revival of the earliest premodern expression of tribal affiliation and rank, has been resuscitated by the left as intentional expression of anti-technological political sentiments. The identification with the rituals, adornments, and accoutrements from premodern, unindustrialized cultures has not been limited to political expressions of body piercing. Scarification, stretching, and other pre-industrial tribal forms of permanent body modification as expression of affiliation, amalgamation, and status are increasingly utilized by body-modified youth as alternative political symbol to communicate acceptance of subaltern status, rejection of western labor market forces, and an orientation toward the nostalgic past in light of pessimistic political sentiments for the future. Many focus their technological criticisms on the larger political arena of social, cultural, economic, and environmental effects of transnational business. Economic world domination, through international corporations often implemented through exploitative technologies, is one impetus among many motivating the use of these politically expressive symbols of embodied outrage. Independent of institutional constraints of conventional apparatus, they are free to pursue a variety of innovative mechanisms of alternative resistance that may even include the occasional use of violent resistance to combat attacks from threatening socioeconomic and political adversaries.

5
Economic Contestation

The approved doctrines are crafted and employed for reasons of power and profit [that] take the form of socialism for the rich within a system of global capital mercantilism in which 'trade' consists in substantial measure of centrally managed transactions within single firms, huge institutions linked to their competitors by strategic alliances, all of them tyrannical in internal structure, designed to undermine democratic decision-making and safeguard the masters from market discipline.

Noam Chomsky

Background

Despite what many apathetic gutterpunks would like casual observers to believe, contemporary barriers facing young people are not simply limited to abusive conditions in the home or brought on by high-risk survival tactics on the street. Some of the most profound impediments to youth development and related ecological communication are found in the current macroeconomic and political conditions around the world (Kozol, 1991; Nurmi, 1991). These deleterious circumstances encourage resistant identity construction through symbolic and non-symbolic discursive opposition among youth. As a result, piercing and other forms of body modification have now become a routine part of international, integrated socioeconomic and political resistance efforts involving sophisticated tactics of community organizing advanced by subversive collectivities around the world. These communities use the body as an important discursive vehicle with which resistance messages against conventional society can be displayed. Though of prime importance, the symbolic mechanism of oppositional identity construction on the body is not the only tactic used by this youth community to demonstrate their outrage at contemporary conditions that hinder their existence. Oppositional communication also simultaneously occurs in digitized territories far beyond the visual gaze. Although public displays of body piercing may initially be inspired by the desire to provoke direct contestation through interaction at the individual level, over time the popularity of piercing has neutralized the potential antagonism inherent in these visual displays. As identity construction takes on more urbane strategies over the life cycle, and as politically oriented individuals with body piercings become more confident in their ability to address their specific socioeconomic and political grievances to more specific audiences, the need to target their expressions of outrage to more diverse publics than those routinely available within chance proximity of the body becomes increasingly clear. To that end, political resistance among those engaged in piercing and other forms of body modification involves a high degree of innovation and knowledge to assure genuine political provocation is capable of reaching requisite audiences. Unlike gutterpunks of New Orleans, who can easily accomplish their goals of fleeting socioeconomic and political resistance by engaging in contestation for public space among circulating elites enjoying their holiday regularly entering into their imminent domain, others with more salient political interests must take more innovative approaches far beyond local acts of visually threatening provocation, to ensure inflammatory interactions transpire with specific audiences driving existing socioeconomic and political arrangements. As aristocratic elites increasingly secure comfortable, sanitized, geopolitical and social distances that allow them to insulate themselves from the economic repercussions of their globalizing policies operating to the detriment of the working classes and other victims left in the wake of their operations, authentically oppositional communities of pierced individuals must engage in novel mechanisms of expressive communication to create opportunities for class-spanning contestational interactions. As law enforcement continues to operate on behalf of elite interests (Ellis and Ellis, 1989), as sanctions continue to be unevenly distributed (Tunick, 1992), and as gated communities and similar insulating privileges continue to expand cognitive distances prohibiting any class integration at even the most superficial levels (Morris and Braine, 2001), body-pierced activists have created new digitized discursive formats to undermine, albeit temporarily, these insular structures of privilege.

> Ironically, most systems of human domination...physically segregate those whom they oppress [whom] are likely to live in geographically segregated communities. Despite even close monitoring by repressive regimes, subordinate communities residing in the most highly segregated spaces...often...present a façade of normalcy that reassures dominant groups while fomenting oppositional cultures and oppositional consciousness behind the scenes.[1]

Body-modified oppositional cultures seek to expose broad nonrandomized audiences to provocative contestational messages by using the innovative mechanism of globalizing resistance involving digitized discourse. Through new digitized platforms of communicative action, body-modified activists are able to identify the participants, processes, and consequences of complex adversarial class relations far beyond the chance limits of the bodily gaze. By highlighting specific entities involved in specific economic transactions responsible for specific socioeconomic and political conditions, pierced saboteurs are able to guide fellow oppositional community members to discern the impact of detrimental global policies at the world systemic, nation-state, and local levels. Information dissemination campaigns and related discursive mechanisms used by politically oppositional body-modification communities now involve a much broader repertoire of defiance to identify increasingly complex adversarial activities disseminated to relevant publics in a wider communicative format offered by digitized technologies on the Internet. The deployment of information and communication technologies (ICT) to formalize political outrage can be construed as part of a larger discursive strategy surrounding alterglobalization efforts occurring beyond the body being used to articulate and integrate otherwise fragmented social, cultural, and political subversion taking place simultaneously around the world.

One highly innovative international community engaging in elaborate globalization resistance strategies simultaneously upon the body and the disembodied digitized formats is the network of Polish anarchists known as the Anarchist Federation [Federacja Anarchistyczna]. Since regime change, East European anarchists have remained such a stable force of the European anarchist infrastructure that the official annual European Black Cross meeting was held in Bialystok, Poland, in 2004.

Today, this politically active community of postcommunist body piercers has evolved dramatically to engage in effective tactics of discursive resistance using digitized ICT platforms available through the Internet to identify and disseminate complex socioeconomic and political information regarding threatening adversaries both locally and globally, as well as report on the specificities of the detrimental effects of their transnational business activities. These information dissemination activities serve to unify the network beyond the local as they develop an innovative discursive platform by which to sensitize audiences to the underlying need for state resistance activities through embodied and disembodied activism. Before we examine the defiant community-organizing features that this information-based resistance activity involves, let us first examine the relevant socioeconomic and political conditions that gave rise to one of the most authentic and powerful body-modified oppositional digitized autonomous activist networks, the body-modified anarchists of Poland.

Profound Deprivation and Marginality

Over two decades ago, Poland's Solidarity labor movement pioneered dramatic systemic socioeconomic and political changes involving an unprecedented ideological working-class revolution that resulted in a variety of unanticipated consequences contributing to the fall of the Berlin Wall, the dismantling of the Soviet Union, neoliberal economic market transformation, shock reforms to stabilize currency under exponential inflation, and a coercive regulatory environment brought on by political integration into the European Union, all at once. These simultaneous upheavals influencing

nearly all facets of social, political, and economic life have resulted in rapidly deteriorating standards of living for many segments of the population
compared to pre-revolutionary levels of subsistence under communism,
reminiscent in many ways of the artificial scarcity experienced under repressive Martial Law. Thus, it should come as no surprise that these tightly knit
oppositional communities of postcommunist dissent have become popular
among disenfranchised youth, assisting them in articulating a variety of
inspirational tactics to reverse the hegemonic socialist legacy and subvert
the savage capitalist markets rapidly replacing it (Romanienko, 2007).

> Why is the West so fascinated by the recent events in Eastern Europe? The
> answer seems obvious: what fascinates the Western gaze is the *reinvention of
> democracy*. It is as if democracy, which in the West shows signs of decay and
> crisis, lost in bureaucratic routine and publicity-style election campaigns, is
> being rediscovered in Eastern Europe with all its freshness and novelty. [T]he
> West looks for its own lost origins, for the authentic experience of 'demo-
> cratic invention'. The reality now emerging in Eastern Europe is, however, a
> disturbing distortion of this idyllic picture.[2]

The profound socioeconomic and political changes associated with postcommunist democratization, as well as the deleterious economic consequences disproportionately affecting youth and other similarly vulnerable
cohorts of an increasingly innocuous labor market, have together provided
a fortuitous environment for anarchist ideologies to flourish under new
"democratic" conditions of Poland. Strengthened through antigovernment
sentiments brought on by the systemic delusions promulgated under both
communism and capitalism, the catastrophic socioeconomic and political
events of the past two decades have fostered legitimating anarchistic dissent on a scale and speed unlike any witnessed before in history. Without
the luxury of poignant naiveté that drives western intellectuals to support
socialist pathways out of unregulated, neoliberal, exploitative global market
economics under late capitalism; body-pierced Polish youth, deeply familiar with both forms of vehement systemic oppression, deductively adhere to
anarchist ideologies as the only rational pathway out of the dystopian abyss
based on their own personal indigenous experiences.

> What should not be lost in the fog of competing loyalties is the similarity
> between capitalist and Communist ideologies: material abundance, rapid
> urbanization, educational facilities, military strength—these indices define
> both American and Soviet notions of development. We are now in an age
> dominated by a common industrial ideology which is just as much the prop-
> erty of the Soviet Union as it is of the West. Soviet and American societies
> share not only an emphasis on technological and scientific achievements but
> they also share a willingness to absorb human losses which will insure them
> world leadership.[3]

Despite the superficial ideological veneers that distinguish capitalism from
communism, the planned and unplanned centralized or decentralized

economies have remained essentially indistinguishable, with pledges for material abundance under both delusional systemic forms of production left largely unfulfilled. This is especially true for marginalized workers such as unskilled laborers, women, and young people.

Anarchy or the Collusive State

Are the anarchist components of contemporary resistance efforts genuinely ideological or, as many have suggested, are they mere superficial, fashionable veneers? Given their survival under both systemic forms of oppression, postcommunist anarchist activists have no choice but to deductively espouse anarchy as a viable alternative to the collusive state. Public-sector entities, after all, figure prominently in the analysis because deleterious economic arrangements are not exclusively driven by private-sector business interests. The reluctance of the Polish government to combat or otherwise mitigate simultaneous exploitation by combined coercive exogenous public- and private-sector forces associated with American and European hegemonic capital serves to demonstrate that exploitative arrangements, and related pacification, remained essentially unchanged since regimes transferred power from East to West. As was the case under the Soviet regime, the placating role of Polish government and its facilitation of trade interests to exploit natural, human, and other indigenous resources was consistently observable throughout capitalist transition. In fact, ex-communists maintained collaborative power-sharing, even under the oppositional presidency of Lech Walesa (Millard, 2000). But unlike conditions under the old system of communist domination, the circumstances surrounding the new system of neoliberal capitalist exploitation was, by many estimates, even more exploitative due to voluntary complicity of the masses brought on by material consumer culture. A powerful combination of dependency profoundly affecting supply and demand, the dual-edged sword of inactivity due to the dismantling of nearly all national economic production activities, patterns of conspicuous consumption exhibited by dilettante consumers, and unregulated predatory lending to provide debt to further perpetuate the delusions of free market success have together resulted in a frighteningly efficient pacification program for the masses, only dreamed of by authoritarian dictators such as Stalin and Lenin.

> Under capitalism people were powerless, personal agency was warped, and communities fragmented. Capitalism's consumer culture with its produced commodities...renders people powerless, without recognition of their humanity / dignity, locating pluralities of enfeebled subjectivities in fragmented moments of social moments of life worlds based on consumer choices. Consumerism and consumer-based forms of commodified identity promise meaning and meaningful selfhood, while at the same time breaking its promise in order to inspire ever more consumption. On the one hand, consumerism creates artificial, encapsulated realms of pseudo-agency as choices between mass produced advertised brands and styles, and limits human

potential for self-fulfillment. Importantly, consumer-based consumption leads to a migration of subjectivity from concerns with political economy to a preoccupation with various sites and modes of hedonism. This resulting indifference to political concerns and political action, serves to strengthen, if only by default, the very conditions of alienation. The problem...is how mass-produced, mass-marketed goods and images homogenize selfhood and erode its capacity for critical thought. The pseudoindividualization acquired through commodity consumption acts as a constraint to genuine freedom and self-constitution.[4]

Contemporary consumer culture has falsely advanced consumptive decision making or pseudoindividualized agency as participatory democracy, under the guise of fulfilling what Poles have come to call western standards. The accumulation of material goods is paramount for the public gaze, whereas private deprivation remains the genuine rule and not an anomalous exception. These paradoxes of transitional capitalism create conflict at all levels of society, perhaps most acutely felt in gendered negotiations within conventional heteronormative families. Underemployment by materially oriented frustrated matriarchs and escapism through alcohol consumption by frustrated patriarchs only exacerbate the deprivation and other material failures of capitalism. As young people witness these family-based material delusions to legitimate the historic turn away from communism, these divisive sociocultural conditions fragmenting society have led to a peculiar laboratory of legitimation fostering revolutionary anarchist ideologies among young body-modified activists, whose parents, more often than not, are disgruntled, unemployed, hard-drinking Solidarity revolutionaries themselves. Never before in the history of ideological resistance to capitalism have socioeconomic and political conditions led to such rapid smoldering discontent and related oppositional identity construction against state authorities facilitating existing exploitative conditions as witnessed in Poland today. The challenge for body-modified postcommunist anarchists, particularly those who experienced both hegemonic structures of subjugation, lies not only in the legitimation of anarchy, but also in the simultaneous delegitimation of both communism and capitalism.

Nowhere is the task at hand more effortless than in a faltering democracy such as Poland. Postcommunist body-modified anarchists are in the process of using embodied mechanisms of discursive dissent to simultaneously delegitimate both systems of socioeconomic and political oppression through public testimony generated on the body and digitized discursive platforms offered through ICT. Two powerful discursive vehicles are thus used in conjunction to authenticate oppositional forces of anarchist dissent. Digitized postcommunist anarchy is advancing the delegitimation project against communism and capitalism via the deployment of meticulous documentation elaborating the exogenous and endogenous causes and consequences of systemic deterioration. Through tactical adversarial alignment expedited through body modification and information technology, anarchist activists

are able to disseminate timely and relevant information regarding the constantly fluctuating socioeconomic and political conditions to stakeholding
audiences largely composed of other body-modified activists. This embodied resistance endeavor serves not only to authenticate anarchy as the only
legitimate form of oppositional dissent that remains a feasible option for
Poland's future, but is also used to discredit the nation-state for its role
in exacerbating the suffering associated with postcommunist neoliberal
capitalist transformation. Moving well beyond antiglobalization rhetoric
vociferously perpetuated by activists in the West who stubbornly adhere to
dogmatic socialist solutions for escape out of the neoliberal capitalist quag-
mire, Polish communities of body-modified activists are carefully elaborating the specificities of oppression ubiquitously inherent in all extortional
forms of hegemonic state-centric rule, regardless of innocuous ideological
underpinnings. Through the tactic of systemic and de facto state delegitimation, coupled with the identification of collusive public- and private-sector
elite who benefit from existing exploitative arrangements, the anarchist
community of Poland publicly constructs ideal types of adversarial relations with conventional authoritative others necessary to authenticate the
utopian liberation project that they embody.

> [T]here is substantial evidence that all this is not inevitable. As projects of
> globalization deepen the inequalities of power around the world, some forms
> of development are starting to suggest that conditions are possible for resist-
> ing the trend. Such blatant and severe usurpations of human rights in favor
> of corporate rights...have been met with fierce resistance.[5]

To begin the analysis to decipher these fierce resistance discourses portrayed simultaneously upon the body and in these digitized platforms, let us
now explore relevant theoretical frameworks that might help to demystify
the inspiration behind contemporary anti-systemic discursive anarchist dissent organizing in Poland and beyond.

Poland in the World System

To better understand the circulation of knowledge driving the outrage
that is articulated both on the body and in technological formats among
anarchists under examination, our analysis must first detail the profound
socioeconomic inequalities that are becoming apparent in Poland and
around the globe. To that end, insights from the international stratification paradigm known as *world systems theory* can assist in providing constructs that are useful in examining the underlying conditions that lead
to such unequal resource distribution and related deprivation around the
world. Although unequal resource distribution is not limited to the nations
experiencing postcommunist transition, some of the most drastic changes
in global history have recently occurred in the contemporary nation-states

located in postcommunist Eastern Europe. World systems theory alone cannot, however, adequately explain all dimensions of the complex phenomena influencing transitional newly-integrated European Union members. In light of the dynamic economic, social, and cultural influences affecting contemporary inequality in Poland, the current treatment will also examine anarchist responses to emerging international stratification through *democratic human agency* theories. This multi-level analytic approach will not only optimally advance the exploration of new transitional conditions of pervasive dependency-breeding downward economic mobility facing Polish youth, but will also identify the powerful revolutionary potential inherent in unleashing political agency through democratic resistance efforts deploying digitized information platforms. The world systems approach demonstrates that as globalizing forces enable exploitative capital to circulate to the detriment of the working classes around the world, so too are resistance tactics similarly circulating globally to destabilize the collusive but fragile consumption and production patterns which contemporary exploitative systemic economic arrangements are contingent upon.

Globalization or Global Deprivation?

Socioeconomic factors have had a profound impact on the character of human solidarity around the globe. One of the most influential elaborations of global relations focusing on international inequality is offered through world systems theory (Wallerstein, 2000; Frank and Gills, 1993).

> Immanuel Wallerstein (1974, 1979) defines a world system as an entity with a single division of labor and multiple cultures, and within this category there are two sub-types: world-empires in which the intersocietal division of labor is encompassed by a single overarching imperial policy, and world economies in which the political system is composed of many states competing with one another within an interstate system. [A]ll state-based world systems can be characterized as operating according to a logic of "capital imperialism" in which core regions accumulate resources by exploiting peripheral regions.[6]

The world system's economic arrangements therefore occur between the *core* [superpower nation-states], *periphery* [dependent less-developed nation-states], and *semi-periphery* [buffering nation-states that demonstrate characteristics of both]. Exploitative relations among these geopolitical entities are thus considered to be the primary conditions that permeate all international relations and perpetuate international inequalities (Luhman, 1982). Analysts of the world systems approach demonstrate that these relations exacerbate cycles of dependency (Ragin, 1983), increase debt and consolidate corrupt leadership (Munck and O'Hearn, 1999), and solidify rather than ameliorate conditions of poverty (Chirot and Hall, 1982). The impact of these social, cultural, and economic power arrangements has been gravely overlooked with regard to the state and certainly neglected in

poignantly optimistic analyses conducted by deregulation-oriented economists supporting neoliberal trade agreements disproportionately benefiting
nations located at the core.

> The state's critical role in unleashing global finance has been well recognized.
> The unilateral decision by the American and British governments in the early
> 1980s to abolish capital controls sparked a competitive dynamic among the
> other advanced nation-states, none of whom could afford the status quo as
> capital poured into those countries that relaxed their regulations. By the end
> of the decade, every OECD nation had removed all significant barriers to
> cross-border movements of financial assets and the unfettered mobility of
> international capital became a reality. The state also has been instrumen-
> tal in creating the institutional foundations of a new global constitutional-
> ism as embodied by transnational accords such as NAFTA, GATT, Single
> European Act. These initiatives have led to massive asymmetry of power
> between capital and other social actors. Globalisation has been accompanied
> by a remarkable ideological campaign, mounted with evangelical fervour
> by transnational institutions such as the WB, the WTO, the IMF, to create
> popular support for an open international order [presenting] a rhetoric of
> powerlessness [involving] a conscious strategy to obscure the way in which
> the world is actively being [transformed] by powerful social interests (includ-
> ing national governments). The scale of international financial transactions
> has grown so vast that governments have effectively lost control of their stan-
> dard instruments of monetary policy. Central banks do not possess sufficient
> reserves to defend a state's exchange rate once the financial markets have
> made up their mind to sell a currency.[7]

There is evidence that the coercive movement of capital operating to the
detriment of small-scale economies in the periphery and semi-periphery has
had an especially devastating effect on young people, who are becoming
globally 'superfluous' and at risk for permanent disenfranchisement.

> We are witnessing epochal social and economic transformations at global
> and national levels. Deindustrialisation and subsequent structural unemploy-
> ment have hit young people disproportionately hard, obstructing paths to
> adult statuses, identities, and activities [who are] at the margins of declining
> labour markets [representing] an apparently surplus population. Capitalism
> in this 'post-industrial' period, has jettisoned its surplus population on an
> historically unprecedented scale. Marginalisation and exclusion have gener-
> ated new forms of urban poverty which afflict those exiled from the labour
> market mainstream in the US and Europe. [Analysts perceive] this dangerous
> class as offering the only remaining threat to the dominance of the capital-
> ist system. Others have talked of anarchy at a consequence of the grow-
> ing chasm. This perspective on the social exclusion and inclusion of young
> people would call for explorations of the variety of ways that young people
> [develop] cultures of survival...as the paths of transition...have for some
> become blocked and for others more circuitous. [The simultaneous] collapse
> of the economic certainties and stable welfare systems...have generated new
> cultures of survival and new strategies of accommodation, negotiation and
> resistance amongst working-class young people.[8]

The current treatment argues that the globalization processes outlined in world systems theory are the singularly most influential determinant in the development of youth resistance identities involving body piercing and other forms of discursive outrage being constructed in Poland and around the world. The reason for this is not simple material scarcity, but rather that postcommunist semi-peripheral nation-states are in the process of experiencing *decomposition into the periphery* [peripheralization] through dependency relations, conditions that profoundly influence the ideological orientation of postcommunist youth. Just as the middle classes of advanced industrial societies are experiencing a decomposition into poverty classes, so too are the effects of the one-world systemic global economy being demonstrated as the erosion of the global middle class known as the world systems *semi-periphery*. The current treatment deems global world system and related deteriorating industrialized relations to be the primary factor associated with semi-peripheral economic collapse known as *third worldization* (Frank, 1994).

> The discussion about the pros and cons of [an EU] core is usually conducted from a Western European perspective. However, the picture is much clearer from an Eastern European perspective, leaving little room for debate. The idea of a European hard core is viewed as an East European nightmare because it condemns the post-communist states to an inferior peripheral status.[9]

Thus Poland's socioeconomic and political deterioration is deeply linked to transnational capitalist processes being experienced around the globe, which "confronts us with the challenge of understanding new forms of partial connection, new experiences of border" (Anderson, 1991).

> Increasingly, social problems are expanding beyond national borders. A shift in one country's economy can have profound effects on the international market and economic health of other nations. As problems are becoming more transnational, so too are movements for social change. Activists are stretching beyond state boundaries to work in solidarity with those with whom they identify in distant countries.[10]

In addition to rapidly deteriorating conditions of material deprivation, regulatory conditions and disadvantageous currency regimes imposed on Poland and other postcommunist states through detrimental European economic harmonizing policies have contributed to dependency on exports and related rapid downward mobility for citizens. Postcommunist nation-state governments have become the new villains as they collude with dependency-breeding hegemonic interests at the core. The strategic dismantling of all production activities in the postcommunist semi-periphery under the guise of efficiency has intentionally created profound economic dependency on imports through two decades of imposition of what was initially known as public–private partnerships and later privatization. The pacification that comes with the lack of economic production, reliance on peripherally produced core-imposed imports, the anomalous absence of a primary-tier labor market, the inability to develop any semblance of systems of meritocracy, and the lack of upward class mobility has led to the unprecedented rise of pragmatic resistance to nation-state government among activists embodying piercing and other forms of modified discursive resistance. These complex oppositional forces are dramatically observable in postcommunist new European nation-states such as Poland.

> The first world has placed obstacles in the way of, if not combated, states seeking to rise from second to first world status. For decades, Western embargoes and other obstacles directed against the East[ern bloc] were covered with the fig leaves of Cold War ideology. Yet, today many of these same Western policies, even some...trade restrictions, continue for reasons of naked economic competition. Should we not regard the Cold War as principally an ideologically disguised yet crude attempt by the West to keep the East, and of course the South, in second place? Of course this strategy, which included an arms race to spend the East into bankruptcy, CIA machinations, and myriad other tactics was successful. With the demise of "socialism," these costs are exacerbated, and the center-periphery structure and conflict is only further enforced, or rather more exposed. The political and ideological changes in Eastern Europe through which its people aspire to join the First World in Western Europe threaten instead to place Eastern Europe economically in the Third World. Many of these regions now face the serious prospect, like Africa, of being marginalized out of the international division of labor [which] threatens to return them to the backwaters of history.[11]

In the midst of these catastrophic hegemonic conditions causing massive rapid downward economic mobility as well as the entire elimination of the world's middle class through third worldization into the periphery, politically oriented networks of activists, many of whom engage in body modification, have shown themselves capable of exerting tremendous human agency in resisting these detrimental processes, even in some of the most remote and fragmented developing oppositional enclaves in Poland and around the world.

> Today, as global elites push for the final incorporation of all regions into a single capitalist system based on neoliberal principles, they are being met by an unexpectedly resilient, far-reaching, and multi-faceted coalition of resistance. Whatever it may be called—the anti-globalization movement—it is clear that a new coalition has emerged to challenge the dominance of political and corporate elites all across the contemporary world.[12]

Antiglobalization efforts in Poland and beyond attract attention to and reverse the consequences of hegemonic conditions imposed by the one-world system economy. According to Wallerstein,

> Hegemony...refers to that situation in which...one power can largely impose its rules and its wishes in the economic, political, military, diplomatic,

even cultural areas. The material base of such power lies in the ability of enterprises domiciled in that power to operate more efficiently...in many instances within the home markets of the rivals themselves [and benefiting from] non-interference of the political machinery. I mean hegemony only to refer to situations in which the edge is so significant that allied major powers are de facto client states and opposed major powers feel frustrated and highly defensive.[13]

The current approach argues that the hegemonic exploitative socioeconomic conditions being disproportionately experienced by young body-modified activist communities on the geographic and political peripheries situated at a distance from the exploitative core creates such geopolitical isolation and alienation that activists are compelled to create highly innovative digitized discursive spaces in order to provoke dialogue with adversarial audiences. This goal is accomplished locally through bodily discourse and globally through participation in digitized communities, transcending beyond space and time to organize persistent collective action including protests. Through a vital combination of dual-edged resistance tactics involving informally organized outrage demonstrated on the body and more formally organized outrage expressed in oppositional activities conceptualized and formalized through digitized information dissemination activities, body-modified anarchists at the semi-periphery are attempting to creatively usurp a variety of systemic structures of privilege. This takes place through a powerful combination of sabotage, including sensitizing the public to the potential threat inherent in exercising their own political agency, as well as the fragile role of consumption and production patterns that facilitate local dependency on core-bartered, periphery-produced, knowledge-intensive goods driving the exploitative global world economy.

Dependency and Political Agency

Although decomposition of the world's middle class through industrial relations elaborated through world systems may indeed be underway for those located in the semi-periphery, the key element of exploitation that is crucial in understanding the rise of anarchist thought and related downward mobility is the process known as *dependency*. Dependency involves exploitation of peripheral and semi-peripheral nation-states by a hegemonic transnational industrialized core.

The father of dependency theory is Raul Prebisch, an Argentinian who headed the UN Economic Commission for Latin America. Foreign capital, allied to a domestic elite, prevents the redistribution of wealth that would extend to the poor through the benefits of modernization. Nor is the government, tied to the international fiscal system, able to direct new investment and spending where it wishes. Instead, it inflates the currency. Thus foreign influence (primarily North American) is more noxious as a barrier to structural change than as a directly exploitative colonizer. The International Monetary Fund is viewed as particularly villainous because its remedies to inflation stifle growth and promote repressive regimes. [Researchers] found a high correlation between repression and the application of capitalist efficiency criteria. This makes bureaucratic-authoritarian regimes the favorites of international finance. [I]mport substitutions [also creates] new forms of dependence and new sociopolitical imbalances.[14]

Changes that have taken place in Poland through a combination of neoliberal market economics, the privatization and subsequent dismantling of all state manufacturing industries, the imposition of food and other imports brought about through common European agricultural policies that give preference to corporate production firms in the West, the dismantling of anachronistic small-scale inefficient farming culture in the East, the exponential devaluation of local Polish currency in favor of the Euro, and the elimination of social welfare programs previously enjoyed under communism have together resulted not only in the informal colonization of the nation by exogenous corporations responsible for the distribution of real estate, food, clothing, and the loans necessary to mask the failures of capitalism, but also extreme deprivation associated with the highest levels of unemployment of all EU states for the past four consecutive years (Narozny, 2006).

> Of the three aspects of transition (economic, political, and social) the one creating by far the most turmoil and disruption in people's lives is the attempt to dismantle the old command economies and move toward greater reliance on market forces. The by-products of this triple process of privatization, marketization and international integration . . . include growing income and wealth differentiation; loss of government subsidies to industry, agriculture, and society; bankruptcy, unemployment; and the erosion of the total social safety net provided by the old regime. [T]he collapse of communism has generally been accompanied by the rapid erosion of social welfare provisions and the retreat of the state from its protective and redistributive role. In opening themselves to world economic forces, postcommunist societies have subjected their inefficient industrial and agricultural sectors to intense international competition, thus intensifying the threat to much of their population. One might expect that the multiple threats posed by international economic integration, globalization, and postcommunist transition would provide more then ample stimulus for the mobilization of egalitarian social movements.[15]

Research focusing on world systems has yet to document with any level of specificity how these conditions of dependency spur human agency to politically resist the forces that lead to such catastrophic social economic and cultural conditions. This is the intended approach of the current analysis, which asserts that young, body-modified, postcommunist anarchist activists use discursive mechanisms of resistance simultaneously upon the body and in digitized platforms to oppose systemic forces of inequality and related dependencies woven across nation-state political boundaries, as well as to identify the collusive exogenous and endogenous elites that contribute to the solidification of these transnational socioeconomic and political arrangements. By attracting attention to these complex processes and their collusive participants who assure the continued devolution of semi-peripheral nations such as Poland into conditions of abject poverty, coupled with strategies to subvert the exploitation, alienation, and cultivated obedience necessary to survive increasingly hostile neoliberal market conditions of dependency foisted upon Poland by core nation-states, the analysis will demonstrate how postcommunist conditions have been fortuitous in enabling anarchist communities in the eastern bloc to thrive with immense popularity. At this point it may be useful to examine the mechanisms driving dependency and peripheralization, to better understand youth receptivity to deploying unique forms of embodied and digitized resistance combating adversarial systemic relations operating to the detriment of Polish society.

Consumption and Human Agency

There are politically oriented, anti-systemic, body-modified anarchists who, in the absence of any effective conventional ideological apparatus, are preoccupied with complex documentation activities involving broad adversarial audiences through knowledge dissemination on digitized discursive ICT platforms at the global level. Postcommunist activists who experienced both forms of systemic oppression under communism and capitalism are a particularly stable community of anarchist opposition engaging in creative resistance activities. Their oppositional strategies tend to encourage the optimization of human potential by highlighting the reversibility of collusive activities surrounding production and consumption patterns upon which dependency relations with core nation-states are contingent. These activists expose the effects of contradictory consumption patterns for the public gaze, while in reality most fellow citizens are experiencing severe genuine deprivation including food and medicine shortages in private life. The concealment and denial of the lack of personal savings and retirement schemes, reliance on high-interest predatory lending for basic subsistence survival, and the perpetual inability to access quality medical care all increase debt, postpone and inflate eventual costly expenditures, and exacerbate cycles of dependency. In attempting to deconstruct contradictions inherent in consumer spending, anarchist activists attempt to empower the masses by creating safe spaces for genuine dialogue to strategize how to resist dependency both locally and globally. These subversive tactics are intended to discourage reliance on goods and services produced at the periphery but imposed and bartered by surplus value-extracting entities in the core. Without the mass consumption of imported goods from the West, dependency relations could be significantly weakened.

Despite the overwhelming evidence that Poland is by any measure a *failed market economy*, the public's preoccupation with consumption activity that fosters the illusion of western success to justify the rather embarrassing revolutionary turn away from communism results in a temporary suspension of citizenship and in statelessness.

> The irrationality of the rational leads to increased productivity accompanied by increased destructiveness. [M]anipulated needs are articulated into men by the power of suggestion through the mass media to keep production stable and to increase it. Needs no longer arise in the individual but in the autonomous technical and economic process. The vicious cycle of irrational [consumption] produces these needs. A system always programs men, it satisfies their needs as they adapt to its needs. While formerly the dominated stood separate from their masters, today domination is no longer exercised by human subjects, but by the anonymous and almighty system itself.[16]

In questioning the taken-for-granted imposition of western material consumption that in actuality strengthens the economic power of an exploitative core, activists are sensitizing the public to the rather excessive transaction costs associated with dependency relations inextricably linked to capitalism. These transaction costs may perpetuate illusions of western material success, but in reality massive unemployment creating overcrowded living conditions in neglected dilapidated communist bloc housing is obscured by a traditional cultural inclination to disguise economic and other failures within families. These cultural arrangements are further exacerbated by the lack of national redistributive justice efforts constrained by tax-free arrangements for direct foreign investment and a variety of other corporate welfare programs that are together manifesting in contemporary society as an emotional state of suspended animation brought on by disbelief regarding the displacement and statelessness experienced in one's own country due to national exploitative policies implemented by party-appointed, perpetually-corrupt government.

> Dependent people, propertyless and usually unemployed, the tradition insinuates, are not committed to community, do not exercise key virtues, and cannot be trusted to make decisions about their own lives, let alone political decisions. This is the flip side of the tradition: if dependency is the problem, what does it mean to be independent, and how do people achieve this status?[17]

Arendt (1958) was among the earliest theorists to advance a theory of political action to describe tactics reversing citizen sentiments of statelessness and its role in facilitating political action and related empowerment.

> According to Arendt, the adherents of "tribal" nationalist movements regard themselves as "stateless" [whose] unique plight...is that they are invariably "outlaws" regardless of where they go or what they do. Because their liberty or even survival depends on the mere indulgence of the police, they live in constant peril. Her concern here is rather the inherently debilitating effects

of political exclusion on one's potential for human agency. In her view, the rights conferred with membership in a formally organized political community are themselves indispensable for living a fully human existence, so much so that to lack them is to be deprived the very basis of human dignity. [A] stateless person is "deprived not of their right to freedom, but of their right to action". What he has lost is not an assurance of noninterference in his affairs, but the recognition of his agency from others that would be needed for those affairs to make any difference in the world.[18]

Though dependency relations are predicated on pacification of the masses to enable unfettered markets to continue their exploitative arrangements, decision making or pseudoindividualization in the domain of commodity consumption has increasingly failed to live up to its alleged satisfactory exchange potential and has demonstrated to the discerning polity that twenty years of pseudoagency brought on by Western consumerism has little to do with genuine civic engagement. On the contrary, the exercise of true human agency and its recognition by relevant publics is crucial to the development of inclusive citizenship and lively political engagement in a democratic society.

> [An] implication of Arendt's stress on the spatial quality of politics has to do with the question of how a collection of distinct individuals can be united to form a political community. What unites people in a political community is therefore not some set of common values, but the world they set up in common, the spaces they inhabit together, the institutions and practices which they share as citizens. To be engaged in politics means actively participating in the various public forums where the decisions affecting one's community are taken. In Arendt's view, only the sharing of power that comes from civic engagement and common deliberation can provide each citizen with a sense of effective political agency.[19]

Thus, according to Arendt, human agency triggered through pluralized, even occasionally conflicting political discourse is the antithesis of dependency. Political discursive agency is contingent on the construction of creative and engaging democratic spaces. Methods used to construct these contemporary discursive spaces have become highly evolved along with available digitized technology to include unconventional political community organizing beyond geographic and temporal boundaries. By providing unlimited opportunities for transnational resistance, these new digitized democratic spaces irrespective of space and time are being carved by Poland's high-tech anarchist activist community in order to facilitate the restoration of human agency, encourage civic engagement, establish the primacy of authentic participatory democratic citizenship over consumptive capitalism, and foster the recognition rights of belongingness that such status confers. These tactics of empowerment are capable of reversing the pacification of the unemployed, debt-accumulating, consuming public, and provide opportunities to maximize human potential through opportunities for civic engagement within the family and community. This active, oppositional, pluralizing, integrating, spatially transcendent form of discursive democracy attempts to combat the isolationism brought on by world systemic arrangements through inclusive and empowering knowledge dissemination, formalized voices for creative and antagonistic state confrontation, and related subversion associated with autonomous living.

> Discourses and the identities produced through them are inherently political entities that involve the construction of antagonisms and the exercise of power. Moreover, because social systems have a fundamentally political character, they are always vulnerable to those forces that are excluded in the process of political formation. The construction and experience of social antagonisms are central for discourse theory. At the outset, social antagonisms introduce an irreconcilable negativity into social relations. This is because they reveal the limit points in society in which social meaning is contested and cannot be stabilised. Antagonisms are thus evidence of the frontiers of social formation [and] occur because social agents are *unable* to attain fully their identity.[20]

Given the vulnerabilities inherent in limitation or their limit points, social systems are not omnipotent and are highly susceptible to a variety of exogenous influences based on unstable, untenable, and unjust operations. Polish anarchists at the semi-periphery, conceptually, temporally, spatially, and geopolitically alienated from these exploitative aristocratic elites, are nevertheless using their experiences in defying both forms of systemic domination promulgated under communism and capitalism through innovative embodied and disembodied resistance simultaneously. They use their oppositional human capital to provide opportunities for participatory democracy by contesting public- and private-sector arrangements on which core-periphery unequal relations are contingent, and encourage discussion and planning on the ways in which dependencies on exogenous hegemonic entities can be steadily dismantled. These tactics often focus on changing production and consumption patterns toward more indigenous local economies of scale, a strategy that is particularly attractive in agrarian-based developing economies such as Poland. Given the landless people's movements in the southern hemisphere, urban homesteading in the West, the global push for small-scale vegetarian slow food production and consumption, and other successful sustainable resistance repertoires nostalgically popularizing underdevelopment around the planet, these and other tactics of liberating anarchist thought are starting to bolster mass social movements against hegemonic states with tremendous ease and success. Before proceding further, it may be useful to explore exchange paradigms that can help to decipher these complex, hegemony-dismantling activities currently deployed by anarchist activists unified in resurgent underdevelopment struggles around the world.

Conceptualizing Dependency

The first study that sought to demonstrate dependency relations and their effects of the elite asserted that resources are routinely used to control and manipulate individuals to align their goals with those in power (Berlew and Hali, 1966). This was the first organizational model of dependency, which demonstrated that the internalization of expected attitudes and standards reinforced desired behaviors among those in lower-status positions. Those striving for managerial ascendancy and other forms of privileged distinction were regarded as agents of dependency, seeking financial and nonfinancial rewards in exchange for reinforced behaviors. Though their analysis was limited to intraorganizational dynamics, the same classic approach can now be applied to explore relations where resource transactions occur across core to periphery within a singular world system. The notion of dependency relations was advanced further through the role of unequal exchanges known as *asymmetry* (Blau, 1964). Exchange theory elaborated on dynamics of power distribution in organizations.

> [F]rom the exchange perspective, behavior of an individual becomes controlled externally when others in that person's environment have power over him and make requests for behavior based on that power. Blau argues that situations of asymmetrical dependence, and hence, asymmetrical power, were not stable in that the less powerful actor would be led to undertake activities to redress that power imbalance.[21]

Through Blau's insight we see the very fragile nature of unequal power exchanges, which by their very nature are highly unstable and tenuous. Resources must constantly be transferred in order for the desired normative effects to be elicited among the collusive elite. This is particularly challenging under conditions of transnational resource exchange from core to semi-periphery during European political integration, because all state industrial production has already been dismantled and privatized in its entirety. With no further industrial resources to be exchanged, collusive elite have no further incentives to continue economic sabotage associated with downward mobility and their collaborative role in indigenous breeding of dependent third worldization in the semi-periphery. In the absence of industrial capital, the continued alignment of elite collaborators with resource-transferring hegemonic bureaucrats at the core is problematic at best. Incentives can be temporarily perpetuated in the form of Western standards of comfort at meetings in Brussels and Luxembourg, but world systemic political arrangements will eventually result in instability in political parties and other collaborating institutions due to widening social distances with the polity. The diminishing intimacy between the elite and the polity in the semi-periphery can be captured through the notion of *social distance scales* (Bogardus, 1926). Social distance was later developed into *power distance cultures* (Hofstede 1984), which highlighted cross-cultural differences in dealing with asymmetrical power exchanges. This

groundbreaking research explored complex authority relations internationally, which viewed high-status elites as *agents of stratification*, who impose
and solidify power disparities and other coercive institutional arrangements in dependency transactions that perpetuate the one-world economy.
The efficacy of power distance measures can be a useful indicator of societal disintegration, but can the prevalence of power distances necessarily
provide evidence of actual collusion among *interlinking hegemonic powers* (Frank, 1966), as advanced in world systems theory? To determine to
what extent these power distances are maximized by *agents of dependency
stratification* to the detriment of vulnerable labor force participants such as
those represented by body-pierced youth communities in the downwardly
mobile semi-periphery, the analysis might now explore traditional safety
net programs historically available to mitigate the effects of failed market
economies through public welfare and private philanthropic efforts.

Unmediated Dependency

Dependencies under conditions of a one-world system are not limited to
trade relations between core and non-core nation-states. Dependency can
also be affected by a variety of public mediating structures (Berger and
Neuhaus, 1996. Research on mediating structures around the world has
described how citizen participation in public and private welfare redistribution schemes has not only fostered civic engagement (Patten, 2002), but also
divided citizens and dismantled national unity in a variety of ways (Mettler,
1998). Reductivist research generally oversimplifies these mediation structures by suggesting that government mediation through welfare functions
divides citizens whereas private nonprofit-sector mediation through charitable activity unites citizens. These oversimplified perspectives hardly capture
global mediation efforts between individuals and their complex superstructures with any level of accuracy. For example, public welfare has been
demonstrated to bifurcate the labor force according to dual labor market
principles (Piven and Cloward, 1971), divide competing beneficiaries by age
cohorts (Wilensky, 1975), deepen existing class factions (Esping-Andersen,
1990), isolate recipients by gender (Scott, 1984), and dismantle the stability of families (Clarke, Cochrane, and Smart, 1987). Private mediation in
the form of nonprofit-sector interventions, on the other hand, has been
described as an instrument of unification based on shared ideological orientation (Meister, 1984), coalescing on political pedagogy (Van Til, 2000),
a centrist influence for marginalized masses (Cohen and Arato, 1992), and
status as the ultimate provider of pluralistic opportunities for participatory
democracy (Ware, 1989). In the case of Poland, the analysis will demonstrate that anarchist pedagogical activities highlight how both public state
welfare and private philanthropy are both failed systems whose operations
do nothing to legitimate neoliberal market economies and provide virtually no mediation for postcommunist societies to mitigate the effects of
hegemonic international trade and its instrumentalizing institutions. The

failure of public and private welfare mediation occurs through detrimental policies instituted by nation-states that simultaneously thwart the ability of charities and welfare programs to buffer the deleterious consequences of failed neoliberal market economics. The innocuousness of private- and public-sector mediation further fuels the popularity of anarchist ideologies among youth, who can perhaps be described as deeply disenfranchised not only from industrial operations, but also from public- and private-sector redistribution efforts that, in the context of postcommunist societies, have never served to alleviate the effects of capitalism on vulnerable marginalized labor market "participants" nor the dependent relations on advanced industrialized nations that accompanies these failures.

The dependency brought on by these asymmetrical relations can perhaps be best explored in light of the resources exchanged through systemic *transaction* paradigms (Handy, 1993, 1999. Here exchanges can be *calculative, cooperative, or coercive*. In this typology, resource exchanges are reduced to their essential relational elements capable of dividing or unifying entities engaging in resource transfer. Because of the pervasive complexity of political, cultural, and economic integration currently taking place, the analysis will explore how transactions among collusive elites are increasingly adversarial, solidified through coercive exchanges, through transactions that breed dependency to the socioeconomic and political benefit of those operating at the core.

Economic Dependency

According to the Critical Dictionary of Global Economics (Beynon, 1988), important measures to determine dependent economic relations involve indices such as import-export trade imbalance, industrial manufacturing, and knowledge scales. Deficits in either imports or exports restrain economic growth in an entity's manufacturing activities, whereas trade imbalance due to overreliance on imported goods is a factor in dependent relations. Competitive industries that make up a significant portion of a nation's independence now require knowledge-intensive manufacturing, and exported goods remain an important indicator of levels of technology transfer in manufacturing and hence overall development.

> Economic theory suggests that there exists a certain pattern...which has been recorded in many countries that nowadays enjoy a level of development. It goes as follows: at the onset, imports exceed exports in a country entering the path of development. In time, the relationship between the import and the export of goods and services is reversed, which make it possible to repay previously incurred debts. In the third phase, intensive export of capital becomes possible, the profits of which in the fourth phase, enable the trade deficit to be overcome. The Polish market economy is still young, which is why it is easier for imports to exceed exports. After all, Poland's partners, particularly in the EU, are able to offer a rich assortment of products.

[The] zloty against foreign currency gives exporters [an advantage in that] imports do indeed become cheaper. Thus in Poland competitiveness understood in this way is falling. Exports should become an important factor in economic growth. The world's major exporters—Japan, South Korea, and Germany—[and especially the] countries of the far East...subsidized export in various ways and introduced strong protectionist policies with regard to their domestic markets. Poland cannot adopt such strategies due to its' striving for membership in the EU. It has to adjust to the rules that are binding in the internal European market.[22]

According to the World Development Report 2000, EU exports between 1990 and 2000 showed a sharp increase for core nations in Ireland, Italy, France, and Belgium and declines in [semi] peripheral nations such as Slovenia (27 percent of GDP), Poland (8 percent), Lithuania (5 percent), and Latvia (4 percent). A decade of "harmonizing" economic policies into the European Union has had a very beneficial effect on the economic strength of core nations through expanded exports, whereas manufactured goods imports have significantly increased in peripheral and semi-peripheral economies.

Technology transfer known as the *embodied technology transmission* theory is another alleged indicator of economic stability. In an extensive study conducted between 1970 and 1991 covering 8 core countries (Canada, France, Germany, Italy, Japan, Sweden, United Kingdom, and United States), 13 UN International Standard Industrial classified industries were examined

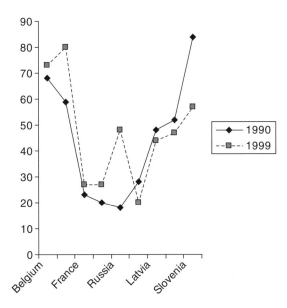

Figure 3   Changes in Exports in EU Nations between 1990 and 2000

Source: World Development Report, 2000

with regard to endogenous and exogenous productivity effects from domestic and foreign research and development. Import weighted foreign research and development along with bilateral import flows obtained from the World Trade Database of the Hamburg Institute of Economic Research were examined to determine if there are any plausible benefits of technology transfer to a nation's manufacturing productivity. The study concluded that the embodied technology transmission hypothesis leads to almost no beneficial impact to a nation's trade of manufactured goods, particularly in exchanges between advanced and less-developed industrial sectors.

> [T]he finding that in research and development intensive industries there is only a relative small gain from foreign same industry research and development is consistent with the notion that market conduct....tends to be monopolistically competitive, with internalization of the return to the research and development investment being a primary concern, and where there is therefore little [transfer of technologies] innovative products among competing firms.[23]

The illusion that technology-intensive industrial manufacturing is transferable to underprivileged firms or across competitive national boundaries is therefore fully disputed in critical economic analyses (Cowen, 1988), and flies in the face of neoclassic economics, which posits that "strong positive comovement of GDP and employment...is generally characteristic of changes in technology to business cycles" (Gali, 1996). In fact, according to research commissioned by the National Bureau of Economic Research, even when a new technology is successfully implemented in manufacturing sectors of advanced industrialized nations, the immediate effects felt within core nations paradoxically manifests as a decline in employment.

> [T]o the extent that technology shocks are a significant source of fluctuations in those variables, we would expect Recognizable Business Cycle models to provide at least an accurate description of the economy's response to such shocks. For the majority of the G7 countries, however, positive tech shocks lead to a decline in employment and tend to generate a negative co-movement between that variable [condition] and productivity.[24]

As far as imports as a dependency measure are concerned, the privatization and subsequent dismantling of the entire nation's manufacturing industry as part of postcommunist 'efficiency' transformation has resulted in the entire collapse of industrial self-sufficiency previously enjoyed under communism, which historically operated for the benefit of an exploitative Soviet economy. To determine from what source these imported goods into Poland originated and if dependency is contingent on core nations as advanced in world systems theory, data from the International Trade Statistics Yearbook were examined and the results are presented below.

According to the data on exports presented above, 92.8 percent of all goods imported by Poles originate in the core nations. Removing the cases of Russia and the United States (together composing 13.7 percent of Polish imports), Poland is dependent on European core nations for 79.1 percent

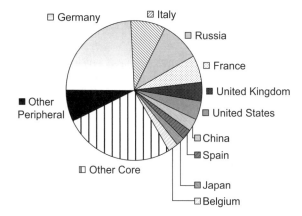

Figure 4   Source of Manufactured Goods Imported into Poland by Core-Peripheral Classification, 2000

Source: International Trade Statistics Yearbook

of all manufactured goods imported. The biggest source of dependency is Germany representing nearly a quarter of Polish imports (23.8 percent), followed by Italy and France (14.6 percent). Goods manufactured in peripheral nations around the world represent 7.2 percent of all of Poland's imports. The evidence therefore supports the assertion that Poland's separation from the Soviet Union and subsequent integration into the EU has been very fortuitous for manufacturing sectors found in the core nations of Europe, resulting in Poland's economic dependency on Western Europe for the provision of nearly all its consumables. These conditions are consistent with world systems theory, which posits that a single world market composed of trimodal geographically distinct regions involving groups pursuing special economic interests composed of uneven production advanced by coercive political structures made up of collusive government elites operating in the interest of hegemonic forces seeking political stability to drive the expansion of exploitative global capitalist empire is detrimental to those outside hegemonic regions concentrated in a geopolitical core.

Knowledge Dependency

In addition to a variety of economic indices surrounding declining exports, the innocuousness of industrial technology transfer, and other types of dependency-breeding trade imbalances, knowledge is another crucial element in the cultural production of pacification associated with domination by hegemonic world system interests. To maintain the tenuous and fragile position of core global superiority, nation-states are now in the process of shifting peripheral and semi-peripheral societies into a pervasive devolutionary phase of disengagement and disenlightenment, leading to a state that Grossberg (2005) calls *antiknowledge culture*. It is argued that the stability of economic systemic domination is reinforced by limiting the public's access to information in a return to the Dark Ages as a normative mechanism of oppression.

> The first symptom of the new antiknowledge culture is the denial of the need for the best information possible, on both the part of the government and the public. Since the late eighteenth century, modern governments have attempted to control the behavior of populations without force, and this has required improving their knowledge of the population. Yet over the past twenty-five years, they have moved in the opposite direction, limiting both the accumulation and the availability of information about the country and its people. This diminishes what one might call the collective intelligence of the nation and alters the accountability of the government.[25]

The avoidance of exorbitant expenditures and risk of delegitimacy associated with militaristic intervention of the masses, coupled with the turn toward highly effective nonviolent collusively engineered means of normative controls surrounding material culture, have together resulted in the solidification of antiknowledge environments through public disinformation campaigns. Not only are economic elites relevant but political entities also figure prominently in the orchestration of inauthentic knowledge as part of the concerted effort to conceal the genuine realities of socioeconomic and political conditions facing most of the world's population entering the twenty-first century.

> [T]echnological revolution perpetuates the interests of the dominant economic and political powers, intensifies divisions between haves and have-nots, and is a defining feature of a new and improved form of global technocapitalism.[26]

Knowledge-driven *technocapitalism* assuring uneven knowledge circulation benefiting the core is further reinforced by disinformation campaigns perpetuated by an educational system that functions largely to socialize obedience and discourage the questioning of authority, venerate state violence (Lewis, 1971), and reproduce the existing class structure (Giroux, 1983).

> From the point of view of truth production, however, the central question is not whether the truth is true or false, scientific or ideological, but how it is produced, circulated, transformed, and used. State educational discourse is a truth discourse in many senses. First, state educational discourse defines what is 'true' but at the same time, what is 'not true'. Second, official discourse tends to define the 'right' and 'not right', creating the basis for certain kind of self-evident, taken-for granted consensus about what kind of practical decisions and actions are accepted, legitimized, and justified. Finally, the official discourse also seeks to determine what is 'good' and 'not good' [and] to define the identity of the subjects—what they have been, what they are, and what they will be.[27]

To advance the authority of public education entities through these *nonobjective truth discourses*, religious institutions, especially in Poland, are offered carte blanche intervention by the state to mutilate pedagogical curriculum with disinformation so subjective as even to deny papal authority and conceal official church encyclicals on the compatibility of science (John Paul II, 1996). Such a subjective, anti-scientific, dogmatic, antiknowledge political agenda is not limited to misinterpretation among conservative Christian political party-driven Poland, but has also led to the dismantling of scientific institutions that have historically collaborated with government to advance complex public policies in Washington, DC. As part of the new cult to restrain upward economic mobility and diminish distinction and excellence among the masses, antiknowledge culture distinguishes and rewards mediocrity, redesigns innovative critical thinking as sanctionable disobedience, and further contributes to downward cultural mobility and third worldization via the dissemination of disinformation discourses. These draconian educational policies disempower the public, discourage independent thought, and prohibit objective scientific curriculum pertaining to sex education, Darwinian evolution, birth control, the laws of theoretical physics surrounding the origins of the universe, rational decision making, and other elements of cognitive, human, and thus collective development.

Dependency-breeding attacks on knowledge do not end with schools and government. The most vehement attack on independent information acquisition is unequivocally the mass media. Dependency brought on by knowledge circulation through mass media is highly biased in favor of dominating elite interests, with optimistic subjectivity significantly coloring economic, political, and financial information. Where economic optimism fails to elicit the requisite trust and obedience in experts, other skilled masters in the art of collusively engineered normative controls generate dependency on authoritative powers through fear campaigns (Altheide, 2002). Those in control of the means of interpretation and communication render innocuous the concerns of the disenfranchised (Chomsky, 1999). Through digitized technologies and the perpetual 24-hour news cycle, the mass media use an innovative combination of false optimism and fear of threatening adversaries to pacify the masses and build trust in experts in order for hegemonic instruments to persistently advance elite interests (Cohen, 1972; Fowler, 1991; Romanienko, 2002).

> The term hegemony refers to a situation in which provisional alliance of certain groups can exert 'total authority' over other subordinate groups, not simply by coercion or by the direct imposition of ruling ideas, but by 'winning and shaping consent so that the power of the dominant classes appears both legitimate and natural'.[28]

Nowhere is the intentional shaping of subordination more powerful than through the foreign-owned postcommunist media. According to a report by the European Federation of Journalists, foreign ownership of print media in postcommunist countries is so pervasive that it "is threatening pluralism and undermining journalists' professional and social rights" (European

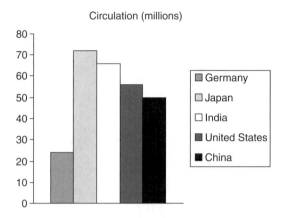

Figure 5   World Print Media Ownership
Source: World Bank and the World Association of Newspapers, 1999

Federation of Journalists, 2003). Media in these countries are now controlled by the largest firms in Europe, all German-owned: Axel-Springer Verlag, Westdeutsche Allgemeine Zeitung, Passauer Neue Presse, and Gruner Jahr. Among postcommunist countries, Poland is no exception, with 80 percent of all Polish media controlled by foreign interests. Fifty percent of all magazines sold in Poland are owned by German firms, 40 percent of newspapers sold in Poland are owned by German, Norwegian, and Italian firms.

Postcommunist media is firmly under the control of German and other aristocratic elites located in old European core states. Due to these systemic arrangements, not only is disinformation surrounding economic, social, political, and cultural life disseminated by foreign-owned core business interests, but perhaps most destructively, inauthentic information is widely circulated intentionally underestimating the power and scale of political resistance efforts currently underway among anarchists and other activists, in order to undermine their popularity among frustrated victims left devastated in the wake of *economic neopograms* known as *shock therapy* instituted by a handful of dilettante experimental economists and resisted by those whose voices were suppressed while trying to demask their destructive outcomes.[29]

> [S]tudents of social movements have not yet fully or systematically considered the suppression of dissent or the demobilization of social movements. Through framing, the mass media depict social movements in specific, and sometimes deprecatory, ways. This has important effects on social movements participants, potential recruits or supporters, and movement adversaries. In a democratic society, where open coercion is not an option that can be used too often without losing legitimacy, the state must come up with subtler ways to maintain social control. In sum, most research on the suppression of social movements considers the direct violence that the state uses to quell dissent while it ignores the myriad ways in which dissent is proactively

challenged through more subtle modes. On the political terrain of crisis, dissent is often framed by the state and mass media in terms of negation, and in terms of criticism and objection, which downplays, if not elides its' regenerative aspects rooted in creativity, conscientiousness, and courage. Dissenting citizens not only speak to perceived dangers and problems in society, but they also speak to the opportunities and possibilities of vigorous political life.[30]

Print and other forms of core-owned media in postcommunist semiperipheral countries such as Poland are therefore the newest technocapitalist instruments used to widen social distances, naturalize asymmetric international trade relations, constrain the public's familiarity with resistance through contemporary collective action, and pursue other suspended forms of truth manipulation. Staniszkis (1995) attributes the evolution of anti-knowledge culture taking place in Poland as part of a larger process associated with pseudodemocracy and failed statehood.

> Firstly, while a façade of parliamentary democracy does exist, the real centers of power (which are dispersed and unable to control the whole process of transformation) are situated below the level of parliamentary and party politics, within the structures of a strongly internalized corporatism. In fact, as has been indicated, this is corporatism of a special type. Its social contours are highly deficient and selective, with the articulation of only certain interests eliciting a response from the decision-makers. [W]hat we are witnessing are explicit attempts to technocratize the decision-making process and exempt it, as it were, from the area of open politics that is subject to public control and conducted by elected bodies of government. The objective of this technocratization of major decisions is to assume control of the sphere of structural power, thereby gaining the capacity to determine the shape of newly-established institutions and rules of conduct. In particular, what is at stake is the ability to influence the components of the market infrastructure that define the opportunities for capital formation, the level of transfer costs and access to institutions that lower that cost, and finally, procedures for redistribution. This [involves] weak political sphere of the state and a weak, atomized society. Its traits include selectivity, the over-representation of interests of the "political capitalists", and a high degree of internationalization (where elected bodies of government are more conscious of their responsibility to the international institutions supervising the process of transformation e.g., the IMF, than to their own electors).[31]

At this point, we can conceptualize systemic relations even further by exploring the third and final construct of dependency, the distribution of occupational rewards in everyday life.

Occupational Dependency

Resource transactions driving dependency relationships in a one-world systemic economy are not limited to economic and knowledge instruments, but are also found in the form of normative controls instituted through *occupational rewards* (Barley, Meyer, and Gash, 1988). Occupational rewards distributed unevenly through coercive transactions within an extremely scarce resource, high unemployment, turbulent postcommunist economic environment has a profound impact in constructing dependency relations, particularly among international employers from highly developed knowledge-intensive production industries from the West. Research in organizations has previously shown that there are significant differences in worker orientation toward managerial attainment and other occupational rewards based on internal and external labor market classifications. Reward orientations can be classified based on external labor market variables such as gender, marital status, and family size, or internal labor market variables such as satisfaction, commitment, managerial attainment, and perceptions of alternative opportunities available. More relevant to the analysis pertaining to anarchist resistance of neoliberal market economics is, however, the fact that a highly utilitarian labor market typology has emerged, bifurcating motivation through either *intrinsic rewards* such as those involving optimizing challenge, talent, recognition, and autonomy, or *extrinsic rewards* involving optimizing wages, security, travel, fringe benefits, and other measurable forms of remuneration (Huang and de Vliert, 2003). These powerful dimensions motivating occupational stability have yet to be applied in examining dependency relations, and not in any work-related context beyond labor markets. Yet the intrinsic and extrinsic reward factors surrounding achievement can be used to advance dependency in socioeconomic and cultural contexts beyond collapsed and innocuous labor markets, particularly in transfers of achievement and related rewards away from innocuous labor market opportunities toward more hospitable, rewards-generating activism. In other words, as postcommunist occupational opportunity structures continue to constrain possibilities for achieving any type of rewards, individuals maintain their orientation toward achievements, but transfer efforts toward resistance tactics found in activist work. The analysis intends to demonstrate that anarchist activist communities such as the saboteur network in Poland provide disenfranchised young people with substantial opportunities for effective achievements surrounding intrinsic and extrinsic rewards through alternative labor known as collective action. To understand the contemporary transfer of orientation toward achievement from remunerated work to unremunerated activism lies in the historical absence of motivating achievement factors under communism.

> Promotions were awarded primarily on socio-political considerations, therefore, workers perceived minimal reward for expending extra effort on the job. In fact, in traditional socialist societies, qualities associated with motivation such as achievement, ambition, and initiative were viewed with suspicion and contempt. Risk-taking was suppressed. Individuals who showed signs of excelling within groups were seen as destructive for group harmony. Historically, the "Red Managers" experienced little pressure to perform, their promotions being dependent on...connections and party loyalty [and were]

identified as "micro-managers" and "macro-puppets." Numerous motivation theories exist, but [e]xpectancy theory suggests that people are driven by the expectation that their behaviors will produce results and that the results will lead to desired outcomes/rewards. [It] assumes that people feel they have control over their environment.[32]

A casual observer might consider how so many Polish ex-communist elites have become such passive and collusive agents of dependency fostering hegemonic interests.

Not only state-owned enterprises are involved in shaping the trajectories of exit, but so are hybrid property forms that combine features of the preexisting governance structure and public property rights to gain competitive advantages in the transition economy. Economic liberalization releases the old communist elite from preexisting organizational controls, enabling them to pursue rents in boundary transactions between the public and market sectors of the transition economy. Because of the continuities in the underlying institutional arrangements, e.g. property rights and work organizations, the communist elite can maintain considerable power and privileges, resulting in persistent or even augmented cadre advantages under conditions of market reform. This is the power persistence argument [where] the old communist elite sought to adapt to regime change by converting its political and social capital—positional power and network ties—into economic capital in the newly privatized corporate economy. [The power persistence paradigm assumes] an ease of convertibility of political capital into economic capital in the transition from state socialism.[33]

To understand the role of corrupt elite in peripheral and semiperipheral societies, referred to above as the *power persistence argument* (which allows exogenous hegemonic entities to occupy and exploit natural, human, and other nation-state resources), realize that a powerful causal factor driving these collusive arrangements is that neither the polity nor its leadership has ever had the benefit of intrinsic rewards under either communism or capitalism. Although a nonmaterial, ideological, intrinsic reward orientation might be useful in cross-cultural analysis in advanced industrialized societies with robust labor markets competing for high skilled workers (Romanienko, 2001), it is unable to capture any postcommunist worker motivation where even the best jobs offered by the most stable international employers offer little possibility for optimization of even minimal intrinsic rewards. In postcommunist society, there is not now, has never been, and likely *never will be* any semblance of a labor market so stable or competitive as to provide opportunities for quantifiable nonmaterial esoteric intrinsic occupational rewards typically available through primary-tier opportunities in advanced industrialized dual labor market economies.

Under the Communist system, young people did not have the luxury nor perhaps the need . . . to explore directions for their future. Education did not have a payoff in extrinsic rewards such as better paying jobs. [T]here were also few intrinsic rewards to education under the socialist system [with] prejudice against advanced education and intellectualism.[34]

Left only with deflated wages distributed in unstable, temporary, coercive secondary-tier transactions from core to semi-periphery with few extrinsic and even fewer intrinsic rewards, the cadre of collusive elites that enabled unregulated business operations to flourish in new European postcommunist nation-states has exhausted any possibility of continuing these exploitative arrangements for the future (Ost, 2005; Kubicek, 2004; Kolinsky and Nickel, 2003). Given the lack of production activities, the skeletal remnants of consumer culture, mass unemployment, and suspended animation of statelessness associated with disenfranchisement within one's own homeland, the profound alienation of young activists is and will continue to be at an all-time high. These arrangements and the anarchist resistance efforts that foment as a result have had significant impact on the successful strategic transfer of rewards from occupations to other action-oriented segments of civic engagement creating an anti-antiknowledge mobilized society demanding reintegration and reversal of systemic statelessness. System theorists consider actions that seek to expand access to valid information and free choice to be formal systemic interventions.

> Intervention may be defined as a process of planned change aimed at helping an ongoing social system to become more effective in determining its purpose, and designing its problem-solving, decision-making, and operational tasks to achieve these purposes. [T]he social system exists independently of the intervening change agent. [The] social system that has [demonstrated] a need for diagnosis and/or change to an interventionist... must be considered as an ongoing, independent entity that controls its own future.[35]

Through this dependency interventionist framework, the analysis will show precisely how digitized embodied and disembodied anarchist resistance efforts operate to combat or otherwise subvert the systemic processes in a profoundly coercive one-world economy.

Image 1 Building Facade in Torino, Italy, by Dr. Alessandra Rusconi of WZB Social
Science Research Center of Berlin

Image 2 "New Species" Suspension Party in Leoncavallo, Italy, by Alex Canazei (see http://www.alexcanazei.com)

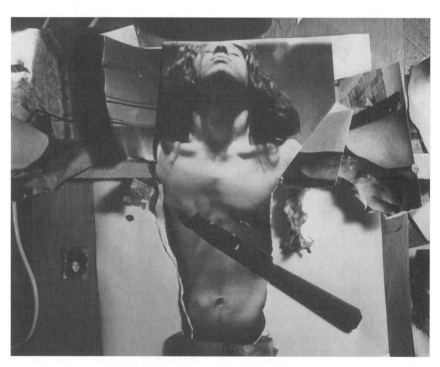

Image 3 *Selfcrucifixion*, I, 1973, performance at One Person Gallery, Wrocław, Poland, photograph, *100 × 75cm, author:* © Andrzej Dudek Dürer

Image 4 Mokry, Lead Singer from the Wrocław crustcore band Infekcjia, photographed by Marta of the Noise and the Fury

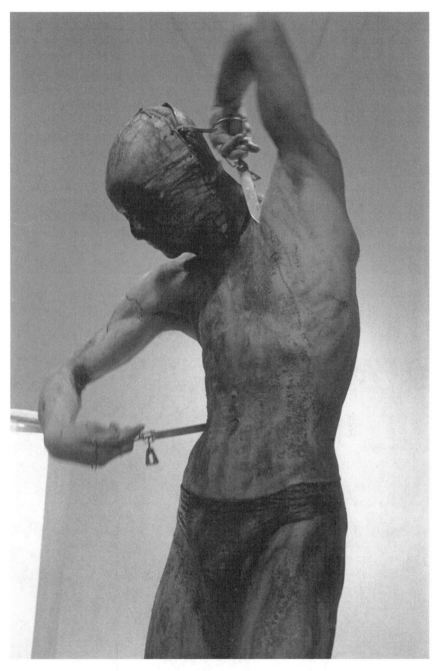

Image 5 Micha Brendel, Performance Artist from Thüringen, Germany

Image 6   Motorcycle club member funeral in Poland

Image 7   Website promotional graffiti at the Wagenburg EcoSquat of Wroclaw

Image 8 World music from Brazil known as the Anti Virus Projekt [Anti_Virus@gmx.de] performing at Wagenburg, Wroclaw

Image 9 Pirate Circus France, performing at the Wagenburg EcoSquat in Wroclaw

Image 10 Bodgo, Resident of the Wagenburg EcoSquat of Wroclaw

Image 11   Guests at the Wagenburg EcoSquat of Wroclaw

Image 12   Guests at the Wagenburg EcoSquat of Wroclaw

Image 13   Guests at the Wagenburg EcoSquat of Wroclaw

Image 14   Dzik [Wild One], Resident of the Wagenburg EcoSquat of Wroclaw

Images 6 through 14   Courtesy of the author's private collections

6
Digital Contestation

According to Habermas, the quest for emancipation and liberation must begin with the achievement of undistorted communication. Habermas identified the institutionalization of domination in the reproduction of distorted communication. Individuals must work to create a dialogue in which all participants are treated as equals.

Wilkie and Bartoy, 2000

Background

Given the lengthy socioeconomic world system and political agency approach presented thus far, the challenge for the body-modified anarchist activist community has rested on the ways the underlying sentiments of alienation, pseudoindividualization, and disenfranchisement can be productively harnessed to reverse these systemic arrangements. This has culminated in the worldwide discursive resistance endeavor known collectively as the *alterglobalization* movement. As this analysis will demonstrate, the effective mobilization of so many disaffected young people has been facilitated through the strategic development of a digitized global saboteur network involving anarchists and other activists who "take possession of a space" online (Bodker and Christiansen, 2006). By offering do it yourself [DIY] alternatives to knowledge and consumption dependency patterns, by deconstructing what I call *failure camouflage* in traditional societal settings, and by providing opportunities to obtain alternative intrinsic and extrinsic rewards through collective action, digitized body-pierced anarchists are in the process of acculturating subversive dissenters into nonoccupational mechanisms of achievement through reorientation away from private goods and toward collective labor. These resistance efforts, simultaneously addressing the global and the local, enable young activists to maximize their political agency, become empowered through diverse opportunities for civic engagement, and develop their human potential by focusing on nonmaterial, esoteric, intrinsic rewards increasingly rare in an unregulated neoliberal market context. The following analysis will demonstrate that anarchist discourse highlighting the uneven distribution of extrinsic and intrinsic occupational rewards provides audiences with valuable insight into the possibility of minimizing power distances, reversing democratic failures, and creating a more hospitable socioeconomic and political environment to foster harmonious cooperative exchanges within a politically mobilized climate of autonomous living. The *sources* of distributed resources, as well as the *method* of distribution (which can both breed dependency), will be shown to significantly influence broad anarchist coalitions throughout the transatlantic activist community. By exploring these factors, our analysis will be able to capture, with some level of specificity, efforts to reverse sentiments of alienation that are inherent in rapidly deteriorating labor markets via the construction of defiant networks of anarchist resistance on- and offline.

The evidence presented thus far has demonstrated that the detrimental effects of dependency relations from a world systems perspective are rooted in a complex series of resource exchanges that are transferred in an environment of artificial scarcity. This environment is constructed using asymmetrical power relations contingent on maximizing social distances through the alienation of a collusive elite away from a fragmented semi-peripheral polity in an unrestricted exploitative neoliberal failing market economy. The situation is exacerbated by the lack of industrial production, and conspicuous consumption without legitimating mediation from either private charitable or public welfare institutions. The result is severe socioeconomic and cultural deprivation camouflaged by family discretion and predatory lending. At this point in our analysis, it might be useful to examine the online elements of political resistance that are attempting to prevent these unequal power exchanges from continuing to take place. These complex deleterious systemic conditions have led to the emergence of a formalized discursive oppositional anarchist online community using communicative resistance strategies that deploy dual-edged tactics of bodily and disembodied digitized mechanisms of dissent. Evidence will demonstrate that failed democracy in lieu of plebiscitary rule by postcommunist elite attempting to maximize power distances through normative transactions coercively transferred from core to periphery in a scarce resource environment perpetuates smoldering discontent among defiant youth. This smoldering discontent leads to the construction of embodied discursive resistance communities on- and offline, building an inclusive oppositional sabotage dialogue project, to ensure that autonomous voices perpetuating independent living are represented. This mobilization approach toward activist cultures falls under the rubric of consensus building.

Why is cultural consensus analysis so popular? Arguably, it is because it addresses a significant problem: ethnographers, although untutored in the truth of the local culture under investigation, desire to properly characterize the beliefs and values of the group they study. [I]t is possible for individuals in a cultural group to show a significant degree of uniformity, despite the lack of socially defined and culturally transmitted system of beliefs about that domain of experience.[1]

This *cultural consensus approach* can therefore be useful to illustrate the distinct ways that stakeholders in dissenting anarchist networks discursively resist processes of political integration, capitalist transformation, and disparate class stratification through online activism. This effort represents the construction of a powerful *system of oppositional consensus* that unifies geographically and philosophically fragmented activists by constructing an alternative to world systemic globalization, or an alterglobalization. The analysis intends to show that body-modified anarchist activists are profoundly affected by an environment that presents significant challenges to their existence based on unequal economic, political, and social power relations in a developing setting. By linking the political and social structure to individual resistance ideologies articulated on the body and through digitized networks, we may begin to understand the ways in which the awareness of deprivation due to emerging systemic inequalities and modernity is vehemently contested by this emerging contemporary digitized discursive resistant youth movement.

> Not only activists and movement scholars but also Western governments are impressed by the Internet as a mobilization facilitator. As evidenced in an official report on the website of the Canadian Security Intelligence Service devoted to anti-globalization protest: "The Internet has breathed new life into the anarchist philosophy, permitting communication and coordination without the need for a central source of command, and facilitating coordinated actions with minimal resources and bureaucracy."[2]

Keeping in mind the lack of conventional mediating institutions (Gillett, 2003) and predominance of coercive transactions imposed by a West-placating hegemonic elite exacerbating the profound inequality found in transitional contexts (Szelenyi, 1988), it might be helpful at this point to focus on the technological factors that enable these popular, powerful, tightly knit, body modified, alterglobalizing anarchist networks to proliferate in Poland and beyond (Jones, 1999; Marham, 1998).

Alternative Media

According to many anarchists interviewed throughout this study, conventional media is construed as tremendously skewed in the interest of economic power holders that own and disseminate biased information to distract the public. And they are not alone in their assessment. Research has shown that very little content is devoted to critical analyses of business or government, and almost no space or time in conventional media is devoted to social problems that economic arrangements create or the social movements that seek to reverse these trends (Dahlgren, 2005). Substantive media coverage has, as demonstrated in longitudinal analyses, actually decreased reporting on socially relevant issues over time.

> [The trend in] levels of environmental reporting are lower [representing merely] two percent of key evening news coverage. Furthermore, in a tightly reasoned study [researchers] have demonstrated that existing media coverage generally reflects the dominant ideological and economic power-structures operating in a particular market. [T]he tendency of the media [is] to rely upon industrial sources of information more than the public relations of [advocacy] groups. In an effort to be sensational, timely, and simple, media formats underemphasize risks and over-dramatize the spin on...disputes. Thus the general public is left with a body of hardly controversial information and very little direction in terms of what one should do with such input.[3]

Given the innocuous orientation of conventional media, ICT has provided a powerful and stable platform for the conceptualization, dissemination, and evolution of independent, unbiased, and uncommodified sources of alternative information benefiting individuals concerned with sense making in an otherwise complex world (Earl, 2006; Bansler and Havn, 2006; Robertson, 2002). Prior research has shown that the key elements in the platform's rapid popularity among communities of activists are primarily user and environmental awareness (Sanchez-Franco and Roldan, 2005) as well as potential opportunities for interaction (LaRose, Mastro, and Eastin; 2001). The Web provides refreshing opportunities to expand awareness of the existence of like-minded others (Leinonen, Jarvela, and Kakkinen, 2005) and for direct interactive involvement among highly motivated users (Stivers, 2004). These are just a few of the many extrinsic and intrinsic rewards offered by ICT that are left completely unsatisfied by conventional content historically made available through passive unidirectional communications offered through television and print media.

> [E]xpectations were significant predictors of Internet usage. [P]ersistence is an inherent characteristic of individuals with high self-efficacy. Self-disparagement and self-slighting had strong negative correlations with Internet usage in themselves. It may be that the interactive nature of Internet consumption makes it more salient than passive consumption of conventional mass media.[4]

How does ICT provide motivated users with the potential for environmental and interaction awareness? Opportunities are fostered through technical filtering, known also as *path and pattern recognition systems*. Through technical path and pattern recognition systems of filtration, ICT is now capable of bringing users the information they demand based on immediate analysis of similar user needs. This technological breakthrough has brought users relevant online information with unprecedented precision, regardless of subject content. In this way, fragmented communities of any type, living in geographically distinct regions, may gain rapid access to content deemed popular with users reflecting similar needs. Through these high-tech pattern and path collaborative filtering systems, users become aware of online tendencies of like users, enabling environmental and interactive awareness to emerge simultaneously. Whether users are rural swingers in search of partners for wife-swapping, religious fanatics who articulate hate in the American "Bible Belt," or industry day trading stock analysts; these path and pattern recognition systems are able to spatially concentrate and deliver tailored content of interest swiftly and with stunning precision.

> Also known as recommender systems, collaborative filtering forms an important approach to the sharing and awareness of information amongst a group of people. In loose terms, collaborative filtering [elicits website activity patterns and] recommends new objects that similar people liked. Patterns to some extent involve awareness of a trusted author, while paths involve awareness of colleagues to draw on. In making such comparisons...we wish to show...how artifacts, human activity involving them, and particular people are represented using the formal vocabularies of computers. This in turn determines what aspects of awareness and interpretation the computer supports, and what is left to human interpretation and language.[5]

Though the role of computers in unifying fragmented communities is a relatively new area for scholarly inquiry, these recommender systems and the egalitarian platforms they provide are becoming the key element in the unification of diverse disenfranchised publics. Technological advances in these recognition systems have leveled the playing field and enabled sabotaging resistance efforts to be integrated just as rapidly and precisely as the strategic circulation of unregulated neoliberal capital around the world. These recognition systems furthermore enable important information to be exchanged among relevant audiences and, in the process, enhance awareness of like-minded users, as well as disseminating the conditions of deprivation and other environmental factors they operate within. According to Ben-Rafael and Sternberg, "[t]ransnational diasporas crystallize lines of social solidarity that cross-cut nations and continents and become a driving power for both the multiculturalism of societies, and for globalization."[6] For our analytic purposes, user and environmental awareness of *diasporic deprivation* will be shown to be the primary unifying concept enabling philosophically diverse, geographically distinct *alterglobalizers* to access the online content they require to advance, legitimate, and unify (through articulation of public dissent) their geographically fragmented but periodically coalesced oppositional consensus movement. In the process, they exhibit highly efficient, technology-driven, defiant community construction capabilities among world system saboteurs around the globe.

> The very term "antiglobalization movement" is controversial and suggests a somewhat artificial coherence. Nevertheless, in the wake of Seattle, this quite diverse and eclectic mix of groups and movements was now lumped together...and there was a broad—if often grudging—recognition across

the political spectrum that this was a politically significant movement. The broad point was that the effort to cast questions of trade as exclusively about trade served precisely to obscure their more wide-ranging connections and contradictions. To privilege the mobility of capital was thus to disparage the mobility of labor and with that to contribute to a sometimes xenophobic anti-immigrant racism. The enhanced capital mobility of neoliberal globalization created competitive pressures that drove down wages and labor conditions. For activists, the project of globalization was less about dissolving boundaries for the greater good of all, but rather in configuring various boundaries in ways that selectively privileged an already global elite.[7]

The interconnectivity facilitated by ICT and the precision of its filtering recognition systems bring integrative content as well as nonintegrative content associated with globalization. Though there may be many geographic, ideological, dogmatic, educational, and philosophic distinctions among its members, the online alterglobalizing platform has provided a discursive space to explore the interconnectedness of contemporary social problems, which in turn leads to discourses on the interconnectedness of solutions, which in turn leads to interconnectedness of a mass societal worldwide resistance endeavor to publicly implement these devolutionary tactics.

> Increasingly, social problems are expanding beyond national borders. A shift in one country's economy can have profound effects on the international market and economic health of other nations. As problems are becoming more transnational, so too are movements for social change. Activists are stretching beyond state boundaries to work in solidarity with those with whom they identify in distant countries.[8]

The precision path and pattern recognition available through ICT platforms sensitizes users to specificities of alterglobalization. Content brings about a level of awareness that has not merely resulted in protests or other participatory democratic attacks on hegemonic agents of dependency stratification on- and offline. Directed content has actually increased cultural capital among resistors as they exchange aesthetic, social, cultural, political, and other informative resources throughout their consensually oppositional digitized network. This has led to a powerful form of insurgency and related community building within the constraints and limitations of different formations of struggle.

> The beginnings of the twenty-first century have been dominated by contradictory and chaotic processes of globalization. Right across the planet there are signs of the changes at work, from globalization of the economy...to the increasing import of global fashion, architectural styles, consumption patterns, and celebrities. Our sense of living in a global world has been heightened by increased awareness of the interconnectedness of new types of problems from pollution, global warming, or failed states. All these cut across borders [enabling] new kinds of networks and flows of communication, action, and experience [called] global movements. [C]ondemnations of

globalization...perpetuate a view of the global as constituted by an active dominant center...forced to defend themselves against a process originating from outside.[9]

This new-century digitized discourse revolves around the articulation of defense strategies against a coercive, hegemonic, dominating other whose demands for obedience from the masses results in oppositional fervor globally (Jordan and Taylor, 2004), while enabling activists to accumulate high levels of alternative cultural capital locally (Nakamura, 2002). Although the amassing of human capital, including defiant displays of piercing and other forms of body modification, may indeed be occurring in distinct ways at the individual level, of interest here are the particular ways that these resistance efforts lead to online interaction known as *interfacing* to facilitate the circulation of resistance capital at the community level (Johnson, 1997). The involvement of individuals in resistance capital circulation occurs through profound familiarity with complex social, economic, and cultural knowledge disseminated by both body-modified and unmodified activists. This provides strong evidence that the pacification, dependency, and antiknowledge campaigns attempted by hegemonic partnerships between big business and big government are already in the process of being significantly sabotaged online. Research suggests there are four dimensions of capital accumulation leading to conventional online community building that are widely in operation (Pinkett, 2003).

> I define community cultural capital as various forms of knowledge, skills, abilities, and interests which have particular relevance or value within a community. Activated community cultural capital constitutes: a.) exchanging knowledge and resources b.) improving technology fluency and the ability of community members to express themselves via technology c.) coalescing around shared interests and d.) shifting individuals' attitudes and perceptions of themselves and the world.[10]

The current treatment seeks to extend this conventional capital argument to suggest that the accumulation of cultural capital among online politically oriented anarchist activists is so high at both individual and community levels that users are not only satisfied by their interfacing integration into existing consensual digitized global resistance endeavors, but are also motivated and gratified by very high levels of intrinsic and extrinsic rewards available through alternative digitized media content. ICT offers users genuine opportunities for subversive activities and a variety of other collective action on- and offline, while providing interactive content to immediately rectify dependency-breeding lifestyles through the do it yourself punk worldview, enabling online alternative cultural capital to flourish through access to relevant literary, visual, music, and other aesthetic accoutrement.

> [U]nder conditions of globalization, it must certainly retain all its former capacity to speak to the conditions of human beings whose way of life is

impinged upon by the pressures of an alien modernization. There are various components of action under this revolutionary narrative: the prospect/threat of irreversible change, the supposition of power on the part of some or other agents to advance, prevent, or divert that change; and some end-state to which that change is directed.[11]

The goals of these revolutionary narratives are explicitly articulated as the reversal of dependency through self-sufficiency and a reorientation of achievement, coupled with the unique independence and empowerment associated with anarchist worldviews and related discourse. Online content enables users to subvert asymmetrical power distances under a one-world economy by obtaining rewards previously available only through participation in primary-tier labor market opportunities. Although online alterglobalization content makes low or no user demands with nearly no normative mechanisms of social control, the willingness of activists to conceptualize and struggle concretely toward an alternative vision for a globalized utopian future is a powerful and efficient motivating factor to coalesce previously fragmented activists under broader universal ideological auspices of self-sufficiency and socioeconomic justice. Thus, conventional community organizing and participation in occupations are increasingly being abandoned for their failures to create needed social change, in lieu of digitized community alternatives to lived activism. User gratification needs remain unchanged, but are instead reoriented and redirected toward nonremunerative mechanisms of achievement involving intrinsic rewards circulated among virtual fellow saboteurs that may be geographically isolated and fragmented.

> The communications field has witnessed an explosion of Internet studies employing uses and gratifications approach. The major assumptions of this theory—that audiences are goal directed and actively seek out media to satisfy specific needs—appears well suited to study a medium with interactive applications. [P]olitically interested Internet users [access] the web mainly for guidance [and] information. [Our] study found that politically interested web users were motivated to go online for different reasons than the general public, and therefore participated in [action and knowledge based] activities online.[12]

If digitized platforms have indeed been effective in unifying distinct voices of systemic resistance around the globe through new awareness of alternative guidance and information (Terranova, 2004), how does it accomplish these political objectives, and what, if anything, motivates users, known as cyberactivists or hacktivists, to engage in these innovative mechanisms of unconventional community building? ICT digitized discursive platforms place low or no demands on users, have virtually no rules and regulations, possess essentially no censorship policies, have relatively no stipulation for participation, attempt no normative imposition of censorship or other social controls distorting communication, perpetuate essentially no hierarchies, and offer no financial remuneration or other immediate tangible rewards for participation. Yet together these online community mechanisms of discursive dissent have enabled these digitized platforms of consensual opposition to become wildly popular among anarchists and other body-modified activists.

> [W]e see how the internet helps to promote what are called alternative or counter public spheres that can offer a new, empowering sense of what it means to be a citizen. [G]iven the fluid character of many of these networked-based movements, and the ease of joining and withdrawing, it is really difficult to estimate what portion of the citizenry is actually involved. Yet contemporary social movements and their use of ICTs constitute a major element in the landscape of late modern democracy. Moreover in the new media environment, traditional hierarchies based on differential knowledge and information access are challenged. Counter-expertise and counter-information, not least in the form of alternative interpretation of current events and access to databanks, modifies to an important degree traditional imbalances of power between elites and protesters. The internet may facilitate the traditional forms of protests such as rallies, demonstrations, and collections of signatures, but it will hardly replace their forms. What the internet does allow is for immediate mobilization. The internet may also serve as a tool to provide information that tends to be suppressed by the more established media.[13]

As an essentially blank slate of potential social constructivist opportunity, this platform is a neutral canvas reflecting a community eagerly willing to integrate creative multimedia input with a variety of multimedia methods and mechanisms useful for exercising human agency in the active construction of an improved world system and alternative forms of globalization.

> Voices from the periphery are now taking their place within the contemporary dialogue, displacing and revealing the ethnocentrism that has characterized modernity. People who have been pushed to the margins often have a particularly acute understanding of processes to which those in the center remain blind. This is because the power necessary to sustain the centre's position has operated against those being peripheralized.[14]

Given the seemingly limitless potential that these digitized discursive platforms provide to the historically disenfranchised, marginalized voices are now using these unique online vehicles of resistance to carve out new spaces for creativity, freedom, and constructivism. This powerful combination of free and creative constructivism falls under the rubric of esoteric intrinsic rewards, where the creation of an alternative globalized DIY world takes precedence over material needs persistently left unsatisfied by faltering labor markets and reinforced by nonmediating welfare systems. Furthermore, the innocuous occupational opportunity structure, even under the most fortuitous of industrialized conditions, operates under such an inhospitable atmosphere typified by consistently coercive and demoralizing exchanges for these young people, that conventional occupations can no longer provide any promise to humanity of even minimal stability or occupational rewards, even in advanced industrialized nations indicative of a strong civil society. Featherstone and Burrows (1995) refer to these alienated online anarchist activist community builders as *cyberpunks*.

> The cyberpunk view of the world is also one which recognizes the shrinking of public space and the increasing privatization of social life. Close face to face social relations...are becoming increasingly difficult to form. As patterns of both social and geographic mobility increase the fluidity of social life they undermine the formation of strong social bonds. The...retreat...into their increasingly fortified, technologized, privatized worlds away from the increasingly remote and ungovernable spaces occupied by the repressed...only serves to further close off the more proximate 'social' sources of identity. All that is left is technology.[15]

For hegemonic systemic arrangements to continue in their present form, the illusion of stability and the circulation of symbolic piecemeal rewards to collusive elites are fundamentally contingent to assure continued pacification of the masses. The redirection of achievement away from a decomposing labor market toward robust networks of achievement-oriented meritocratic activism creates increasingly fragile circumstances for coercive institutional arrangements that benefit an ever-smaller cadre of clandestine elusive industrialists and their cooperating agents of dependency stratification.

> To the extent that employees do not perceive themselves controlling their own work, they will be in no position to receive intrinsic rewards, develop intrinsic satisfaction. Job orientation is based on one's personal value system, with intrinsically-oriented people being more interested in job content and extrinsically-oriented people more interested in context.[16]

In the hope of stabilizing the tenuous position of privileged elite left highly vulnerable by these fragile institutional arrangements secured through the strategic distribution of ever diminishing rewards and the dissemination of illusions of optimism and stability from collusive agents from below, scholarly inquiry has explored employee satisfaction from nearly every international angle (Huang and Van de Vliert, 2003). Organizational theorists have identified ways of extracting more and more labor surplus from workers while distributing fewer and fewer rewards (Pinder, 1977; Eisenberger and Cameron, 1998). Conspicuous consumption, greed, and colonization continue to expand power distances between the bourgeoisie and an increasingly alienated proletariat on a global scale unlike any witnessed before in history. Worker alienation has become so ubiquitous, rewards so miniscule, and working conditions so irrelevant, that competition among disposable workforce participants creates superfluous veneers of collegiality at the most superficial levels (Appold, Siengthai, and Kasarda, 1998).

As a result, dissention and discontent is fomenting in nearly every corner of nearly every workplace in Poland and around the world.

> Corporate individuality is the new rational and privileged form of individuality. The struggle over the coming American modernity is…a program for breaking up of society itself, and ultimately for breaking up of any collectivity that cannot meet the criteria of corporate individual. In the end, it is the social bond that must be broken, allowed to continue only in the form of the contractual reciprocity of the market. The family, in its obligation to the corporation and the market [is] materially attacking its' ability to survive.[17]

With the breakdown of authentic social bonds among laborers and other conventional communities, the prevalence of consumptive pseudoindividuality, failure camouflage, paternalistic obedience that permeates nearly all aspects of social life, and the increasingly coercive role of the state, fewer and fewer opportunities are presented in which the modern human feels free to allow his or her genuine self to surface.

> Now the key resources that governments use to suppress opposition are of two broad types: violent means of coercion, persuasion, and inducement, typically wielded by military and police forces; and nonviolent means of coercion, persuasion, and inducement, or, as they will be called here, socioeconomic sanctions, chiefly in the form of control over economic resources, means of communication, and processes of education and political socialization. The circumstances most favorable for competitive politics exist when access to violence and socioeconomic sanctions is either dispersed or denied to opposition and to government. The least favorable circumstances exist when violence and socioeconomic sanctions are exclusively available to government and denied to opposition.[18]

Perpetually under threat from state violence, these alienating conditions of double-edged modernity coupled with hegemonic capitalism have caused such profound disenfranchisement among youth that digitized anarchist activist platforms have become extremely popular by providing on and offline forums for a return to authentic living that encourage critical thinking and provide opportunities for lived political action that satisfies nonmaterial esoteric intrinsic needs driving alternative social constructions of society. The orientation toward achievement, left persistently unsatisfied by disingenuous fragmented conventional communities, increasingly unregulated markets, coercive states, and welfare systems incapable of any redistributive justice, is an innate drive that encourages reflexive thought among even the seemingly most obedient of workers and motivates new forms of social bonds and lived activism online and at the picket line.

> [T]he great intensification of the reflexivity in the current advanced societies…is explained by the rational and reflexive nature of the human beings integrating society. These individuals, as rational thinkers, do not act

mechanically inside social structures or in front of them but, to a greater or smaller extent, tend to discuss, reconsider, or think continually about their vision of these structures and their place in them. [This may be] why some local societies are capable of devising competitive responses to globalization processes, and other local communities are subjected to intense socioeconomic erosion as a result of these processes.[19]

Nowhere are these online anarchist activist communities more authentic and lively than in the cultural context of Poland. With these theoretical, technical, and cognitive caveats in mind, the analysis will now focus on discursive digitized consensus systems of opposition created by body-modified anarchist activists in urban areas throughout this defiant developing nation of deprived and demoralized youth.

Digitized Content Analysis

To conduct the content analysis of websites of interest to the politically oriented body-pierced community of Poland, a snowball sample was identified and relevant body-modified politically active individuals were interviewed in three phases, first between 1999 and 2001 next between 2005 and 2007. and finally during the author's full-time residency in the Wroclaw anarchist ecological squat known as Wagenburg between 2009 and 2010. The website that was consistently reported as the primary contact point for all matters pertaining to political activism among those engaged in body modification is the site of Anarchist Federacja [the Anarchist Federation]. This has a subtle double meaning in the Polish language, as "racja" means "right" or "justice' and "federacja" means "rights at the federal level." Though "Anarchist Federation" is a loosely accurate translation, it does not capture the nuances of the Polish version, which could better be described as "the federation for national rights through anarchy." FA's subtitle further describes their website as "the one that's NOT for government." A preliminary examination was conducted within a user-oriented framework where the delivery of information for broad audiences appears to be an important part of activism web design. For the casual user investigating the site at even the most superficial levels, there are a variety of aesthetic, artistic, political, and ideological interactive services offering extrinsic rewards such as concert information, protest invitations, downloadable brochures, downloadable books, downloadable music, and numerous other sophisticated multimedia bells and whistles. For the committed returning user, this main national source for information deemed relevant for all anarchists is updated almost daily, with intrinsic and extrinsic rewards offered through access to new information, current events, news content, invitations to national and international events, and colorful multimedia. Though the links were numerous and offered a wide variety of information representative of the global anarchist worldview, website designers made a tremendous effort to assure that users are exposed simultaneously to regional indigenous justifications for alterglobalization for tangible purposes at local community levels. Thus, website designers bifurcated sites as either representative of FA's endogenous activities through knowledge categorized in the current analysis for our purposes as *internal content*, or exogenous activities and knowledge beyond the imminent Polish anarchist network considered for our analytic purposes as *external content*. This approach, coupled with stable and timely provision of information and other services offering a variety of extrinsic and intrinsic rewards, has resulted in FA becoming Poland's primary and most significant *virtual anarchist umbrella organization* for all communication necessary for community construction among politically oriented body-modified activists throughout the nation.

Internal Content

There are nine internal links, the first of which offers an English-language version for international guests. The second internal link is called "Propaganda," which offers four main ideological documents or organizing principles that justify the need for FA. The third is a geographic link to 26 regional headquarter affiliates within Poland. The fourth provides official addresses, emails, and procedural information for contacting the members at regional levels. The fifth provides an official mission statement and manifesto with the title, "Plastic Majority" [English translation attached], which includes FA position statements on topics such as creating alternative futures, the illegitimacy of societal control by government, the alternative status and distinct privileges associated with marginality, unethical taxation, punk independence strategies, and institutional problems associated with defense industries, religious institutions, and criminal justice systems. Documents advancing FA's organizing principles further advocate their vision of an ideal green lifestyle that maximizes freedom of speech and encourages members to participate in frequent collective action such as strikes, demonstrations, boycotts, refusal to pay taxes, strategies to resist obligatory national military service (for males), and other mechanisms of human empowerment. The sixth and largest link from the main page of this virtual anarchist umbrella organization website provides relevant news from around the world, which is updated frequently. The seventh link discusses the history of anarchy and the evolution of FA in contemporary Poland (discussed elsewhere in the current treatment), and includes documents pertaining to membership obligations and other regulations. The eighth link has 15 lengthy articles written in the original Polish or where necessary translated into Polish, including works by American-born contemporary theorists of Polish-Jewish ancestry such as Noam Chomsky, as well as historical figures in the evolution of anarchist thought of Polish ancestry, such as Rosa Luxembourg[20] and Jozef Edward Abramowski. There are also works by anarchist theorists beyond Polish culture. The website concludes with a final link offering a short self-test to determine if a given user might be an anarchist, and an archival gallery of photographs, flyers, party invitations, protest invitations, theatrical performances, brochures, alternative art gallery shows and openings, and other visual examples of community construction that have already taken place through political and aesthetic activities.

External Content

There are also over 40 external links to relevant websites outside the FA. The first link directs users to the General Network of Anarchy in Poland website [Ogolnopolska Siec Anarchistyczna], which is the nonvirtual organized network of regional squatter residential and organizational bases located throughout Poland. The second link offers a free subscription to an online information service, known as the FA Internet Bulletin [Internetowy Biuletyn FA]. The third link directs users to helpful advice and other procedures on becoming formally and informally affiliated, ranging from full-time residential squatting to the most casual participatory support of cultural capital accumulation in the form of attending punk rock music performances at one of the many alternative cultural centers found throughout the national network. The fourth link directs users to officially endorsed websites of political, aesthetic, and subversive interest. The fifth link offers a discussion area on where subscribed members can post messages or information that advance FA-related activities, submit personal commentary, or make other discursive contributions.

The next link directs users to nine regional sections of FA geographically distributed throughout Poland. These regional sections usually concentrate their activities around a geographically tangible cultural center or anarchist squat or both. The remaining 25 external links can be characterized as ideologically substantive links, including one website offering an online critical theory "zine" called "Idea Recycling" [Recykling Idei], enabling users to submit articles for publication. The second link offers direct access to the now world-renowned alternative source for media information and beyond known as "Indymedia" (i.e., independent media). The third external link offers free around-the-clock access to an online library composed of anarchist-oriented literature translated into Polish. The fourth and fifth links explain the FA's integration into the worldwide anarchist movement by offering users access to activism opportunities inherent in the international anarchist network known as Anarchist Black Cross [Anarchistyczny Czarny Krzyz]. The sixth is an online anarchist bookstore [Ksiegarnia Anarchistyczna], the seventh is an organization called the Official Automatic Red Rat [Oficyna Automiczna Red Rat], and the eighth offers a link to an organization known as Another World [Inny Swiat]. Link nine is another "anarchist solidarity" website, ten directs users to a "freedom activism" website, eleven through fourteen offer direct access to four anarchist-endorsed pacifism and anti-war websites, sixteen to a neighboring German anarchist website, seventeen to an international "alternative social thought" website, and finally a "radical action through creativity" website.

The links conclude with other FA anarchist-endorsed websites advocating alternative visions of globalization in the form of aesthetic, feminist, anti-dogmatic, or ecological community [re]construction.

Methodology

A qualitative approach was then used to capture the efficacy of community building and information dissemination under observation. Because the current analysis seeks to demystify knowledge-generating and other resistance activities of body-modified, politically active, anarchist youth on and offline, the website's internal network content was a primary concern and was approached within a social constructivist perspective, where member beliefs and sentiments are perceived to construct their social realities and hence operational activities in regional centers. This approach led to the conceptualization of four categorical independent variables that are believed to influence the kind of operations occurring at regional centers. These independent variables capture dimensions of (1) network connectivity, (2) ideological orientation, (3) transaction exchange types, and (4) motivating rewards. Thus the distinct operational activities occurring in each regional headquarters are hypothesized to be dependent on member capabilities of embedding the center within the larger network, on articulating relevant ideology, on the method of resource exchanges, and on the distribution of relevant rewards. To that end, high or low network connectivity was examined based on number of links. Ideological orientation was assessed by evaluating local adherence to a variety of anarchist-endorsed paradigms articulated nationally in the FA anarchist-organizing document known as the "Plastic Majority" manifesto. These were then examined in light of how the resources are exchanged among users based on transaction types (either cooperative, calculative, or coercive). Use of this contract typology is based on the expectation that anarchist philosophies are highly antagonistic, to match their perceptions of the environment. The final dependent variable involved opportunities for rewards to motivate achievement among users so that high levels of satisfaction are capable of being experienced by participants within the online anarchist-activist framework. These were hypothesized to manifest either as opportunities for tangible material needs, no rewards, or expected to be likely found in intangible esoteric intrinsic nonmaterial rewards. Anarchist operations occurring at regional headquarters are thus deemed to be dependent on a combination of these four variables involving connectivity, ideology, exchanges, and rewards. The current hypothesis suggests that the more embedded a regional anarchist network is, the more salient their adherence to multiple ideologies, the more cooperative their exchanges, and the more successful they are in offering opportunities for achieving intrinsic rewards, the more active and lively will be the resistance activities that they offer. Because prior research suggests that the more institutionalized activities an organization engages in, the more formal and stable its operations (Tolbert and Zucker, 1983; Dobbin, 1994), the current treatment theorizes that activities occurring at each of these nine regional centers (residential squats, culture centers, pubs, meetings spaces) are a reflection of the community sentiments of the digitized and nondigitized local operational network, the adherence of members to anarchist ideologies, the flow of resource exchange among the network, and orientation of members toward intrinsic rewards. These independent variables are local determinants that are indicative of the extent to which each of the nine regional anarchist centers offers the local oppositional *alter community* a variety of opportunities for lively action and activism. Thus, online dimensions of community constructions based on network centrality, ideology, exchanges, and rewards are expected to reflect the frequency and breadth of activities offered locally at these regional oppositional consensus centers. Furthermore, regional fluctuations regarding local networks, local philosophies, local transactions, and local rewards are advanced to be independent factors that influence what activities individual centers offer in terms of local opportunities for squatting, expansion of cultural capital, concerts, pubs, and regular gatherings. The salience of anarchist operations on and offline by region is therefore believed to provide some representative levels of the genuine scale of socioeconomic and political resistance that has been steadily perpetuated among activist youth in Poland since the fall of communism.

Given this conceptualized model extracting relationships among categorical variables, the first part of the analysis explored the nine regional headquarters where resistance operations tend to be concentrated around a variety of alternative culture production. According to data presented on websites, coupled with triangulation through direct observations in the field, anarchist activities tended to concentrate around full-time residential squats, and/or centers for alternative culture providing the forum for music-spoken word-performances for the expansion of relevant cultural capital, and/or noncommercial pubs, and/or through regular meetings to articulate the need for and organize political actions that advocate anarchist philosophies. These centers as well as the websites they produce offer authentic evidence of active, ongoing, social and political mobilizing among members. By comparing regional differentiation regarding tangible operations in these lively viable collective venues (our dependent variable), the analysis can accurately portray how anarchist activists' connectivity, ideology, exchanges, and rewards operate together to influence the efficacy of resistance activities offered. The analysis intends to show that the extent to which participants are able to access existing networks, ideological information, resource exchanges, and satisfactory rewards together determine the diversity and stability of authentic local anarchist resistance activities reflected on and offline. This approach will demonstrate that these websites and the online collectivities that they represent not only offer users knowledge surrounding globalization and unique alternate philosophical anarchist strategies to combat the contemporary deleterious conditions it imposes, but does so through a variety of motivational rewards delivered through complex transactional mechanisms that authentically capture the alienating sentiments, adversarial institutional relations, and other minutiae needed to clarify the complex contemporary struggles of our times. The analysis will qualitatively demonstrate that network activity, ideological orientation, transactions involving political, aesthetic, and socioeconomic exchanges of human capital, and access to alternate sources of achievement greatly influence the activities offered by saboteurs concentrated around these unique regional centers of resistance in Poland and around the world.

Results

With these modeled constructs surrounding operational authenticity in place, seven centers and their websites were examined in light of network interconnectivity. There was significant differentiation in regional centers with regard to all four dimensions of operations. Network connectivity results ranged from the smallest number of links in the capital city of Warsaw (with only 5), to the largest created by the squat and cultural center located on the Eastern border in Bialystok (with 35 links). The oldest and largest anarchist cultural center and squat located in Poznan had fewer than 25 links, despite the fact that they, in actuality, had the designation of being the national contact point for the international global anarchist network. Thus, high or low regional website connectivities may not necessarily reflect the genuine depth and breadth of regional or international integrated action, and may actually run the risk of underestimating the political, social, and cultural capital circulating in these centers. Low connectivity platforms such as Warsaw and Gorzow did not necessarily disclose all the resistance activities occurring in their catchment area. The Warsaw website, for example, failed to mention another nonresidential anarchist center for critical thinking loosely affiliated with Warsaw University, in existence for almost 20 years. Specific activities regarding residential squatting were also underrepresented nationwide, perhaps due to police attacks on the rise on squatter settlements in Paris, Copenhagen, and other cities throughout Europe (see Bennhold, 2005; Squatters Practical Network, 2005; Isherwood, 2007). Archival data regarding evidence of past protest action were also incomplete and did not tend to capture the full scale nor the measurable successes of past world systemic globalization resistance efforts in which regional members were involved. Thus it appears that online digitized platforms provide users with only a vague indication of resistance activities, offering a preliminary but discrete road map to explore the broad brush of anarchist ideologies, transactions, and rewards that are truly motivating this unique community. Portrayals of past mobilizing activities may be only partially disclosed in order to avoid the risk of participant recognition by law enforcement officials, or perhaps to make an atmosphere for new activists considering participation as inclusive as possible. Nevertheless, digitized website platforms can capture some of the depth and breadth of resistance activities on and offline, and should primarily be used to augment a fuller inquiry triangulating data to fully capture the genuine extent of collective action. Studies of online resistance communities and other forms of digital activism might perhaps best be used in conjunction with participatory action or other forms of direct observation in the field.

Ideology was found not to fluctuate significantly, with little vacillation evident in promoting specific combinations of ideology that each regional collective advanced as crucial to their resistance vision. Although each offered their online version of what anarchist priorities might take precedence over others, it was notable that all approaches, though working to advance local interpretations, tended to deviate little from the national anarchist manifesto, "Plastic Majority." Warsaw and Lodz presented primary orientations toward ecological concerns, advocating bicycling and vegetarian lifestyles. Poznan and Bialystok tended to focus on Food Not Bomb activities to reverse the deprivation of the surrounding community. Use of military or other forms of state violence by dominating institutional powers was widely documented by nearly every regional center, with little evidence to demonstrate that anarchists espoused use of violent means to achieve their own political goals individually or collectively. On the contrary, nonviolent protest and harmonious peaceful living with all living beings (including animal species) regardless of ethnic, racial, gender, sexual, and religious diversity was consistently advocated. In fact, there are many anarchists who espouse such universal egalitarian lifestyles and are so opposed to violence in any form that they use these digitized platforms to discourage consumption and exploitation of animals either through experimentation or as a source of food. Regardless of ideological orientation, no regional site advanced any approach to resisting world systemic globalization employing any necessarily coercive polemics or discursive imposition. Instead, audiences were encouraged to explore, at their own pace and comfort levels, the underlying philosophies that drive these alternative lifestyles, and to personally consider them as viable options to resist the status quo. One methodological complication regarding online ideological analysis did, however, arise in the question of validity with regard to *sequentiality*. It may be methodologically flawed to advance the sequential order of a given variable online (in this case ideology), thus running the risk of misrepresentation. No research to date has demystified what significance or primacy, if any, the sequential content patterns represent for designers or the community members. In other words, when a given anarchist center (or any other entity) positions one form of anarchist ideology first on its online content, does it necessarily means that the ideology holds a similar salient location of primacy among members of that community offline? The significance of sequentiality as an accurate indicator of community offline sentiments may be methodologically problematic and require further study to determine construct validity.

The mechanisms by which anarchist websites sought to portray their ideologies and activities to users were, nevertheless, surprisingly cooperative, with excessive enthusiasm articulated in all but two sites. The newest community, less than a year old, was Szczecin, which displayed the most coercive exchanges, with anti-fascist defiance firmly articulated throughout. The most provocative was their assertion that members support "war among classes, not wars among nations" and the notion that "theft from the rich is ethical." The second most defiant was found in Wroclaw, with anti-fascist mobilization also a strong element prioritized among their activities. It is interesting to note that the two cities where the most coercive forms of resistance against fascism and nationalism were articulated online, Wroclaw and Szczecin, were the very same cities located on territories annexed after World War II due to the Yalta Agreement implemented by Roosevelt, Churchill, and Stalin which exogenously redesigned Poland's borders and resulted in the forced transfer of Polish, Ukrainian, and German war survivors. As such, these repatriated regions, and Wroclaw and Szczecin in particular, are under constant attack by German elite in the courts, in museums, in the media, and other institutions (Lutomski, 2004).[21] Given the levels of coercive dialogue online, the institutionalized threats from aging nationalist German adversaries in the courts and conventional media manifest as equally defiant resistance on and offline. Among those with highest network centrality, Lodz was highly cooperative and oriented toward providing users access to literature online. This center also used their interactive platform as an opportunity to conduct technologically and methodologically sophisticated surveys on the needs and orientation of users, and found that 35 percent adhered to unlimited anarchy principles (as opposed to specifically green anarchy [17 percent], anarcho-syndicalist anarchy [12 percent], socialist anarchy [11 percent], or capitalist anarchy [only 6 percent support among users]). These disseminated results describing Lodz anarchists may indicate that users have highly generalized and salient anarchist identities and want to see the freedom this ideology espouses infiltrate all aspects of public and private life. When the current analysis was being conducted, Lodz was in the process of gathering data for tolerance of violent tendencies among members. The most balanced and thorough delivery of information overall was also the oldest squat in the country and the oldest Polish anarchist website in the country located in Poznan, which is also distinguished with having the largest anarchist library in the nation, and the largest squat. Rather than advance any necessarily informative literary role that Lodz seems eager to fulfill, Poznan, which is the oldest and most established anarchist squat in Poland, was oriented more toward dissemination of legal and other rights-based tactical knowledge.[22]

Rewards were perhaps the most surprising element of the analysis, as all regional headquarters offered new and returning users concrete opportunities for both intrinsic and extrinsic rewards. Through paths and patterns that brought users highly relevant internal and external content, nearly every region had a "public relations" component, explaining activities in very fundamental terms so as not to contribute to misunderstandings or

Table 4 Anarchist Websites in Poland; Internal Content Analysis by Region

	Resistance	Network	Ideology	Transactions	User Satisfaction
	Operations	Centrality	Articulation	Exchange Types	Reward Types
WARSAW http://alter.most.org.pl/infoszop/	bicycling meetings	5 (3.7)	ecological anti-war animal rights women's rights	cooperative	intrinsic extrinsic
WROCLAW http://www.wroclaw.ibw.com.pl	live concerts/performance publishing formal membership subscriptions downloadable graphics/stickers	8 (6.0)	anti-fascist anti-nationalist anti-education indoctrination adversarial relations w/Parliament	coercive calculative	
LODZ http://www.czsz.prv.pl	research publishing strategic events (calendar) lobbying for jailed activist (murder) public relations	32 (24.0)	ecological animal rights labor rights anti-war anti-fascist	cooperative calculative	intrinsic extrinsic
POZNAN http://www.rozbrat.org/fa.htm	national anarchy library live concerts/performance strategic events (calendar) publishing downloadable graphics/stickers	25 (18.7)	Food Not Bombs anti-war homeless property rights (squat) national legal right updates ecological	cooperative calculative	intrinsic extrinsic
SZCZECIN http://www.faszczecin.most.org.pl	subscription philosophy dissemination	15 (11.2)	anti-war anti-fascist	coercive calculative	intrinsic extrinsic
BIALYSTOK http://decentrum.bzzz.net	member website publishing live concerts/performance downloadable graphics/stickers/music	35 (26.1)	Food Not Bombs anti-missile anti-dogma ecological	calculative cooperative	intrinsic extrinsic
GORZOW http://www.fa-gorzow.prv.pl	protests strategic events	14 (10.5)	international historic founders national historic founders chat/guest book	cooperative	intrinsic extrinsic

Note: 2 missing cases due to technical construction. Column percentages in parentheses. Network connectivity data excludes links to external sites.

perpetuate moral media panics. There were very profound explanations for casual users, and an effort was made whenever possible to universalize the goals of anarchist alterglobalization project to appeal to political moderates and other broad sympathetic audiences. Thus, Polish anarchists used their digitized platforms to describe the continuum of available anarchist resistance efforts (ranging from libertarian to complete stateless anarchy) by stressing the universality of the social benefits they struggle for through the tactic of minimizing or completely eliminating state intervention in civil life. Rewards were not merely limited to the intangible or the esoteric to be realized among future generations, as originally hypothesized through an orientation toward intrinsic rewards, but were consistently stressed in the form of cultural capital accumulation, access to knowledge, the opportunities inherent in residential squatting, and other short- and long-term benefits that anarchist lifestyles provide. Furthermore, DIY punk paradigm and the empowerment that comes with it was a constant theme of nearly all regional headquarters. Users were heavily encouraged to feel free to interface their creative actions with the integrated regional activities already under way. This included encouraging users to participate through formal members, in order to articulate and construct individualized visions for the anarchist project by providing opportunistic spaces through personal blogs, recommendations on how to produce or consume independent music (usually punk), venues for independent publishing, encouraging audience participation by attending upcoming concerts and other political or aesthetic resistance efforts that increased cultural capital. This included impressive levels of transparency such as procedures useful in starting another independent squat, legal assistance when met with police intervention at protests or while on the street, and ways to start "Food Not Bombs" actions in local communities to nourish, empower, and reverse diasporic deprivation closer to home.

Summary

Although certain methodological complications did arise, content analysis of anarchist activist websites was particularly fruitful in augmenting the larger inquiry surrounding this unique defiant community. As expected, internal content did provide a platform to demonstrate systems of oppositional consensus, particularly by sensitizing users to environmental awareness of the universality of diasporic deprivation brought on by world systemic globalization. By providing users with a variety of ideological alternatives for approaching the project of deconstructing hegemonic empires, users were exposed to many philosophical activist frameworks through which they could participate to contribute to resistance endeavors. Internal content did not, incidentally, strive to represent the full depth and breadth of past, present, or future resistance activities. This lack of transparency may be an indication of the limitations of online dialogue, or it may be inherent in the need for discretion to combat persistent attacks by violent state militia and members of the postfascist movement operating in the interest of dominant groups to dismantle these increasingly powerful subversive social justice networks of worldwide dissent and subterfuge. Digitized discursive content was, nevertheless, able to provide even the most casual users with a plethora of resistance tactics capable of transferring a variety of desirable intrinsic and extrinsic rewards. By expanding members' access to aesthetic, political, literary, and visual accoutrement through information, events, and downloads of music files, posters, stickers, and protest brochures, individual and community accumulation of alternative cultural capital was fully operational. Dependency-reversing strategies were a salient feature on many regional sites, where failure by conventional standards was rewarded, independence was highly encouraged, and alternative consumption patterns advocated. In this way, online content was able to advance, empower, legitimate, and otherwise unify fragmented anarchist activist communities through concrete tactics of resistance on and offline. In the process, the Polish anarchist activist community perpetually exhibited highly efficient, technology-driven, defiant community construction capabilities, and carved an admirable digitized space indicative of innovative use, providing users unlimited potential for rewarding experiences of discursive dissent through integrative, interactive, independent interfacing among geographically isolated saboteurs around the country and around the world.

7

Biker Contestation

For our purpose in general, and our attempt to determine with some measure of certainty the essential character of the revolutionary spirit, the specifically American experience taught men that action...can be accomplished only by some joint effort. [P]ower comes into being only if and when men join themselves together for the purpose of action, and it will disappear when, for whatever reason, they disperse and desert one another. Hence, binding and promising, combining and covenanting are the means by which power comes into existence; where and when men succeed in keeping intact power...they are...in the process of [building] a stable, worldly structure to house, as it were, their combined power of action.

Hannah Arendt

Background

There is nothing that personifies the ideology of freedom more profoundly than the American biker gang. America by her very nature has her origins rooted in defiance of state authority, and as such, the revolutionary principles of freedom of movement, construction of social networks, protection of personal resources, use of markets for free trade, and the willingness to engage in violence if anyone should constrain these activities in any way are uniquely American freedoms vigorously coveted and strenuously celebrated among body-modified biker gangs. This unique philosophic combination of doctrine has been so religiously observed and successfully disseminated by biker gangs throughout history that it has recently been appropriated and to some extent *diluted* by inimical mainstream-conforming motorcyclists. Despite weak attempts to usurp the revolutionary spirit of these, by necessity, *rebellious* expressions of American idealism among painfully dull, conforming, bourgeoisie patriarchs, biker gang culture is alive and well in America's urban environs in the Deep South.

Because their personified revolutionary spirit is in constant cultural competition from disingenuous rebellious factions of society, biker gangs are increasingly threatened and coming under inordinate scrutiny by law enforcement officials. (Davis, 1984; McGuire, 1986; Thomas-Lester, 1991) Rather than prioritize precious criminal justice resources by focusing enforcement efforts on racist, genocidal militia groups among U.S. citizens, or perhaps others who articulate extremist, fundamentalist political aspirations among foreign nationals, law enforcement has instead attempted to cripple biker gangs by weakening highly organized cooperative networks.[1] These attacks by law enforcement officials have not only led to conflict between weekend warriors and one-percenters,[2] but has also contributed to unprecedented levels of tension among various biker gangs across America. This tension has led to such bloody conflict that gang leaders have become involved in a formal mediation capacity to reduce frequencies of increasingly violent altercations among these historically harmonious groups. The tension is further exacerbated by drains of club resources to combat legal attacks (Hernandez, 1990).

Though relations at the time of this writing are somewhat quiet and uneventful, bikers themselves are reluctant to admit but certainly fear further retaliation through miscommunications brought on by convoluted involvement of law enforcement officials. This is particularly egregious in the South, where discontented local law enforcement authorities compete precariously for civil service glory with border interdiction, immigration authorities, highway patrols, and other highly decorated authoritarian segments of state apparatus. This institutional complexity, coupled with the relative lack of complex criminal activity on a mass organized scale in rural areas of the South, leaves members of local police departments free to focus an inordinate amount of resources on the activities of biker gangs. Though anthropologists and criminologists have argued that biker gangs pose little threat to public safety of law-abiding citizens at large (Wolfe, 1991), law enforcement continues to unnecessarily and illegally intervene in these isolationist social networks. Reflecting the usual case with big-budget American military intervention around the world, infiltration of law enforcement into biker culture has caused general fear and instability (Burrell, 1998), has heightened simmering historic group tensions (Murphy, 1996), has contributed to dialogue complications resulting in miscommunication and misunderstanding (Rowe, 1989), and has resulted in unnecessary loss of life due to protection of turf, expression of minority rights, preservation of masculine pride and identity, and refusal to submit to dictatorial state authority (Gibson, 1995).

This is not to suggest that the level of law enforcement scrutiny hasn't, to some extent, been occasionally warranted. The role of some biker gangs with regard to human trafficking for the sex trade (Newman, 2000), egregious exploitation of drug-abusing women (Hopper and Moore, 1990), and elaborate distribution systems of controlled dangerous substances has already been well documented (Werner, 1985). There is certainly evidence to suggest that criminal activity among local motorcycle cultures in and around the city of New Orleans is consistent with global trends (Broach,

1993). Due perhaps to geographic opportunities, there are even indications of pervasive leadership among New Orleans motorcycle gang members in constructing nationwide drug distribution systems spanning the country from Los Angeles to Daytona Beach (Perlstein, 1999). This chapter does not intend to glamorize or elaborate further on the role of local biker gangs regarding criminal activity throughout the South, but rather intends to examine this evolving subculture in relation to the increasingly hostile social structure in which they are embedded.

Defiance Epitomized

As threats to their existence and their ideology become more ominously pervasive, biker gangs have become exceptionally creative in the cultural repertoire of political and ideological expression available to them. To that end, members of biker gangs increasingly appropriate body modification to express defiance messages and to distinguish themselves from less defiant ideologically neutralized motorcycle enthusiasts. Because Americans have more experience constructing, manipulating, and eliminating defects associated with formulations of the schematics of freedom than any other civilization of the world, U.S. subcultures often run the risk of bordering on anarchistic political expression, and a willingness to engage in the protection of rights and freedoms by any means necessary.

The vehemence with which biker gangs protect their ideological, economic, and socio-political sovereignty, self-determination, and minority rights has been shared with many important groups in American history.[3] Continued attempts by state authorities to cripple motorcycle gang culture will not necessarily serve to bolster the state's institutional legitimacy, thus fulfilling objectives to increase already sky-rocketing budgetary criminal justice system allocations, but may paradoxically cause severe managerial criticism (as in the case of Waco) or worse, enable other opportunists to fulfill necessary distributive functions of vice in society (as in the case of the dismantling of stable and loyal ethnic crime syndicates of New York). There is even evidence to suggest that law enforcement is so determined to destroy motorcycle gang reputations in the eyes of the public, that they recently prohibited one club from engaging in charitable activities benefiting sick and abused children (Hardy, 2002). Despite persistent attempts by the state to weaken members of these loyal social and economic biker networks, the strategy of cultivating tensions to justify increasing criminal justice involvement has not been effective. In the face of these coercive challenges from powerful elites, biker gangs have not only maintained their camaraderie and cohesion, but strengthened and expanded their construction of social ties in defiance of such overwhelming adversity. This is particularly apparent when examining innovative coalition-building across geographic, racial, and ideological biker gang boundaries. Coalition strategies to combat the excessive levels of financial, emotional, and technological resources devoted to legal defense against these persistent and harassing judicial system assaults are becoming more and more sophisticated.[4] In the wake of power struggles between law enforcement (who traditionally operate in the interest of conventional economic elites) and rebel biker clubs with no intention of discontinuing their alternative market activities nor dismantling their ideological apparatus (which serves as a crucial expression of their identity), it is no surprise that conspicuous, defiant facial piercing, tattooing, and other forms of body modification are observable among these men with increasing frequency.

Independent Clubs

Much has been written about the "Big Four" motorcycle clubs with large numbers of members in the United States, Europe, and beyond. Composed of Hell's Angels, the Banditos, the Outlaws, and the Pagans; these clubs have been vilified and glorified by journalists, criminologists, and social scientists. Although these highly complex organizations are of substantial sociological interest, they approach motorcycling from a franchising, multinational perspective, operating through the imposition of distant, standardized rules within a hierarchical decentralization management philosophy inconsistent with the organizing principles of their founding forefathers.[5] As these clubs get bigger and more territorial, their rapid growth, explosive membership, expanding institutional structure, geographic dispersion, and fictitious "ghost club" façade have resulted in deleterious consequences that may not serve their interests or survival in the long run. Complexity, competition, and coercion have resulted in unprecedented challenges to their administration and even weakened their ideological orientation to some extent. An organizational theorist evaluating any of the groups composing the "Big Four" would conclude that these gangs are beginning to exhibit an inability to adapt to change, are preoccupied with minimizing overwhelming levels of uncertainty, are experiencing diluted loyalties associated with brotherhood among new members, and have loosely affiliated ancillary associates engaging in (authorized and unauthorized) clandestine activity without concern for club interests but with substantial legal implications nevertheless.[6] Given the precarious changes threatening massive, global, increasingly commodified clubs, it is no surprise that independent biker brotherhoods have remained a stable and unwavering force in the tapestry of biker culture in New Orleans and across America. Law enforcement officials estimate that there are 800–900 independent biker clubs in the United States alone (Kelly, 2000). Thus, it was refreshing to have an opportunity to explore one such autonomous club originating in the city of New Orleans, called the Banshees.

Banshees of New Orleans

One sunny afternoon, I was invited to attend a party in honor of new recruits to be inducted into the Banshees, a motorcycle gang whose clubhouse was located just beyond the New Orleans city limits. I had heard of their existence before from French Quarter men boasting of their masculinity through ties to such an exclusive, closed, and dangerous organization of motorcycle enthusiasts. The Banshees, I knew already, were a profoundly tough, masculine subculture.

But they also had a reputation for fun

A friend once revealed to me that she had lost her out-of-town house guest and first-time visitor during Mardi Gras. When he returned only in time to grab his suitcase for his return flight back home, she was furious that he had not contacted her since his arrival. He begged for her forgiveness as he told how he had been kidnapped by a friendly motorcycle gang. My friend was suspicious of his story, so he revealed that he had been absconded during a parade by members of a friendly biker gang because his blue long hair was a perfect match to the color of the exterior paint of their clubhouse. His abduction was to mark his temporary role as their club mascot, and they believed that it was destiny that he should enjoy the Carnival season with their exclusive company. They bathed him, fed him, and gave him drinks to keep him at the house, but at no time was he allowed to leave the week-long party or make any contact with the outside world. On the way back to the airport, he was so determined to prove his amazing experience that he drove his friend right back to the clubhouse to demonstrate that his hair was precisely the same shade as its exterior. My friend's out-of-town houseguest had the most enjoyable celebration ever, and the Banshees had made a new friend of their seasonal mascot. It was a bizarre experience for all parties, to say the least.

Could one then typify this network as nothing more than your average fun-loving weekend warriors who drive Harley-Davidson motorcycles just to annoy their ex-wives? Was there anything to distinguish these gentlemen from your average fraternity house pranksters found at universities throughout America? To answer this question, I solicited contacts within the criminal justice system conducting undercover surveillance on biker gangs throughout Louisiana. They made allegations that the Banshees are currently among the most feared and dangerous motorcycle gangs in the United States, because, as the informant quoted to my contact, "…they blow shit up." My contact inquired further from his contact, who inquired further from his contact, but all I could surmise was that they periodically sought retribution of their enemies use of highly sophisticated explosive weapons.

As I prepared to meet this fun-loving but presumably dangerous New Orleans biker gang, I wondered if their motivations were political, territorial, financial, or some other factor that would not come to the mind of an outsider. And so, with their joyful but dangerous reputation already familiar to me, I agreed to be a designated driver for some raucous French Quarter folks to the Banshee indoctrination party out of town. This, I knew, was a rare invitation, as the Banshees were not usually so accommodating to individuals outside their subculture. The only reason that they even considered expanding their guest list to include such outsiders was because the Banshees' president was romantically involved with a heavy-drinking French Quarter stripper named Suzy who needed transportation to the party. Suzy had difficulty remembering my name, so she referred to me as "Weird Girl." Because I was sober, drove a motorcycle, could construct cohesive sentences, and did not use my body for survival, I was considered unusual by stripper standards. My assessment of Suzy, on the other hand, was that she was vulnerable, sweet, emotional, and lucid, despite attempting to advance an identity intentionally to the contrary. Her friend who gathered us together was Doc, an emaciated cocaine-abusing Vietnam Veteran who I had met through Painless Paul years earlier. The third guest was Bill, a recreational crack user and architect who designed multi-billion dollar commercial real estate projects in the CBD.[7] Together our eclectic group set out to spend a day with the Banshees Motorcycle Gang.

Cold Reception

When we arrived, I was instructed by Doc to pull directly in front of the yard as close to the parked cars as possible. I protested that those spaces might be reserved for bikers, but he insisted. Our strange ensemble of misfits emerged from the car, and we were greeted very coldly by some brothers of the club. I stayed in the back, but could see that such a large group of outsiders was unexpected. Our presumptuous parking right next to the building was not helping, so I introduced myself and inquired if I should move the car. The brother stared at me coldly and did not even acknowledge that I was present. A chill blew down my spine, and I considered leaving immediately. Another brother came along and invited us inside the clubhouse, enticed us to the keg area, and pointed us in the direction where food was being prepared. He told us to make ourselves at home, and excused himself to attend to party logistics. The radio was broadcasting a hard rock station, and people were spread evenly around the property. I stepped inside the clubhouse, and found the walls adorned with images of nude women. A pool table stood to the left of the entrance, and a biker lay sleeping on the couch to the right. A sign indicated that videotapes and audio recordings were prohibited at all times on the premises. One of the young recruits was working behind the bar and enthusiastically greeted us. A tiny donation for cocktails was expected, but food was complementary. I could not shake the feeling that my presence was totally undesired, so I declined any alcohol and settled in to meet people, hoping to change my initial impression. Two friendly women were seated at the bar, and warmly introduced themselves to me, while Suzy met her president with a warm embrace. Nostalgic photographs of a long history of good times lined the walls of the single-story house, and it got darker and more mysterious the further I followed the pictures of hard-drinking Banshee bikers and babes interacting at parties. Except for jackets and colors, similar pictures could be seen posted in any pub in town. Although the hyper-masculine decorations were not necessarily unique, I had the distinct feeling that this group of people was unlike any I had ever met before.

Determination and Resilience

Under the inviting cover of swaying moss hanging from old oak trees near a raging fire, I reluctantly sat down with some brothers around a table. As we started to chat, I was surprised to find several myths were immediately shattered. The Banshees had been in existence for over 30 years, and they were not limited to the city of New Orleans. The club was actually a part of an elaborate network of Banshee brotherhood spread across several states, who were highly organized and integrated among other motorcycle clubs. As such, guests were not limited to brothers of Banshees, but also expanded to include members from at least two other clubs. In addition, the Banshee members themselves were not limited to the New Orleans chapter, but included brothers that had arrived for the gathering from all over the South including Texas, Arkansas, and Florida. As we sat and discussed the history of the club, bikers arrived on loud Harley-Davidson motorcycles, and were met with warm hugs and kisses from the brothers. The bikes were loaded and it was obvious that many of the riders had traveled very long distances to get to the indoctrination. How arrogant and presumptuous of me to expect such a warm welcome, when these sentiments were reserved exclusively for loyal members of their own brotherhood. Theirs was not a world of false civilities or courteous veneers. It was precisely their absolute disregard for politeness, their maintenance of social distance, and their reserved aloofness that made me secretly desire their acceptance. The warmth and camaraderie I observed among the men was so genuine that I actually felt envious. I wondered how such profound loyalty and camaraderie had developed, and wished that I could earn such respect and acceptance from this exclusive group of people.

To get the attention of the men gathered around the table, I tried to impress them by revealing that I owned a motorcycle.

"That's cute." replied Biscuit condescendingly. "What kind of ride?" Biscuit was very attractive by any standard. He had shoulder-length blond hair and bright blue eyes. He was smiling at all times, and I found myself attracted to his wit and sarcasm. He seemed to have the lowest guard of all the brothers when talking to me.

"Well, I like to ride distances and so I have a vintage touring bike. Not as vintage as I would like, but it's a red 1979 BMW R65."

And thus began a wonderful evening chatting about our respective differences with regard to risk and motorcycle safety. They were poking fun at BMW rider tendencies for an overwhelming preoccupation with safety, and I made fun of Harley-riding biker gang members who routinely traveled highways at speeds of 70 miles per hours with no eye protection. We accepted the polarization among biker culture at the table, and agreed that there must be some rational mediation in between. I felt the need to explain why I did not drive a Harley. I went into a long diatribe at a volume that could be heard across the party.

"Look, I am a woman with no mechanical ability whatsoever, and furthermore I don't want any. I have no illusions that I can even begin to understand the complexities of the inner workings of these magical machines. But I love to ride. Yet somehow after all these years, I can barely figure out where the gas goes. So, as a result of this technical handicap, I am completely committed to riding BMW motorcycles for the rest of my life !!!"

I looked around. Every brother had heard my monologue, appreciated what I had to say, understood the deference I was giving to all of them who were mechanically inclined, and were pleased with my public acknowledgement of low status with regard to technical capital. Two brothers who were taking apart one of the bike engines while I was speaking seemed particularly rejuvenated by my speech, and everyone smiled and returned to their activities. By now, brothers were cooking, people were eating, the girls were drinking, and I was getting cozy with Biscuit. I started to inquire about their exclusivity regarding membership and related restrictions.

"So if I came here with my BMW, you guys would let me park it in the clubhouse area with the rest of the bikes?"

"Absolutely. Without a doubt." he replied. The older brothers around the table from Texas and Arkansas nodded in agreement, and sunk another beer.

"Pledge. Bring us a round of beers on my tab. Young lady, would you care for a drink?" asked the elder Banshee from Texas. I declined, and soon one of the young brothers preparing for indoctrination returned with several beers. Then the public hazing began.

Degradation Rituals

"You forgot to take care of this lady. Why are you such dirt?" the Banshee inquired.

"Sorry Ma'am. May I get you a drink?" asked the young inductee with a southern accent..

"No, that's not necessary." I replied timidly.

"Show the lady how talented you are, dirt. Stand on your head." With this command, the pledge dropped his empty tray on the table, and stood on his head. Dirt was falling from his combat boots all over his face, but he maintained his position, unwavering. I marveled at his control, remembering that he had been drinking alcohol throughout the day. This would be only the beginning of a series of tests to break the pledges' pride. They tested the pledges' willingness to oblige every whim of the brothers, and these trivial humiliations resulted in raucous but fun-spirited laughter among the guests at the party. Everyone was aware that the two pledges would be indoctrinated into the club that day, except for the pledges themselves. The juvenile cruelty was limited to tasks associated with the consumption of alcohol, and as such never really got out of hand. For example, they were told to stand on their heads and drink beer upside down. This they did with such urgency that their boots, upon elevation, shattered the glass windows on the clubhouse façade. This lead to more raucous laughter. When one pledge vomited, they quickly stopped the activities and immediately allowed him to leave the public space of the party and readjust himself in private. These tasks, the brothers explained to me, were the necessary acculturation activities required to foster true loyalty and brotherhood.

"I could never do that." I confided.

"Of course not, you're a woman." replied one of the elder brothers I had come to like so much.

"What's that supposed to mean?" I inquired.

Gang Eligibility

He then went on to explain the rules of membership. First of all, a Banshee had to be a man. Only a man can embody the spirit of the club, or epitomize the levels of loyalty and friendship. Women were considered more suspect, fleeting, fickle, and incapable of fulfilling the occasionally excessive obligations of membership. An unusual smirk came across his face as he squinted and studied my expression.

He intentionally wanted me to ponder whether he was inferring murder. After he let me squirm in my seat and catch my breath for a moment, he continued.

A pledge also had to be white. It was not a rule to discriminate, but one that minimized risks for miscommunication and provided brothers with a maximum degree of understanding. He could see that I was having a difficult time comprehending.

"Look, you're a Yankee, so let me lay it straight out on the line."

He went on to explain that black biker gangs had their own biker associations, and there was mutual respect and admiration between them. There had to be a healthy amount of distance to keep that respect alive, however. He impressed me by revealing that he had very close ties to some members of black clubs, and that they sometimes participated in rituals such as funerals together in his local community.

"So don't go off looking for racial problems where they just don't exist." he stated bluntly. "Besides, the black biker brotherhoods are the least of our problems." Here he alluded to the Bandito–Banshee rivalry, particularly egregious in Texas. I could tell by the abrupt change in our environment that this party was not the proper place to discuss such matters of political importance. He would only state that other clubs, and there were three or four present at this party, were in solidarity with the Banshees. Dangerous simmering animosities between rivals had resulted in deep divisions and unprecedented coalition-building among gangs who historically never had much interest in one another. And here they were forging ties among each other, some for the first time, in my presence.

I was also starting to understand that the atmosphere of danger was not entirely of their own construction. As I was talking to Biscuit, though he made me feel that I had his undivided attention, he would discreetly be on alert watching each and every car that periodically passed before the club-house along the winding public road following the meandering Mississippi River. I also noticed that every time Biscuit and I started to engage in a conversation of any substance or depth, he would invariably be called away to some task. Surprisingly, he would excuse himself formally from the table, and apologize when he returned. Because I was asking a lot of questions, I felt that perhaps some of the brothers were anxious about my intentions. The oldest brother from Texas did not fear me, however, and trusted my intentions immensely. When Biscuit was again called away, I noticed that he was brandishing a large handgun in the back pocket of his pants when he stood up. No holster, just a gun sitting comfortably in the back of his jeans. I was shocked. Then I started looking around, and noticed that many, many of the brothers had what looked to me like large handguns plainly in view. This was perfectly legal, as the state of Louisiana has some of the most liberal firearms laws in America.

"Man, there are a lot of guns here. Is it always like this?" I inquired to the elder Banshee from Texas, who was quickly becoming my paternalistic favorite.

"Yes, just in case girls like you get too wild or comfortable and we have to keep you in line." The elder apparently did not have the same paternalistic feelings toward me.

"Well, I suppose I can tolerate the guns, it's this weird stuff about your women that is freaking me out," I said. I noticed that I was the only woman who was allowed to address anyone. The other women all had symbolic leather jackets that announced the spirit of the relationship of women to the brotherhood. Their leather uniforms screamed their formal affiliations boldly, with "Property of John" or "Property of Jack" or "Property of T-Bone."[8] Such explicit objectification of women in modern culture is becoming increasingly harder to find. I found this cultural expression of appropriation of woman as property highly intriguing. Biscuit returned. I had to know.

"So what's the story with that whole 'Property of..' thing ya'all have going...you know...from a *feminist* perspective."

They all burst out laughing, and slapped the table or their knees, whatever was in closer proximity. Their raucous laughter was so over the top, immediate, and unanimous, that I had to wait a long time for the chaos to subside. I had to admit that these guys were charming and seductive, even though they were sexist, domineering, and obnoxious chauvinists. They ordered the pledges to bring over another round of beer, this time on another brother's tab.

The Role of Women

"The status of women in our club differs from couple to couple," revealed Biscuit as he began to unravel gender relations in his club subculture simply and candidly." Some brothers exchange their women as sexual objects in necessary transactions for our club, while others are highly territorial and do not allow any other brothers near their women, even in informal conversation. In any case, no man who is attached to a woman is allowed to speak to another women at a party like this, in order to minimize the likelihood for internal disorder. In exchange for protection and the other privileges associated with affiliation, the men are expected to maintain a high degree of loyalty to her in her presence and are not allowed to interact in any way with other women at social functions where alcohol is served. So there are substantial rules of interaction between men and women, and varying degrees of respect based on the norms unique to that particular union." Despite the overwhelmingly defiant gait, the big gun haphazardly protruding from his pants, and the suspicious gaze he periodically cast on the passing cars, Biscuit was very attentive. As he spoke, I was surprised that he described Banshee relationships with women in relatively conservative, traditional, monogamous terms. He studied my face and prepared for my reaction when the other shoe dropped.

"On the other hand, when women want to come around for trouble, we give them the kicks they are seeking. We occasionally have female guests that want to take on *all* the Banshee brothers, and we definitely give them what they are looking for." He shot me a look of serious defiance. The thought of Biscuit participating with the rest of the boys in gang-raping some drunken stripper made me profoundly jealous. How irrational, considering I had just met him a few hours earlier. I must have looked disappointed, because other brothers jumped in to lighten the conversation, assuring me that ladies get treated like ladies, and that the women who demand and earn respect get respected.

"Don't forget, after all, that we are the Banshees. Fucked up women come to us all the time hoping to make strange dreams come true. Whatever women are looking for, they won't be disappointed. But not all of us are compelled to participate in all these incidents." a brother interjected.

They were so incorrigible, I had to laugh. It seemed that whenever I started to develop an understanding of their club that vilified them, they would quickly convince me that they were really sweet, kind, and giving men. Just as I started to get comfortable in their midst, complacent about my safety, and minimized the extent of their sexual deviance, they would invariably show me how very dangerously sexual and coercive they could be. As long as I walked a fine line of respect, joy, fear, warmth, and intimidation, they seemed confident that they were being properly understood. And they actually wanted to be understood.

I followed Biscuit into the house. As he prepared to take over cooking duties for the huge barbecue that was underway, he changed into another shirt and I noticed his amazing tattooed torso. Because I had worked in numerous prisons including New York's Rikers Island, I was an admirer of prison tattoo artwork, which was difficult to acquire outside institutional walls. I absorbed his body art incrementally as my gaze followed the beautiful, elaborate, uncommodified artistry to the nape of his curved neck. As my vision traced his symbolic prophecies of Armageddon to his smooth shoulders, I was shocked to discover a horrifying death scene in hell surrounding a skull that floated above an explicit, inch-wide, colorless swastika. As a first-born American of Polish descent who had lost nearly all of my family during World War II, including both paternal and maternal grandfathers, the symbol made me instinctively recoil in horror and astonishment. My eyes filled with tears and I turned my head from the gruesome sight. He grabbed me and wanted to engage me in a discussion. I was profoundly disappointed, and realized that no dialogue could intellectualize what I had just witnessed. Surprisingly, I had seen the non-Nazi version in tattoos among the Houma Indians of Louisiana before, but this particular portrayal seemed to convey all the hatred and fear that the symbol truly embodies. Biscuit went on to explain that when he was a homeless youth living on the streets in a very bad neighborhood, he had obtained the tattoo because he feared sleeping in abandoned cars and buildings throughout the 'hood. He further stated that he did not believe in white or Aryan supremacy, and that he had considered having the tattoo removed for a very long time. He explained it was a childish prank that he obtained while in a juvenile institution that he deeply regretted. I explained what effect the symbol had on me given my political orientation and personal family circumstances. I looked again at the swastika in the context of its contemporary meaning, and wondered how such seemingly good people can overcome such personal adversity and yet still maintain such hatred in their hearts without regard for historical ramifications. The Americanized swastika, juxtaposed against the beautiful gold crucifix illuminated by the hot Southern sun sparkling against his skin, seemed an anomalous and ignorant contradiction that flew in the face of motorcycle gang anti-fascist history and the club's apparent warmth and generosity. Biscuit and the other chefs had to attend to preparations for their feast, to be shared with the other biker gangs now arriving by roaring motorcycles in large numbers. Realizing that there was much work to be done, I shook my head and joined the rest of the guests.

Induction Ritual

As the sun went down and the indoctrination party started to get into full swing, there was suddenly a call for a closed meeting inside the house limited to members and apprentices of the Banshee brotherhood. After they met for nearly half an hour to participate in secret indoctrination rituals, the door of the clubhouse suddenly burst open and utter chaos filled the yard. As the swarthy brothers burst out of the tiny entrance, the screams of running brothers, jiggling metal chains, and the pounding of heavy boots filled the grounds. The apprentices had apparently been awarded their colors and their brothers were running after them in a last-chance public spectacle to take back their fraternal symbols. One pledge, when surrounded, took a stage dive over a chain link fence to show how important his colors were to him so that no one would attempt to remove his hard-earned insignia. He and his sponsoring brother fell into each other on the grass exhausted from the elaborate private ritual and subsequent chase. The apprentice was so overwhelmed with emotion that he jumped up with his jacket and pounded it into the chain-link fence several times, screaming with delight. As if to assure him that his acceptance to their brotherhood was finalized, the Banshee gently stopped his new brother's pounding fists and encouraged him to examine his colors. The pledge burst into tears and sobbed profusely, while the senior brother warmly embraced him. They stood this way for some period of time. The apprentice seemed mystified that he had successfully been granted full membership unanimously from all the brothers of this magical motorcycle club with a prestigious local legacy spanning a thirty-year history. The sponsoring brother helped the new recruit compose himself, and together they slowly returned to the rest of party. The other pledge was equally moved with emotion. An entirely new atmosphere could be felt on the clubhouse grounds, and there was a revitalized sense of importance and belonging observable among the members, both old and new. The fire seemed brighter, the atmosphere was warmer, and the Banshee brothers had all become even more mysteriously unified in whatever secretive rituals and incantations had taken place in their private domain away from the rest of their supportive associates. Lovers, brothers, and friends embraced as they returned to the club house in the direction of the raging fire under the canopy of swaying oak trees. The warmth and peace of genuine friendship and camaraderie gently descended on this group of unique people, as they prepared to settle in for an enjoyable autumn evening in the glow of a crackling bonfire along the winding banks of the Mississippi River.

8
Sexual Sabotage

Popular culture is permeated with ideas that erotic variety is dangerous, unhealthy, depraved, and a menace to national security. Popular sexual ideology is a noxious stew made up of sexual sin, concepts of psychological inferiority, anti-communism, mob hysteria, accusations of witchcraft, and xenophobia. The mass media nurture these attitudes with relentless propaganda. I would call this system of erotic stigma the last socially respectable form of prejudice if the old forms did not show such obstinate vitality, and new ones did not continually become apparent.

Gayle Rubin, 1992, in Vance

Background

Evidence presented in this book indicates that body piercing is dichoto-mized along two distinct typologies, the public and the private. Within the group of individuals who acquire *private* piercings, impalements on the most intimate parts of the body are quite ordinary in both men and women. This practice is referred to as erotic or *genital* piercing. Among males, genital piercings are commonly obtained anywhere along the shaft of the penis, as well as the scrotum and tip. Women also have freedom in terms of impalement potential, and are capable of acquiring piercings on the hood of the clitoris, the clitoris, and along the length of the labia. Though theoreti-cally possible anywhere on the genitals, professional piercers maintain spe-cific standardization of anatomical sites based on impalement experience and pragmatic experimentation. Though there are complexities based on intended purpose of the genital piercing, the specific location of the genital piercing, the object of genital adornment, and technical limitations based on anatomical considerations, the individuals who obtain private piercings in the most intimate areas of the body have one ubiquitous characteristic. The primary purpose of genital body piercing consistently reported by those who obtained these impalements and who were interviewed throughout the course of this study indicated that the acquisitgion of genital piercing serves as a mechanism to exercise erotic agency for the purpose of facilitating intense sexual expression.[1] These expressive "primitive" piercings, found with increasing regularity throughout the modern industrialized West, have substantial societal ramifications. Before exploring the phenomenon further, it may be useful to examine the current cultural sexual atmosphere within which these piercings are sought, to determine what impact the conservative erotic sentiments of the American public has on this phenomenon.

Hidden Resistance

In her discussion of conservative political attitudes and intolerance, Mary Jackman (1996) illustrates the effect of dominant group ideologies in influencing cognitive processes invoked to develop evaluative conservative sentiments toward an innovative, oppositional social phenomenon. She eloquently describes the seemingly contradictory processes by which members of dominant groups (particularly within a democratic system of government) are capable of espousing sentiments of discrimination against any element of society based on fear, dislike, distrust, disagreement, or those who otherwise represent a conflicting ideology in opposition to one's own. Conversely, she argues that membership in subordinate power groups produces feelings of alienation that lead to innovative reactionary responses, often employing discreet tactics of resistance when a given political climate prevents more overt oppositional mechanisms.

> Although individuals are the bearers of beliefs, feelings, and behavioral dispositions, they do not hatch these thoughts and feelings independently. Instead, they borrow from the cultural repertoire that is available to them. The concept of political tolerance...is concerned with the ability of democratic citizens to grant full civil liberties to groups whom they disagree or whom they dislike. In this way, we can delineate the intersection of the two basic parameters of intergroup ideologies—the expression of hostility or friendship [in] the pursuit of group interests. In the theoretical literature on intergroup attitudes and group consciousness, two different ideological modes have been posited. One of these, known as "hidden" or everyday resistance, is described as [acts of] minor infractions of the dominant will...masked by visible acts of compliance.[2]

Within the context of ideological innovation, she reiterates the concept of *hidden resistance* to illustrate subtle but powerful mechanisms of oppositional group consciousness, existing concurrently but delicately woven within a given dominant ideology. These concepts are highly applicable for the current analysis, which suggests that genital body piercing is an innovative but pervasive form of *hidden resistance* and strategic discretionary mechanism to subtly combat the growing sexual conservatism of America. Hidden resistance includes patterns of behavior that discreetly express feelings of alienation by a subordinate group that typically manifest as acts of "...petty sabotage [that] lie behind the *grand theater of compliance*."[3] The mechanism of genital impalement, I would argue, is one such example of hidden resistance, and an innovative expression of otherwise collectively repressed human sexuality.

Why would an individual chose such an invasive, dramatic, and presumably painful method of political expression on the most intimate areas of the human body? Due to the inability of the subordinated public to articulate opposing sentiments *openly* based on fear of retribution, the lack of available discourse fostering the exploration of alternative sexualities, as well as the reluctance and avoidance of association with more radical sexual subversives among subordinate group members,[4] those individuals who are in direct opposition to the conservative sexual ideologies dominating the political fabric of America have turned to the creative, effective, and aesthetic practice of genital body piercing as an expression against the repressive American sexual status quo.

Contemporary Sexual Repression

Influenced by the Puritanical origins of the nation's founding fathers, solidified through religious dogma, and fueled by the social terrorism disseminated by public health bureaucracies throughout the AIDS epidemic, societal expectations regarding sexual behavior and the related statuses associated with such activity have resulted in the construction of a virulent hierarchy of inequality and political oppression based on sexual behavior. The highest status sexuality in the United States currently requires an alliance involving a heterosexual dyad between two individuals of the same age within a legally recognized, monogamous, offspring-producing, cohabitational living arrangement. Mere participation within such an exact alliance is not, however, sufficient to obtain membership among conforming elites with the highest sexual status. Achieved prestige within the requisite monogamous union is predicated or contingent on mandatory capitalistic sequential consumption patterns typically involving, but not limited to, the accumulation of pets, vehicles for transportation, an ostentatious dwelling, its ostentatious contents, accoutrements for breeding, additional vehicles for accommodating clan-like transportation needs (irregardless of environmental consequences), stock for future tuition payments, an investment portfolio for retirement, and finally, the requisite interment insurance. Not only does the dominant group impose strict regulations as to what characteristics sexual linkages should typify, but it also dictates *what* is consumed by the compulsory heterosexual dyad, *when* these consumables should be appropriated, and *in what order.*

Furthermore, the assault inherent in these compulsory sexual sanctions is ubiquitous. No one in industrialized society is exempt from these sexually-stratified, status-producing, consumptive customs and expectations (Romanienko, 2008). The imposition of this lifestyle model and its' related prospects are so deeply engrained within the American collective consciousness, that coercion by the dominant group is endured by all levels of society, regardless of race, class, ethnicity, or gender. Many researchers (Pareto, 1963 and 2000) have highlighted the institutionalized permanence with which these oppressive conditions of moral myopia are imposed upon an amoral minority. Zafirovski (2003) refers to the phenomenon as the Pareto Theorem, which

> can be reformulated in this way: undemocratic tendencies expressed in such abuses of power as arbitrary restrictions, violations and negotiations of civil liberties, individual choice and human rights are likely to be stronger in conservative societies that try to reinforce morality by legal rules and government coercion than in others. [Hedonistic resistance], far from deterring social conservatives, appear to have increased their intransigence by further multiplying, expanding, and intensifying their efforts to impose a sort of universal and permanent Prohibition on American society cum moral hyper-control. Such endeavors resemble in part Nazi efforts "both to exterminate 'objective enemies' and fabricate the 'model citizen' of the totalitarian regime." The aggregate effect of American conservatives' endeavors to recreate human nature in a Puritanical-conservative image is transforming society into a gigantic monastery characterized by moral oppression as well as extreme asceticism. The main of these is the conservative dualism of economic minimalism and social maximalism in terms of state interference, or the contradictions between "license to be licentious" in the market and denial of liberty in social life by moral repression—i.e. Anarchy in economy and Leviathan in society. [S]ocial conservatism consistently promotes individualism in the economy via minimalist governmental policies but persistently restricts or denies individual choice and responsibility in private life through maximalist moral regulation by legal sanctions.[5]

The excessive economical, biological, and psychological pressures on both males and females to contribute to the production of these milestones of sexual conformity has led to substantial deleterious consequences to society, which are too profound to contend with in the current treatment, but are, nonetheless, worthy of identification. Incidence of divorce, increasing rates of white-collar crime, robbery, theft, and other utilitarian street crimes, infidelity, business misconduct, reductions in charitable giving, greed, tax evasion, domestic violence, life dissatisfaction, post-partum depression, parental child abduction, geographic isolation, emotional withdrawal, and gay/straight/bisexual suicide and domestic violence rates are all inextricably linked to the forces that construct and maintain the sexual inequality, compulsory heterosexuality, coerced consumption patterns, and related capitalist sexual repression and exploitation.

As with other economically based systems of political oppression such as those predicated on ascribed or achieved characteristics of race, gender, and class, the system of sexual stratification enables those fulfilling dominant sexual ideological expectations to derive a variety of socially sanctioned societal benefits, whereas while those who do not or cannot fulfill these expectations must endure socially sanctioned punishments and low sexual status for preferring ascetic/asexual solitude, for preferring an "open" marriage, for preferring to practice an "alternative" sexuality, or for developing an "alternative" consumption pattern. There are a variety of mechanisms utilized by those dominant group members to produce and maintain these systems of sexual repression.

> As with other aspects of human behavior, the concrete institutional forms of sexuality at any given time and place are products of human activity. They are imbued with conflicts of interest and political maneuvering, both delicate and incidental. In that sense, sex is always political. For over a century, no tactic for stirring up erotic hysteria has been as reliable as the appeal to protect children. The success of the anti-gay campaign ignited long-simmering passions of the American right, and sparked an extensive movement to compress the boundaries of acceptable sexual behavior. Laws and regulations making it more difficult for teen-age girls to obtain contraceptives or abortions have been promulgated. It is unlikely that the anti-sex backlash is over, or that it has even peaked. Unless something changes dramatically, it is likely that the next few years will bring more of the same. In the last six years [however], new erotic communities, political alliances, and analyses have developed in the midst of the repression.[6]

The emergence of these new communities that challenge dominant sexual ideologies is becoming increasingly apparent, particularly in urbane cosmopolitan areas throughout North America. The individuals who engage in the practice of genital body modification have together constructed one such *innovative sexual community* as a responsive backlash to the *sexual myopia* found in America today.

> Hindrances to pleasure [such as] an antisensual culture...inhibited the mind's ability to act on whatever hedonistic urging it received from the brain. The antisexual messages from the village community, from the church, from life itself screamed so loudly that the neural signals were deafened. In a profoundly antisexual culture, biology does not transmit itself into action. Desire is a...longing for sensuality, one that ultimately prevails over all previous social limitations, pushing us ever more relentlessly toward the maximization of the positive sensations that come from [the sensory receptors] on our bodies. But the spectacular drive towards [pleasure] would accelerate only in the 1960's and rush past the year 2000 with all the players—gays, lesbians, and heterosexual men and women—finding new forms of pleasure in exactly the same ways [such as fetish which] are mechanical contrivances that add to the enjoyment of sex. 'Mechanical' may be understood as...something that nature itself does not originally bring to the sex scene. In terms of the erotic potential of the body, the differences among the sexual orientations have become trivial. All respond to the same deep neural drives. [T]ogether these hedonic changes are creating a society oriented toward personal gratification in a way that previous generations could have never imagined.[7]

Gayle Rubin (1992) refers to these communities as *erotically stigmatized populations*, and calls for the extinction of repressive sexual injustice that they suffer at the hands of social forces seeking to regulate them. For the purpose of analyzing genital modification, it is imperative to keep in mind that these same forces that systematically and intentionally produce the complex, coercive, and hierarchical structure of sexual stratification, also produce the innovative, subordinate, symbols of hidden resistance that genital piercing embodies.

Specialized Expression

Given the tremendous pressure to produce conforming sexual behavior, individuals with alternative sexual lifestyles use genital piercing to discreetly formalize their group membership, as well as to inconspicuously identify one another within the coercive, dangerous, sometimes fatal environment of ultra-sexual conservatism.[8] Because strategies employed by *sexual innovators* such as genital modifiers are diverse and often seek to explore traditional power relations within society among men and women, men and men, and women and women, similarly complex expressions of genital piercing have been developed to reflect these complex alternative sexual practices. A casual examination of the wide variety of genital impalements currently available today would leave a sexual conformist in complete confusion as to the meanings or motivations intended by such dramatic symbols of sexual expression. however, as bizarre and outlandish these practices can sometimes appear to be, they have substantial symbolic, political, and ideological meanings to those who participate in these practices. Genital piercing, therefore, is a socially constructed, network-embedded, linkage-facilitating mechanism of ideological opposition, reflecting a predictable, reasonable, and suitable evolution of postmodern sexual expression that seeks to subtly defy the sexual hegemony of American culture.

> Individuals adopt various ideological elements that float their way according to the exigencies that bear on them and the information at their disposal about the behaviors and experiences of participants in the intergroup relationship. Fragments that become inconvenient are dropped, and new ideas that are compelled because of altered exigencies gain currency. In this way, various ideological packages are constructed and reconstructed as they are, transmitted through dominant and subordinate groups. Those packages are spread eagerly or they fail to gain a following, they persist over a long period of time or they fade quickly, depending on their success in addressing the political problematics that beset [their emergence].[9]

Other sexual expressions embodied through genital piercing do not necessary involve the exploration of existing power arrangements among the genders, but are analogously interpreted through the acquisition of genital piercing. In many cases, genital piercing is used to help signify the gender(s) of intended sex partner(s) among those who consider gender not to be a binary code, but who view gender as a *continuum* instead. Genital piercing can also expedite intended *combinations* of sex partners, signifying the desire for multiple partner arrangements that are sometimes required in order for specialized piercing effectiveness to be maximized.[10] The *length* of commitment, as in casual interaction or one reflecting a longer term relationship, can also be captured by the specific genital piercing acquired. Finally, and perhaps most expeditiously, genital piercing expresses the *types* of sex practice(s) desired, which commonly transcend far beyond the standard missionary position with male dominant on top and female as submissive on bottom commonly espoused by sexual conservatives for procreative purposes. These specialized piercings on the genitals express, often with impressive levels of specificity, the categories of sexual coitus personally preferred by sexual innovators.

> We have learned to cherish different cultures as unique expressions of human inventiveness rather than as the inferior or disgusting habits of savages. We need a similarly anthropological understanding of different sexual cultures.[11]

As such, genital piercing clearly symbolizes an individual's commitment to, and expedient facilitation of, oral, clitoral, vaginal, and/or anal production of sexual stimulation, with specific intended partners, under specific intended circumstances, within specific intended commitment levels to sexual interactions or relationships, and to do so discreetly within an increasingly threatening environment of conservative, often lethal, coercion.

Relevance of Experts

One may wonder how all of this anatomical specificity and sexual expression is even physiologically possible. In an effort to expedite the expression of alternative sexuality, professional body piercers as leaders of these alternative, sexually pluralistic communities, maximize the likelihood of enhanced and expanded sexual possibilities associated with genital piercing, through their private consultations. They behave as expert practitioners who disseminate information throughout these alternative sexual communities, while also laying down rigorous recommendations and strict guidelines involving previous experience that have led to the development of erotic, stimulating, highly effective, aphrodisiacal, genital piercing standards and specializations that their professional community offers. Furthermore, the historical premodern and contemporary anatomical, neurological, physiological, and epidermal knowledge that is required to implement these sex-enhancing impalements safely, assure that genital modifications function effectively, while balancing the need to minimize the risks for infection, with a concern for the particular practices of the participants necessitates a level of mastery and command of the sexual-psychological-libidinal functioning of the human body that can only be compared to the knowledge found among a handful of biological, neurological, and psychiatric sexologists. Expressing the unique sexual practices of the progressive sensual innovator seeking the genital piercing, while incorporating professional piercing standardization to safely implement those desired practices, genital piercing is beginning to exhibit characteristics of an actual profession.[12] Despite this increasing specialization, in stark contrast to their comfortable financial remuneration, and in light of existing sexual stratification in society, however, it is unlikely that body modifier's occupational prestige will ever be formally recognized in conventional society. Professional piercing, nonetheless, remains an overwhelmingly influential (albeit underground) social force that facilitates alternative "premodern" expression of sexual pluralism and erotic variation throughout "modern" industrialized North America.

Exceptional Motivations

There are also genitally modified individuals who do not subscribe to these aforementioned ideological motivations, but who also warrant scrutiny. Although they are cognizant of the political environment that facilitated the emergence and widespread popularity of the genital piercing phenomenon, these individuals outline their personal motivations for obtaining genital modifications as *essential to their occupations*. These individuals maintain that appearance is their primary motivation. Those who obtain genital piercings for purely aesthetic purposes as adornment or beauty aggrandizement strategy are predictably sex workers and strippers. These body modifiers engage in genital piercings exclusively for their clients, who have an aesthetic predilection toward genitals that exhibit these decorative adornments displayed as metallic and sequined hoops, rings, plugs, bars, and chains. The clients of these genitally modified people view these impalements as "exotic," and as such, sex workers and dancers are able to increase their revenue precisely as a result of exhibiting genital body modifications.

In these circumstances, members of the sexual status quo are willing to reward and pay a symbolic premium for a prostitute/dancer's membership among nonconforming, sexually alternative communities, to which they are seeking temporary membership. Here, for a fleeting moment (or occasionally even an entire evening), the existing social/sexual/economic power arrangements are challenged, where the client (who under "normal" circumstances has membership among the hegemonic, socially rewarding, dominant group of sexually conforming elites) temporarily crosses over the dichotomized chasm into the other world, and seeks temporary acceptance among those representing sexually challenging, alternative, erotic communities.

Less popular but requiring identification all the same is a small subculture of individuals who engage in genital piercing with the expressed intent of *preventing* sexual interaction. This occurs through genital mutilation and other extreme forms of genital contortion (with or without surgery or piercing) to express a lack of sexual activity and an imposed inability to participate in any sexual expression whatsoever. The practice of genital mutilation for purposes of imposing sexual impotency is known collectively as *sexual negation*. None of the subjects interviewed for the current analysis expressed these destructive sexual sentiments or acquired piercing that renders the sex organs incapable of functioning, but these individuals do exist (see extreme body-modification websites). Their genital mutilations, implemented ritualistically, intentionally, or purposefully by sex partners, the self, or with the assistance of medical professionals, are some of the most extreme, self-destructive, irreversible, and incomprehensible genital modifications imaginable. These practices include dissection of the penis along the length of the shaft, surgical insertion of cartilage to alter epidermal textures, skin grafting and adhesions of the labia, and other mutilating procedures that sometimes (intentionally or unintentionally) permanently render the sex and/or excretory organs dysfunctional.

After conducting over a decade of research on body modifications of all kinds, these submissive mutilating procedures appear, in my view, to have no aesthetic, utilitarian, communicative, expressive purpose other than to repulse and horrify their audiences, and to do so at a substantial cost to one's own physiological, gynecological, or urological well-being. I suspect, however, that these individuals are *sexual conformists par excellence*, engaging in self-mortification as punishment for their inability to fulfill conventional society's sexual expectations. Regardless of the motives for the apparent destructive and pathological practices found among those who participate in *genital mutilation*, it is important to note that increasing numbers of submissive individuals partake in these agonizing procedures to indulge the sadistic momentary whims of dominating sex partners. As these practices of sexual negation become more widespread, further research will be needed to explore these unusually obedient, sensually-negating rituals of *body modifying extremists* in order to demystify, with greater specificity, the unusual practices of the members of these newly emerging, sexually pluralistic, erotically variegated, genitally modified, sadomasochistic, alternative sexual communities.

9

Political Sabotage

It is a heterogeneous rather than homogeneous group in many respects yet its disunity appears largely in the more obvious aspects of its' nature. Actually there are many forces making for group cohesion and many traits, though not easily apparent, which are shared by its members. The very determination to be different is part of a code of behavior which makes individualism the group's primary virtue. Thus the group serves to perpetuate these qualities which characterize its incoming members and to provide both environment and technique, whereby the social dissenter may achieve a sense of dignity and social importance.

Barbara Chartier, 1950, in Grana and Grana

Background

Piercing and other forms of body modification are an important contemporary practice signifying membership in diverse constituencies that resist, undermine, or are otherwise immune to inauthentic principles and practices needed to actively participate in a one-world systemic conventional society. Be they apolitical gutterpunks, strippers, alterglobalizing anarchists, unemployed postcommunist youth, or murderous motorcycle gang members; they all have much in common. First, they deem conventional society to be utterly disingenuous. Second, they are in the process of solidifying and constructing authentic alternative communities on the margins of conventional society. Third, they employ premodern practices of body modification within a new modern aesthetic that signifies affiliation within their chosen alternative resistance networks. Fourth, these modifications on the body are understood as designating affiliation and rank regardless of geographic location, as their elusiveness and self-imposed exile enables them to lead highly rewarding, migratory, politically engaged, libertine lifestyles. Fifth, they demonstrate a willingness to use a variety of creative tactics to resist coercive institutions attempting to impose conventional worldviews and related obedience on them, often through similarly coercive means such as physical force or judicial institutions if and when necessary. Finally, their investment of personal resources to build these alternative networks results in significant return on rewards regarding the accumulation of valuable alternative capital simultaneously at the individual and community levels. Using these mechanisms, diverse constituencies have, over time, gradually constructed an ideologically diverse but powerfully resistant strategic network of contemporary bohemians, unified and driven by the desire to construct their own sexual, political, aesthetic, and organic utopia through the accumulation of these alternative forms of resistant political capital.

> They do not accept the cultural impositions of the ruling actors who define the framework for the development of individual and collective existence. These individuals and groups challenge these impositions and are determined to start defining autonomously the construction of the meaning of their action. They are builders of their authenticity, because they know who they really are and because they want to be recognized by others for who they are and for what they do.[1]

Though they take what may be considered by some to be rather peculiar paths that involve a variety of bizarre, even painful, rituals to create such highly specialized subcultures, these bohemian forms of a new political and aesthetic utopia are part of a larger project of authenticity that seeks to undermine the isolation and fragmentation imposed by a coercive world system attempting to pacify the masses by destroying all forms of human creativity, distinction, and individuality at many levels of existence. Mirowsky and Ross (1986) refer to economically imposed powerlessness as rational *fatalism*, which often leads to resistance of the dependency it breeds known as *instrumentalism*.

> Powerlessness, defined as an objective condition rather than a belief, is the inability to achieve one's ends. Alienated labor is a condition under which the worker does not decide what to produce, does not design and schedule the production process, and does not own the product. Dependency is a situation in which one partner in an exchange has fewer alternative sources of sustenance and gratification than the other. In addition to its direct, demoralizing impact, the sense of not being in control of one's own life can diminish the will and motivation to cope actively with one's own problems. [T]he fatalist has a reactive, passive orientation whereas the instrumentalist has a proactive one. Instrumental persons are likely to search the environment for potentially distressing events and conditions, to take preventative steps, and to accumulate resources or develop skills and habits that reduce the impact of unavoidable problems. In contrast, the reactive, passive person ignores potential problems until they actually happen [thus failing] to limit the consequences of problems.[2]

The utopian project to [re]construct a body-modified bohemia is predicated, in many ways, on the ability of alternative communities to provide opportunities for members to accumulate forms of resistance capital that facilitate opposition to the homogenizing and neutralizing elements of globalization (Giele, 2002). This *instrumental resistance*, though taking many divergent paths, serves to amalgamate and unify an *imagined community* of unconventional saboteurs that includes strippers, gutterpunks, biker gangs, the homeless, fashion models, anarchists, musicians, artists, performers, and other superfluous disposable people with piercings, tattoos, stretchings, brandings, excessive thinness, and other body modification indicative of adherence to unconventional production and consumption patterns. The camaraderie among them could be observed on any given night in any pub in any bohemian enclave throughout Europe, the United States, and beyond. Researchers are just beginning to chart this unprecedented amalgamation of urban dissidents in their own homelands.

> Among the most striking features of the world in the early twenty-first century are peculiar (yet conspicuous) links between: globalization as a multifarious process driven by narrowly defined economic considerations, the many different ways in which this process impacts the lives of people everywhere, the growing difficulties of those same people to reconcile its impact on their lives with its purported benefits, and finally the dissipating ability of individuals, including most social scientists, to verbalize the contradictory nature of the process.[3]

It may be fortuitous at this point to examine some of the oppositional political paths these communities make available for members to authenticate the contemporary body-modification project of building the new system-sabotaging bohemia utopia *in situ*.

Political Paths to Bohemia

Political resistance is one of the most important pathways to distinction that many body-modified individuals use to achieve their bohemian status. Even among fatalistic gutterpunks who choose to approach conventional authority using apathetic disdain, fluency and familiarity with different tactics of political sabotage remains a powerful determinant of bohemian status. As such, an important mechanism through which a given community can provide members with swift access to authentic bohemian political capital is competency in anarchy and other ideological philosophies to minimize or eliminate state intrusion into public and private life. According to Touraine (1995), the principle of constraining state power is one of the most important fundamentals for any democracy.

> Democracy is a combination of three competing elements: the limitation of state power, the representation of conflicting or competing interests, and the political participation of fully-fledged citizens. We have lived through the rapid disintegration of last vestiges of democratic utopia.[4]

In urgent response to democratic disintegration, body-modified alternative communities provide opportunities for members to engage in all three of Touraine's constructs for participatory democracy. Through the accumulation of political oppositional capital and lived activism, the new bohemians limit the encroachment of the state into citizens' private lives, embody conflicting interests of conventional economic capital through their disobedient displays of defiance, and foster an alternative urbane civic engagement that together perpetuates independent living and alternative consumption patterns to reinvigorate participatory democracy and concurrently cripple unregulated markets and the dependency they breed. The link between human dignity, nonconformity, and coercive institutions has been established by many philosophers.

> Most of us are not free. We are slaves to Hinduism, to Communism, to one society or another, to leaders, to political parties, to organized religions, to gurus, and so we have lost our dignity as human beings. There is dignity as a human being only when one has tasted, smelled, and known this extraordinary thing called freedom. Out of the flowering of human dignity comes freedom. But if we do not know this freedom, we are enslaved. The discipline of conformity, which is created by fear of society and is a psychological part of the structure of society, is immoral and disorderly, and we are caught in it. Creation can be only when there is total freedom.[5]

One pathway to liberty and freedom that is offered is through democracy or, in the Greek, *demos-kratein*, meaning the system of rule by the people. Democracy-building through direct participation focuses on action and the exercise of human agency among fellow citizens, which can be conceptualized as the systemic security to assure individual and collective liberty and freedom.

> I am not free if you, too, are not free; my liberty must be 'reflected' in the freedom of others…liberties are complementary—indispensable to each other—not competitive. Liberty cannot occur in solitude, but is a form of reciprocity. I am free and human only so far as others are such. Liberty…consists of universal reciprocal recognition of the individual's liberties.[6]

Individual freedom is therefore contingent on collective freedom. The extent to which one is willing to work toward maximizing the freedom of others is correlated with the belief regarding how much state authority or "external control" is desirable to manage these liberties and the autonomy that comes with them.

> Philosophers have differed widely about the character of man's nature and its ends; what kind and degree of control of the external world is needed in order to achieve fulfillment. The 'positive' sense of the word 'liberty' derives from the wish on the part of the individual to be his own master. I wish my life and decisions to depend on myself, not on external forces of whatever kind. I wish to be the instrument of my own, not of other men's, acts of will.

I wish to be somebody, not a nobody; a doer—deciding, not being decided for, self-directed and not acted upon by external nature or by other men as if I were a thing, or an animal, or a slave incapable of playing a human role, that is of conceiving goals and policies of my own and realizing them.[7]

The struggle for liberty, freedom, and autonomy within the contemporary democracy-disintegrated framework places severe constraints on life choice (particularly for the young) and compels involuntary engagement in disingenuous activities that alienate us from our own essence and serve to benefit dominating hegemonic others. Many seek to reverse these unprecedented levels of Marxian alienation making up the misfortunes of modernity by constructing a body-modified bohemian utopia built on a desire for genuine living that reflects a high degree of authenticity, no matter how unusual these constructions appear to exogenous others. Authenticity is, after all, intertwined with genuine freedom and success. Unfortunately, those who highlight disingenuousness in society and advocate authenticity in its place are often ostracized and vilified, sometimes fatally. One of the earliest advocates of authenticity was Socrates.

> The contrast between apparent and real success...is absolutely central to...ethics, metaphysics, and in the philosophy of art—the difference between what is authentic and what is fake, what is genuine and what is at best an imitation. Socrates not only went unrecognized by his contemporaries, but he was put to death as a criminal—condemned of the opposite of everything he stood and lived for.[8]

The vilification of philosophers adhering to authenticity has been in operation since the days of antiquity. The threat of authenticity to dominant members of society who control socioeconomic resources has always rested in the fact that the reclamation of one's own human individuality unleashes profound revolutionary potential that contradicts this pacification, complacency, and violence to the self required to perpetuate the status quo.

> Rousseau...understood the political implications of...a social system which manipulated and exploited men...which worked to eliminate all human individuality by denying its very existence. The ideal of authenticity...generated a form of individualism that can only be called radical, for its aims clashed sharply with all forms of authority that existed at the time. [C]ulture served—just as politics did—to reinforce and legitimate a social system whose whole structure did violence to the self. Along with its potentialities for self-expansion, culture had given rise to new modes of self-alienation. Thus the desire for authenticity has emerged in modern society as one of the most politically explosive of human impulses. The search for authenticity, nearly everywhere we find it in modern times, is bound up with a radical rejection of things as they are.[9]

Today it is not so easy to persecute Socrates and Rousseau and body-pierced others who advocate for the critical thinking and minimal government necessary to advance the genuine living project. Russinow (1998) calls these marginalized advocates for genuine living exercisers of *radical political agency*. He calls the turn toward authenticity through political opposition *existential politics*, and sees it as a highly effective mechanism to reverse increased alienation under modernity.

> The poles of alienation and authenticity define existentialism, and existential politics spins political analysis and action between these two poles. It is not merely a historian's conceit to call this politics existentialist. The vocabulary of existentialism became widely popular [among] the young people [who] talked all the time about becoming "real" or "natural" or "authentic" and about transcending their generation's "alienation". This therapeutic quest for authenticity did not lead away from the world of politics, quite the contrary. [The] synthesis of democracy and authenticity always took shape in particular communities, often locally. Over time, the radicals' focus shifted away from identifying and demanding the conditions that would qualify the United States as a social democracy and towards attempts at creating democratic and authentic experiences in their own lives.[10]

Beyond the political, many social scientists argue that the exploration of authenticity is also rooted in the social. The rejection of attenuated social bonds and other forms of isolation and fragmentation brought on by a coercive capitalist modernity is another crucial part of the new bohemian project of contemporary genuine living. West (1990) suggests authenticity arises when the dissident acknowledges that personal dissatisfaction has social dimensions, and that others suffer in a similar way. Widdicomb and Wooffitt (1995) also apply the desire to forge social bonds with others exhibiting similar identities as an important element of authenticity in youth cultures.

> We are interested…in the ways they construct their own authenticity as members of subcultures. [B]y constructing the enduring nature of their interests, speakers imply that their status as members of subcultures is a simple expression of an intrinsic self-identity. The authenticity of, and the motivation for, group membership are deemed to be tied to the presumed need or desire of the individual to acquire the collective identity on offer by the category.[11]

Although the literature on youth cultures describes the many creative ways that young people exercise radical political agency, the fact remains that social structures are increasingly hostile to their efforts toward autonomy. Kum-Kum et al. (1998) call this the phenomenon of *constrained agency*.

> [T]here is virtual invisibility of the voices and concerns of adolescents and young adults in academic debates. [Scholarly inquiry should therefore] interrogate how the lived experiences and cultural products of youth articulate, reflect, and transform…discourses and practices. We use "constrained agency" to refer to the idea [that youth] are still not agents with absolutely

free will—their agency is constrained within matrices…contemporary and historical.[12]

Others consider the alienation felt by youth as a permanent feature of modern social exclusion based on diminishing access to societal resources (Perry, 2006; Baldwin, Coles, and Mitchell, 1997). Given the creation of alternative bohemian communities that inculcate oppositional capital to usurp the persistent social exclusion and other forms of alienation experienced by youth, it may be useful at this point to examine the mechanisms that coercive institutions use to create conditions constraining agency.

Media Attempts to Dismantle Bohemia

Because it is impossible for states to suppress all powerful sources of opposition simultaneously, the media has served as a coercive instrument to disseminate moral panics among the public against these new bohemians. Body-modified utopianists who are exercising their right to democratic discourse by highlighting the coercive and detrimental policies implemented by the state through embodied discourse have their human agency significantly constrained by the media. Because of their numbers, their widespread popularity among youth, their ostentatious presence at alterglobalization gatherings constructing a permanent lived resistance movement, and the lack of long-term ramifications associated with short-term sanctions such as jail or imprisonment for frequent participation in nonviolent protest activities, it has been difficult for the media vilification project against them to take hold with any permanence.

> [T]he greater the conflict between governments and opposition, the more likely that each will seek to deny opportunities to the other to participate in policy making. However, a government must also consider how costly it would be to suppress an opposition, for even if toleration is costly, suppression might be much more costly and hence obviously foolish. Thus the chances that a more competitive political system will emerge, or endure, may be thought of as depending on…costs of suppression.[13]

While conventional media attempts to vilify the activists who participate in collective actions highlighting the deleterious consequences of hegemonic activities happening around the world, the general public has not accepted these judgmental portrayals and attempted moral panics. Ezrahi (1990) attributes this independent thinking to plurality within the American public that is generally reluctant to accept such unmediated criticisms from powerful groups at face value.

> In America, a radically egalitarian refusal to grant any individual or group the claim to privileged authoritative view of the entire society…has apparently contributed to less unified notions of society. It is perhaps due to such

differences that [citizens prefer] a more fluid decentralized concept of society as something which diverse individuals encounter and experience differently in the context of action.[14]

Whether or not one concurs with the author that observant audiences in the West are really so egalitarian, it is interesting to note that the tactic of vilification used by media to discredit the body-modified anarchist activist community, is the very same one they use to vilify young urban Black males, young sexually objectified females, and more recently, young Arabic Islamic males from the Middle East. This might be an indication that these moral panics are used so often that they have become innocuous, neutralized, and no longer capable of invoking the requisite fear upon which disingenuous culture is predicated.

> Increasingly denied opportunities for self-definition and political interaction, youth are transfigured by discourses and practices that subordinate and contain the language of individual freedom, social power, and critical agency. One of the most incessant and insidious attacks waged by the media have been on poor and urban black youth in the United States. If not demonized, youth [especially females] are either commodified or constructed as consuming subjects [using] emaciated youthful models with dark circles under their eyes as part of an advertisement campaign that combines the lure of fashion and addiction with an image of danger and chic bohemianism. [T]he popular imagination is being fed a steady diet of racial panic and right wing extremism. At stake in such representations is not only how American culture is defining the meaning of youth, but also how it constructs children in relation to a future devoid of the moral and political obligations of citizenship, social responsibility, and democracy. Caught up in an age of increasing despair, youth no longer appear to inspire adults to reaffirm their commitment to a public discourse that envisions a future in which human suffering is diminished while the general welfare of society is increased.[15]

Here the author focuses on the lack of intergeneration commitment to youth on the part of parents and other elders. Parental responsibility that once universally aspired to leave behind a better world to a new generation is utterly lacking in contemporary society. This plays out in every socioeconomic aspect, from the rapid consumption of the planet's petroleum products and other fossil fuels as quickly as is humanly possible, to the refusal to leave anything of material value behind through inheritance when familial resources were accumulated under more prosperous economic conditions. The abandonment of younger generations by some parents, grandparents, and others in this new century has indeed been alarming. This lack of intergenerational social cohesion, its deleterious effects on human development, and the family weakness that accompanies it together contribute to isolation and alienation under world systemic conditions. With the anarchist worldview and the struggle for human autonomy in the face of constrained agency exacerbated by the breakdown of families comes a profound sense of moral social responsibility among members of the alternative family unit found in the global anarchist activist community, which media portrayals flippantly underestimate.

> The defining mark of the state is authority, the right to rule. The primary obligation of man is autonomy, the refusal to be ruled. It would seem, then, that there can be no resolution of the conflict between autonomy of the individual and the putative authority of the state. Insofar as a man fulfills his obligation to make himself the author of his decisions, he will resist the state's claim to have authority over him. The fundamental assumption of moral philosophy is that men are responsible for their actions. The obligation to take responsibility for one's actions does not derive from free will alone, for more is required in taking responsibility than freedom of choice. Only because man has the capacity to reason about his choices can he be said [to have] an obligation to take responsibility for his actions. Since the responsible man arrives at moral decisions which he expresses to himself in the form of imperatives, we may say that he is...self-regulating [or] autonomous.[16]

Despite the camaraderie and moral obligations that arise with these alternative anarchist body-modified families, the media nevertheless persists in its attempts to homogenize and reduce all collective action by pierced activists to violent unjustifiable rebellion and dangerous non-ideological anarchy. As desired by certain vulnerable publics such as dominating elites, this media misrepresentation serves to delegitimate the activist community among some, while preventing the transmission of any genuine substance inherent in resistance endeavors to conventional audiences. Despite the failed attempts at obscurity, the general public tends to perceive anarchist activism with misplaced suspicion, ambivalence, and uncertainty. As a result, anarchist thought driving persistent civic engagement remains widely misunderstood, but tolerated, by observant audiences.

> Anarchists have always been accused of a special addiction to violence as a mode of revolutionary change. The accusation comes from governments which came into being through violence, which maintain themselves in power through violence, and which use violence constantly to keep down rebellion and to bully other nations.[17]

What the media fails to mention is that the foundation of anarchist thought that drives many of these body-modified bohemians to participate in these resistance endeavors on the streets and behind closed doors is quite simple and universal. In Miller's (1984) view, this can be paraphrased as follows:

> First the state is a coercive body, which reduces people's freedom far beyond the point required for social co-existence. Second, the state is a punitive body, which inflicts cruel and excessive penalties on those who infringe its

laws. Third, the state is an exploitative body, which uses powers of taxation and economic regulation to transfer resources from the producers of wealth to its own coffers or into the hands of privileged economic groups. Finally, that the state is a destructive agency which enlists its subjects to fight wars whose only cause is the protection or aggrandizement of the state itself. Although the state is the most distinctive object of anarchist attack, it is by no means the only object. Any institution which, like the state, appears to anarchists as coercive, punitive, exploitative, or destructive is condemned the same way. Anarchists have also been severe critics of existing economic systems [and] equally critical of the state socialist system. Their argument, reduced to its essentials, is that a socialist state is still a type of state, the change in economic system not altering the inner nature of the state itself. Coercion, draconian punishment, exploitation, and destructive warfare all continue [through an undesirable] ruling class controlling the rest of society.[18]

Academic Attempts to Dismantle Bohemia

Misrepresentation and mutilation of anarchist ideologies to perpetuate moral panics is not, incidentally, limited to the state or mass media. The social sciences also disseminate research that is detrimental to the relationship between communities of resistance and the watchful public these pedagogical protest messages are intended to sensitize. The research disseminated by collusive intellectuals who regularly compromise their objective scientific integrity by legitimating and aligning themselves with hegemonic interests despite the absence of incentives or rewards further misrepresents the genuine tenets of anarchist thought. Existing research that is sympathetic to the interests of bohemian saboteurs hardly approaches the topic with any gravity or seriousness. The paucity of anarchist thought in the research of the most progressive social scientists claiming expertise on social movements and other forms of collective action is alarming. Among specialists in oppositional collective action, anarchism is cited in chronicles of defiance, whereas genuine antagonist activist relationships with the state are hardly ever documented. The dismissal of Ward Churchill from the University of Colorado for criticizing American foreign policy that contributed to the anti-American sentiment inspiring the attacks on the Pentagon and World Trade Center is expected to produce an even greater chill on authentic political discourse and autonomous movements in the social sciences.[19] Professional associations such as the American Association of University Professors, the American Association of University Women, the National Organization for Women, the American Civil Liberties Union, and disciplinary associations are virtually innocuous and have essentially no legal defense to assure that even tenured scholars documenting genuine social phenomenon will have their free speech protected under current systemic hegemonic conditions. The academic community and the body of literature that they produce represents one of the most disingenuous and collusive cultures of modern times, serving to perpetuate the pacification of the masses and render critical thought innocuous, thus solidifying existing coercive institutional arrangements.

> Studies of social movements frequently ignore the state. This is partly because those who study social movements...underestimate the importance of the state authorities against which they are often making demands. It is also because 'social movements' and 'state theory' have developed as relatively independent branches of sociology.[20]

Intellectuals not only turn their backs on the objective and measurable detrimental changes that are underway, but also routinely vilify and reductivize the broad history of anarchist thought in lieu of the poignant naivete that continues to adhere to delusions of the socialist pathway out of the current savage capitalist abyss. The prolific production and consumption of this vapid myopia on the left greatly underestimates the authentic sentiments of body-modified activist youth, and advances power disparities that exist in society.

For example, advocates for world system governance provide the most vehement attacks on human autonomy from state domination, suggesting that worldwide violent anarchy will be unleashed around the globe if hegemonic core countries do not imminently facilitate a centralized structure for world governance (Bell, 2002). Advocates for obedience to a centralized form of global governance, known as the *realist paradigm*, are not limited to conservative political scientists, but can be found among left intellectual thinkers as well. From this point of view, state anarchy either in the form of national or international structures of violence is viewed as highly desirable, whereas anarchist citizen self-autonomy is considered highly suspect. These alleged progressives, along with racist conservatives dreaming of fostering continued development in the unruly Third World, advocate for a system of global governance through formalized power at the core. They are typically armchair socialists and other affluent American leftists who refuse to even visit an ex-Communist country but, nevertheless, use their comfortable social and economic distances to deter the accurate dissemination of anarchist principles through anachronistic support of big government, ideally through the return to a socialist apparatus. One transparent exchange on global governance was offered by Wendt (2003).

> If [the one world state is not developed] and anarchy [prevents collective security], then it makes sense to define one's sovereignty and interests in egoistic terms and act on that basis. International law is irrelevant or an impediment to the national interest, and one should pursue a unilateral policy whenever possible. [I]f a world state is inevitable...then rather go down with the ship of national sovereignty, states should try to 'get the best deal' they can in the emerging global constitution.[21]

In a rebuttal, Shannon (2005) argues that

> states and people may not share the author's woeful view of life under anarchy. Surely many have suffered from war and insufficient 'recognition', but enough to compel all humanity into submission to a global government? One wonders if [groups with a history of oppression] are comfortable with such forfeiture of autonomy, placing trust in the benign nature of an overarching superstate to uphold their identity."[22]

Shannon thus highlights the absurdity of attempts by intellectuals to bifurcate all global governance choices as either a submission to core hegemonic central governance, or acceptance of the suffering associated with the inevitable lawlessness and violence if more autonomous forms of governance are created.

What the moral panics on anarchy emanating from both conventional media and social and political scientific communities fail to capture is that the desire to dismantle state hegemony is usually accompanied by humanism, or in the Latin *umanisa*, which is the profound belief in human potential. Varela (1999) calls this the *recovery of human agency*, a will to put into motion group, individual, and embodied action.

> A helpful way to address the issue of differing conceptual solutions to the problem of…embodying human agency is to place it within the framework of the general question of agency and structure. In this context it can be seen as a specific problem of the proper *location* of agency with reference to the body, the person, and society.[23]

Because the focus among contemporary anarchist activism stresses the primacy of individualized bodies facilitated by the acquisition of piercing and other distinguishing forms of body modification, human agency with all its distinctiveness and creativity is seen as taking precedence over and benefiting from the dissolution of oppressive governing superstructures. Insofar as mainstream media and the social scientific claims of the necessity for global centralized state governance and the ineffectiveness of human autonomy and self-determination known as humanism are concerned, Leeson and Stringham (2005) remind us that self-rule under anarchy has not only been plausible, it is the oldest and most effective social system in existence.

> The ubiquity of government today causes us to forget that many societies were stateless for most of their histories and that many remained so well into the twentieth century. More striking yet is that the world as a whole has operated and continues to operate as international anarchy. The continued presence of numerous sovereigns creates massive underground interstices for many of the interactions between the inhabitants of different nations. Many of the stateless orders [of indigenous tribes] disappeared with the colonial rule in the nineteenth century. However, the international sphere remains anarchic and shows few signs of coming under the rule of formal government soon.[24]

Thus, attempts to falsely portray systems of stateless self-governance as alien and unfamiliar to society are usually disseminated by representatives of institutions located in the hegemonic core who stand to benefit tremendously from a centralized one world system of governance dictating policy that operates in their interests. Many argue that such debates are innocuous anyway because plans for the coercive centralized system of world governance have not only begun, but the Kafkaesque nightmare is already well upon us.

> If popular reaction in this case takes a really organized form, it can undermine and reverse the highly undemocratic thrust of the international economic arrangements that are being foisted on the world. And they are very undemocratic. Naturally one thinks of the attack on domestic sovereignty, but most of the world is much worse. Over half the population of the world literally does not have even theoretical control over their own economic policies. They're in receivership. Their economic policies are run by bureaucrats in Washington, as a result of the so-called debt crisis, which is an ideological construction, not an economic one. That's over half the population of the world lacking in minimal sovereignty.[25]

Given increasingly coercive centralized governance clandestinely operating without transparency due to dependency associated with international debt and related *market failure camouflage* at the nation-state level, coupled with the dual-edged attacks by collusive conservative and progressive intellectuals that seek to consolidate power at the core, body-modified bohemian utopians provide opportunities for resistance by encouraging the accumulation of oppositional political capital among members to urbanely contest these totalitarian arrangements. With the state, media, and academia colluding to suppress the genuine tenets of anarchist thought, why do these ideologies remain so popular among body-modified activists and why is there more interest than ever unifying embodied alterglobalizing resisters around the planet? The extent to which these utopian bohemians are able to successfully socialize new members with the requisite oppositional capital is determined by many factors embedded in context. At this point it may be useful to explore the historic underpinnings of the ideologies circulating through authentic anarchist activist communities today.

Political Conditions Conducive to Bohemia

Bohemian is actually an historic reference to the migrating ethnic groups of unconventional travelers circulating adventurously throughout the wildly autonomous Duchy of Bohemia located in the borderland regions of the Czech Republic and Germany around present-day Wroclaw, Poland.[26] But there are numerous conditions found around the world that are, even today, just as conducive to this self-imposed transient life of unconventional exile.

> The term 'bohemia' implies a loosely-bound community of artists who disregard conventional dress codes, sexual taboos, and work habits. In France the

word 'bohemian' originally referred to wandering gypsies who supposedly came from Bohemia, a kingdom in Central Europe. The 'bohemian' label was appropriated by nineteenth-century Romantic artists who called themselves vagabonds. By the end of the century a bohemian tradition had evolved in the Latin Quarter, a development which in part explained why Paris became the experimental center of the art world. Reacting against the insularity and pretense of missle-class society, [bohemians] upheld the superiority of a simple life. Since materialism, injustice, hypocrisy, and repression seemed pervasive in America, [bohemians] agreed that their community should promote art, radical politics, freedom, and sexual equality. But few rebels considered how these lofty goals could be achieved. [They] thought that removing the customary restrictions was sufficient to generate creativity and community. Villagers hoped to build a sanctuary for rebels and to revolutionize society; they wanted to live freely and influence public policies. Their first priority was unstructured existence. The creation of an open and supportive colony required some sacrifice of individual interests to the needs of the group. But these [bohemians] refused to impose restrictions on their behavior. [T]hey celebrated self-gratification as a praiseworthy attack on social repression. The deficiency in their vision was not in wanting to replace conventional society with a better one, but in failing to see the magnitude of the task.[27]

Czech Republic, France, and the United States are not alone in cultivating the modern bohemian spirit among their citizens. Nation-states currently in the process of integrating into the European Union, such as Poland, have relatively few barriers to acculturate activists toward transient lifestyles and other contemporary tactics of defiant working-class consciousness demanding reductions of state intervention into citizen public and private life. Transient lifestyles among Poles is due, in part, to push factors surrounding unemployment and reduced borders within the EU. Defiance is another important element and natural component of bohemian life. Based on centuries of colonization by hegemonic neighbors, attempts at re-colonization by hegemonic core interests, and the historic role that Poland's Solidarity labor movement had in contributing to the dismantling of the Soviet Union, evidence suggests that the working class of Poland is the singularly most defiant labor force of all postcommunist nations, based on the frequency of collective actions, types of resistance, and protest participants in attendance (Kubik, 2001).

Poland...had the highest level of mobilization during regime change. During the [postcommunist] period, collective protest in Poland was [also] intense. Our research indicates that Poland had the highest incidence of protest among the East Central European countries. The most protest-prone groups included various sections of the working class, young people, and state employees. Post-communist collective protest in Poland was decidedly nonviolent [with] violence occur[ing] most often when the youth participated in protest actions: 23.4%. The Polish repertoire of protest has proven to be significantly different from [other postcommunist countries]. In sum, our study demonstrated that many Poles who were uncomfortable with routine parliamentary democracy and dissatisfied with party politics, turned to contentious collective action as a mode of public participation. [P]rotest in Poland [has become] a routine thus institutionalized form of participation in public life.[28]

Poland's workforce has therefore created social and cultural conditions that are highly conducive to oppositional tactics, even to the degree that they are integrated into the daily repertoire of mundane life. Such success in acculturating oppositional collective action is not, of course, limited to the defiant working classes of Poland. Evidence suggests that collective action is now part of the common fabric of urbane cosmopolitan civic engagement around the world. Meyer and Tarrow (1998) call this routinization of oppositional collective action and related civic engagement evidence of a *Movement Society.*

> Proponents of the Movement Society hypothesis argue that protest and other activities typically used by social movements have become widespread and "normal". Drawing on observations about the ways in which social movement actors make claims against their targets, these researchers have noted that the protest activities of social movements...are becoming institutionalized as part of the standard repertoire of political participation. [T]here has been a general upward trend in the number of participants reported at protest events,...the number of claims articulated by social movements over time has expanded, [and have a] fairly continuous [less] sporadic nature.[29]

Body-modified oppositional bohemians with high levels of political oppositional capital fully embody the lifestyle of *lived political activism* that composes the Movement Society. Expedited by persistently displayed defiant body modification, there is no moment of potential oppositional action within the Movement Society that is not fully utilized. Either through embodied resistance on the skin or disembodied resistance found on digitized platforms, political opposition is continuous, ubiquitous, and enduring. The new bohemians perpetually infuse Movement Society with ostentatious displays of body modification and other aesthetic but defiant signifiers of creative resistance, displayed either on the street in more formal oppositional endeavors, or in more informal (even the most intimate) egalitarian activities in private. Among the new bohemians in the Movement Society, personal is still political, and so it was only a matter of time until public oppositional resistance, or what Edelman (1971) called "mass arousal through protest" would eventually infiltrate the bedroom for a widespread "democratization of sexual privilege" (Schwartz, 2000).

> [Anarchy] acquires not only a new sense of urgency, but a new sense of promise. In the...free sexuality of millions of youth, in the spontaneous groups of the anarchists, we find forms of affirmation that follow from acts of negation. The absolute negation of the state is anarchism—a situation in which men liberate not only "history" but also the immediate circumstances

of their everyday lives. The absolute negation of the city is community—a community in which the social environment is decentralized into rounded, ecologically balanced communes. The absolute negation of the patriarchal family is liberated sexuality—in which all forms of sexual regulation are transcended by the spontaneous, untrammeled expression of eroticism among equals. The absolute negation of the marketplace is communism—in which collective abundance and cooperation transfom labor into play and need into desire. It is not accidental that at a point in history when hierarchical power and manipulation have reached their most threatening proportions, the very concepts of hierarchy, power, and manipulation are being brought into question.[30]

In the new body-modified utopian bohemia, oppositional agency now infiltrates all spheres of movement society, the public and the private.

The antisexual messages from the village community, from the church, from life itself screamed so loudly that the neural signals were deafened. In a profoundly antisexual culture, biology does not transmit itself into action. The steady removal of previous barriers—medical, social, and cultural— encouraged millions of people to pursue sensuality. [T]ogether these hedonic changes are creating a society oriented toward personal gratification in a way that previous generations could have never imagined.[31]

Political resistance in the form of lived activism that manifests through egalitarian or other sensual relationships exploring power through the exercise of *sexual human agency*, does so in the most intimate contexts of the movement society. Yet the phenomenon is not new. Political resistance, sexuality, and authenticity have been thoroughly intertwined in early philosophic and political thought.[32]

[Montesquieu]'s approach to sex is deeply moralistic; but because his morality is the morality...of authenticity, he comes to the radical conclusion that sexuality has a positive moral value. Sexuality is the most vivid expression of nature—and hence of individuality—in man. As such, it is integral to the formation of personal identity: sex is the medium through which every individual can not only enjoy himself, but actually define himself.[33]

The turn toward hedonistic sensualities and related gratification among genitally modified bohemians composing the utopian movement society exhibits an innovative mechanism of oppositional cultural capital against regulatory sexuality externally imposed by coercive institutions such family, church, and state. Responsibility for sexual activities and their consequences is considered by the anarchist activist community to rest solely in the internal workings of the participants themselves, which should not be regulated or otherwise brokered by the state.

[E]very ethic of authenticity starts from the assumption that human beings inevitably have contradictory internal forces which pull them away from their self-chosen principles. In order to be a fully moral being, according to the ethic of authenticity, we must not deny or try to suppress, but rather acknowledge the presence and the force of the urges which deflect us from our principle, while at the same time continue to orient our conduct to a moral point of view.[34]

Though not necessarily a new tactic, the *urgency* with which these utopian insurgents adhere to sensual cultural production is certainly a novel part of the larger project of oppositional aesthetics among the new bohemia, facilitated on an unprecedented scale by the formalization inherent in the acquisition of genital piercings and other forms of sensuality enhancing, hedonistically oriented, arousal-enhancing, defiant body modification.

[T]he subculture of gratification model says that social change creates within individuals a positive desire for sexual liberation, and creates a subculture in which these individual sentiments receive group sanction and reinforcement.[35]

The popularity of *sensual resistance* and the widespread infusion of hedonistic pleasure into politics by the body modifying community have indeed served to solidify utopian subcultures of gratification, but this is not to suggest that these contestational activities occur smoothly without attacks by conservatives outside the movement society. On the contrary, as members increasingly demonstrate the hedonism, enjoyment, creativity, and fun that accompanies what is known as *tactical frivolity* that drives these now routine community-based utopian resistance activities (Chesters and Welsh, 2006), governments and other institutionally imposed regulatory moral authorities are increasingly coercive in their efforts to eliminate or otherwise suppress the alternative production-consumptions pedagogy inherent in the new bohemian utopia constructing the Sensual Movement Society.

Political Conditions Destructive to Bohemia

The new sensual libertine bohemians (Pelling, 2006) are constructing the utopian movement society through a variety of creative tactics including the reduction of camouflage surrounding personal and market failure, the reversal of reliance on personal and collective predatory lending, the demand for states to reduce interference in autonomous exercise of human agency, and the support and encouragement of other conditions that demystify the illusion of normalcy that are crucial to perpetuate the taken-for-granted domination by hegemonic elites in all spheres of life, public and private. As resistance efforts to inculcate bohemian values to observing publics become more and more creative, states are also exercising a variety of tactics to perpetuate the illusion of state control while suppressing content of oppositional messages. State suppression of resistance is not limited to attacks on these radical anarchist activists, but is instead a formal, integrated system of suppression used to cripple any attempted activity representing nonhegemonic viewpoints by labor unions, vocational associations, or political parties.

> [State efforts] to attract and retain direct foreign investment not only results in the exclusion of [small entrepreneurs] and organized labor from the polity, but also in the active suppression of protests challenging political exclusion and economic deprivation. Given the importance of political and economic stability to the state's development strategy, increased resources are devoted to expanding its repressive capacities. To ensure a steady stream of hard foreign currency to pay off debts, states must stimulate…export[s]. This "stimulation" often entails union-busting and wage suppression.[36]

State suppression of resistance activities often uses violence to cripple the scale and substance of collective actions. The tendency to use violence and other forms of coercive suppression by governments usually leads to the use of equal if not more excessive violence by anarchist activists, particularly when engaging in civic engagement through protest and other collective action to strengthen deteriorating democracy.

> The association of anarchism with heinous acts of violence has, as I have already observed, become well established in the popular mind. From a historian's point of view this may appear quite unwarranted. Only a small proportion of anarchists have advocated terrorist methods—and only an even smaller proportion have tried to practice them. A word must first be said about distinction between violence and terror. I take violence to be the broader term covering all illegal acts that involve damage (or the threat of damage) to persons or property. Acts of terror, on the other hand, are clandestine acts of violence carried out to create a climate of fear which will lead to political changes. This distinction is important, because many anarchists who would accept certain acts of violence as part of insurrectionary strategy…would nonetheless strongly oppose terrorism.[37]

Studies of violence in social movements suggest, however, that incidents tend not to induce fear, but rather are largely *reactionary* as *defense* tactics used by activists in response to government aggression.

> Aggressive interactions between movements and institutions are not likely to occur at the emergence of a new issue. When the movement challenges the political system through mass protest, [authorities] first attempt to resist changes and thus provoke further radicalization. In the long run, however, individual movements and movement families as a whole tend toward more pragmatic and cooperative strategies. Once violent actions have been used without significant success during or after the peak of the conflict, the more professional and moderate movements prevail.[38]

The use of violence by powerful adversaries who prevent anarchist activists from participating in licensed and state-sanctioned demonstrations and other forms of political action is, therefore, not the arbitrary and impulsive modus operandi as claimed by false portrayals disseminated by the media and social sciences to vilify activists, but rather represents a judicious process of decision making in reaction to violent suppression usually instigated by the state.[39] This judicious decision making is invoked by political activists with significant oppositional wisdom socialized through direct immersion in creative sabotage networks composing the new Movement Society.

> This view of the relationship between coercion and protest is consistent with the initial assumption that dissidents think and are capable of implementing different strategies that are alternated according to the level and type of coercion with which they are confronted. [R]epression encourages [dissidents] to adapt their tactics. Through adaptation, dissidents switch to different protest activities in their repertoire or formulate innovative strategies that are designed to surprise the regime and thus improve the productivity of their tactics.[40]

The willingness to use violence to expedite political goals during resistance activities is therefore a situationally specific, complex phenomenon that typically involves an analysis of costs and benefits that eventually succumbs and yields to the collective needs of the ideologically diverse holistic coalitions of moderates and pacifists that construct the modern Movement Society.

> Anarchy has many masks which are all important, and this diversity cannot be united under one banner. It is not so much that anarchy offers blueprints for a liberated egalitarian and sustainable future for all of us, but it poses difficult questions right now about power, the relationships of human beings to each other and to the rest of the world. In essence, the real strength of anarchism lies in its critiques of power relationships which exist interpersonally and between people and institutions and in its mistrust of any person who would wish to wield such power. In acknowledging and criticizing these power relationships, however, anarchism is not merely reactive. The terrains and theory of action have changed, and now there are activists operating in fields of protest for whom the works of Kropotkin, Malatesta and Bakunin are distant. Modern anarchism has long since needed a major overhaul,... new theoretical and practical tradition[s have] started to develop over the last few years.[41]

Although violent suppression instigated by the state remains a constant reality in the lived activism of bohemian subterfuge, tremendous restraint is exercised by anarchist activists in order to achieve oppositional consensus among diverse saboteurs for the good of the entire collective. This restraint is notable, considering the many formal tactics of violent and nonviolent suppression routinely used by the state to quell collective actions, particular at alterglobalizing events. Some of these contemporary tactics used by the capitalist state have been well documented by Boykoff (2006), and now include the use of "...direct violence, public prosecutions and hearings, employment deprivations, surveillance and break-ins, infiltration and use of agent provocateurs, delegitimation though black propaganda and creation of schism, harassment and harassment arrests, extraordinary rules and laws, mass media manipulation, bi-level demonization, mass media deprecation, and finally, mass media underestimation, false balance, and disregard." It is interesting to note that these are many of the same tactics described by Czeslaw Milosz (1990) to describe crippling deprivation of life under Soviet totalitarianism.

Even though many body-modified activists are pacifists who may have a lower tolerance for violence than society at large, it does not necessarily mean that they are not willing to use violence to defend themselves if instigated by the state through direct confrontation in the course of state-sanctioned collective action. Furthermore, activists who articulate a willingness to use violence for political expediency may not necessarily be eager or enthusiastic to instrumentalize this willingness with any frequency. These ambivalences are not a new phenomenon of political resistance associated with alterglobalization. On the contrary, violence to combat state violence used for suppression of democratic participation has historically been a divisive issue in rights-based resistance endeavors. For example, the nonviolent Christian ideologies of Dr. Rev. Martin Luther King, Jr. frequently clashed with the "by any means necessary" Nation of Islam ideologies of Malcolm X, fracturing strategies to advance a united American civil rights movement (Branch, 1998). To complicate matters further, the mere articulation of willingness to expedite political goals through violent means serves to unify in-group relations among defiant saboteurs, is effective in provoking fear among naïve audiences, and accomplishes much to convey to distant observers the sense of purpose and urgency with which social justice is needed to imminently create a new world order (Hozic, 1990). With the exception of Timothy McVeigh, who bombed the federal building filled with civil servants in Oklahoma City during regular business hours, and a handful of religious fundamentalists who crashed airplanes into the Pentagon and World Trade Centers, genuine pathological violence against innocent bystanders has remained the exclusive modus operandi of the militarized state known as the USA to impose the economic interests of its ruling hegemonic elites around the world.[42] Compared to these insidious forms of systemic mass murder and torture through militarized state mechanisms in Iraq to secure U.S. control of the last vestiges of the Earth's dwindling petroleum reserves, sporadic small-scale violence among protesting anarchists is completely incomparable. If and when anarchist activist violence does occur, it usually takes the laughable form of burning garbage, overturned automobiles, or barricaded squatters in abandoned residences preventing "eviction notices" from being served by police through their now customary brutality. Yet before we discount these petty forms of sabotage that small-scale anarchist violence fosters, keep in mind that the subtle allusion of the willingness to use violence as part of the arsenal of creativity advancing the resistance repertoire of the new utopian Movement Society remains an important and desirable component acculturating disenfranchised bohemians in the fine art of political opposition. Beyond its sporadic use at alterglobalizing resistance endeavors, it remains a discursive tactic among body-modified anarchist activists intended to instill fear in naïve publics and communicate the urgency for social justice to reverse the severe deprivation indicative of our times. Whether or not violent resistance is actually used, these articulated tendencies threatening conventional elites symbolized defiantly on the body, in networks, and in online communities are together an important mechanism of subterfuge demonstrating proficiency and salience of oppositional cultural capital among body-modified members of the alterglobalizing new Movement Society.

10

Aesthetic Sabotage

Now all this is very tentative and generalizing. I would agree with Park that Bohemias are great centers of change. Oddly enough, the only people who have given attention to Bohemias have been Marxists. Lenin...took [them] very seriously, in part because [he feared] them. The only body of social theory that has had an integral place for the Bohemia is in Marxist theory. This is exemplified by the fact that the article on Bohemia in the Encyclopedia of the Social Sciences is a very meager and almost nonexistent one. In the Russian encyclopedia that came out in 1930, there is a forty-page article on them, very elaborately theoretical. But certainly, there seem to be grounds for proposing that as a source of social change Bohemias are worth our closest attention.

Mark Berney, 1955, in Grana and Grana

Musical Cultural Capital

In cultural enclaves such as New Orleans, a powerful indicator of authentic Bohemian status is competency in musical aesthetic capital. In both industrialized and less-developed nations, musicians are capable of uniting members of fragmented culture, play an important role in the implementation of rituals, establish order amidst chaos, and provide the discursive vehicle for socially sanctioned emotional expression. Whether through the frenzy of bongos ceremoniously pounded to awaken beneficent spirits in a voudouin ritual, the screeching melodies of bagpipes proudly played by men in skirts in a Scottish parade, the soul-searching sound of the tuba playing a dirge during a second-line procession to a Vieux Carre cemetery, or the creation of hard-driving breakbeats during programming of techno riffs in a Nottingham sound studio, the talent, expression, and fortitude required by these unique artists to create music telling a cultural story is very important in our social world. Music, as both production and consumption activity has many functions, including its use as a mechanism of cultural expression.

[Music as]...communication and its ideology as a mass culture derives not just from the organization of its production, not just from the conditions of its consumption, but also from the artistic intentions of its musical creators and from the aesthetics of its musical forms.[1]

Through the discursive potential of music, emotions and feelings of social participants are often expressed in ways that words otherwise could not. Dealing with themes of love, hate, hurt, fear, rejection, happiness, sadness, strength, weakness, loss, or anger, music is a culturally produced artifact that expresses human authenticity through unmediated discursive mechanisms of communication that unify listeners under the rubric of shared understanding. Not limited to expressing mere emotion, music is also a powerful mechanism of genuine political oppositional consciousness, which has been historically feared by representatives of established order.

> [M]usic has been seen as an important social force in many different ways. [A]ttention is drawn to the connections between pop and politics along two different dimensions. First, there is the way in which [contemporary alternative music] is seen as oppositional to the established values in the broadest sense. Second, there are interconnections between [the music] and politics...which opened up new possibilities for self-expression, something that authority did not like.[2]

Music has often represented societal struggles rooted in racial, class, and gender identity. Rose (1994) refers to political music such as rap as *oppositional transcripts*, which chart a variety of contentious struggles by providing "a contemporary stage for the theatre of the powerless." Music as an artifact of contestational culture enables us to engage in an oppositional discourse that might otherwise not be permissible in conventional society.

Bennett (2000) has argued that music is also an important determinant of geography. In his view, when interracial interethnic communities are patched together in any given urban environment, the inevitable concentration results in elective affinities bound up in space and place. In the process of located identity construction, understanding shared experiences of other races and ethnicities invariably gives rise to empathetic camaraderie. As such, it is only a matter of time before a subculture of understanding rooted in different struggles taking place in the same (or different) geographic locations emerges in these oppositional environments. Hence, the desire for artistic expression inherent in crossover and other hybrid musical forms serves to integrate previously fragmented communities across racial, ethnic, and gender chasms. Rooted in deleterious socioeconomic conditions that inspire diverse audiences to discuss the difficulties of coming to terms with the depths of deprivation brought on by modernity, music serves to further reverse failure camouflage and unify previously competitive factions of youth by providing the platform to genuinely express the universality of their struggles.

> The process of localization...may rely on local affinities...at the level of experiential and which, in turn, demands a more abstract form of analytical

engagement. A general supposition of those who have attempted to account for the appropriation of African-American musics by white British working class youth is that the structural position of white working-class Britons and African Americans is sufficiently similar to allow for...oppressions experienced by each group to be simultaneously addressed. [W]hite working-class youth's experimentation with black music and style occurs in a range of differing local contexts and thus against a variety of socio-cultural backdrops which may or may not include an established black population. Within the group then, there was a carefully fashioned sensibility which dictated that in being frank about their dedication not only to African American hip hop but also to the stylistic and ideological forms of address they deemed to be a part of it, they were in turn revealing and honesty and integrity within themselves thus setting the group apart.[3]

Unity in music and the struggle for shared articulation across racial and ethnic divides have not always, incidentally, been met with widespread receptivity or enthusiasm. To the extent that communities of color recognize any elements of white hegemonic [re]production or [re]consumption of Black liberation music as a disingenuous interpretation, members of innovative communities of color can create significant barriers to the use of their ethnicity-based culturally expressive art form and style.

[A]frican...youth culture was monitored by those neighboring white youths interested in forming their own subcultural options. Of course, in both Britain and America relations between black and white youth cultures have always been delicate, charged with a potentially explosive significance, irrespective of whether or not any actual contact takes place between the two groups. The profound subversion of white man's religion which places God in Ethiopia and the black 'sufferer' in Babylon has proven singularly appealing. This appeal requires little explanation. Clothed in dreadlocks and 'righteous ire' the Rastaman effects a spectacular resolution of the material contradictions which oppress and define [these] communit[ies].[4]

The question of white appropriation of bodily accoutrements of communities of color, including hairstyles, was highly contested in the earliest days of musical crossover, and its authenticity remains suspect and reluctantly tolerated on a case-by-case basis. Mercer (1987) points out that interracial style diffusion leads only to more innovation among genuinely aesthetic members of subcultural communities.

[W]e have to confront the paradox whereby white appropriation seems to act both as spur to further experimentation and as modified models to which black people themselves may conform. Yet hair is never a straight-forward biological fact, because it is always groomed, prepared, cut, concealed and generally worked upon by human hands. Such practices socialize human hair, making it the medium of significant statements about self and society. What is at stake, I believe, is the difference between the two logics of black stylization—one emphasizing natural looks, the other involving straightening to emphasize artifice.[5]

The real struggle for racial and ethnic authenticity in music was made more problematic by music industry executives, who commodified and neutralized cultures of opposition by subsidizing white elite interpretations that diluted the ethnic and racial elements of political outrage exemplified in these indigenous musical art forms, often exporting a sanitized version to enthusiastic masses. Insidious aesthetic and oppositional neutralization through commodification is, of course, not limited to musical genres expressing Black community struggles. Like the blues, ska, and jazz preceding it, punk has also been usurped by the music industry since the earliest days of its highly authentic origins.

> [S]ubcultures are objects of 'authentic' expressions only as long as they remain undiscovered by the market. Thus, to take again the example of 'God Save the Queen', it is possible that this song's message became incorporated into the sensibilities of divergent range of disaffected social groups. The frustrated adolescent, the political activist, the atheist, the anti-royalist would all have comprehended the message...in a similar fashion, but the significance they attached to it would have been very different. Indeed even within the more immediate punk movement, it is arguable that a number of different sensibilities were patched together by the media to suggest a coherent 'subcultural' affiliation.[6]

After becoming commodified, resistance through music that once reflected oppositional transcripts turns instead into routine repetitive craftwork. Through this process, music's powerful revolutionary aesthetic potential is rendered impotent. As a result, much of the original contestational inertia gets lost in its *corporate translation*. We need to look no further than Elvis, the Rolling Stones, and many other avant-garde artists who were exploited by music industry executives in the early phases of their careers to advance the long history of corporate theft of ethnic intellectual property rooted in the white exploitation and neutralization of musical genres of resistance.

> The relationship between the spectacular subculture and various industries which service and exploit it...inevitably lead to the diffusion of the subculture's subversive power. Thus as soon as the original innovations which signify 'subculture' are translated into commodities and made generally available, they become 'frozen'. Once removed from their private contexts by the small entrepreneurs and big fashion interests who produce them on a mass scale, they become codified, made comprehensible, rendered at once public property and profitable merchandise. [Commercialization] defined the subculture in precisely those terms which it [originally] sought most vehemently to resist and deny.[7]

Despite the deleterious consequences to oppositional aesthetic capital inherent in music's corporate commodification, various artistic genres of music still serve as an important aesthetic vehicle by which oppositional consciousness and related musical authenticity among and within diverse groups flourishes underground. Paradoxically driven by the alternative consumer demands found in the now substantial body-modified market segment of youth, emerging politically oppositional world music fusing techno, ethnic, punk, alternative, rock, and trance dance music render the strict artificial divisions of the old orthodox musical genres (and the anachronistic purists attempting to maintain them) obsolete. Thus, the challenge for oppositional communities in the face of these new musical hybrids turns to strategies to maintain the music's expressive defiance and liberating revolutionary potential that originally inspired its production.

> Pretending that bohemia exists apart from its own commodification is futile. The goal is to figure out what it means to be a self-styled outsider when there is no outside. It forces us to admit that we are linked to the larger world in ways that we despise as well as those we might accept.[8]

The increasing demand for authentic oppositional music eventually went underground to encourage the reluctant, sometimes grudgingly congenial unification of scientific, technological, and artistic communities of all racial and ethnic origins, enabling them to come together to produce the unprecedented artifacts of musical hybrids through new aesthetic-oriented computer technologies (Romanienko, 2001).

> When outsiders appropriate content from a disadvantaged minority culture, the source of the appropriated material ought to be fully and publicly acknowledged. This will especially be the case when outsiders lack opportunities to express themselves in their own style. I have in mind the situation of African-American blues and jazz musicians. Not long ago, white musicians who appropriated musical styles from African-Americans had the opportunity to record and perform that minority musicians were denied. Artists ought to be as respectful as possible when appropriating content. This imperative is particularly strong when artists borrow from an oppressed minority culture. The members of such a culture will reasonably be particularly sensitive to further indignities and artists ought to strive to avoid giving offense where possible. Presumably, artists who appropriate content from a culture do so because they find something of value in that culture. An artist who engages in cultural appropriation ought to be sensitive to the plight of [those who] have been subjected to cultural imperialism.[9]

The elective affinity among technical and artistic communities who finally started to acknowledge the mutual beneficial relationships fostered by the new transparencies, provides unprecedented opportunities for 'sampling' music from around the globe, which resulted in the fusion of rap, ska, hip-hop, and rock. These circumstances provided new forms of artistic freedom and unique [re]interpretation of culturally situated (albeit occasionally overprocessed) oppositional world music. These commercial and technological circumstances, while reducing to some extent music's overall innovative capabilities, nevertheless fulfill the voracious appetite for politically resistant internationally mixed dance music demanded by transient oppositional youth with a penchant for travel. Through a combination of self-imposed and economically compelled exile, transient body-modified refugees seeking socioeconomic and cultural environments more hospitable to their presence become inadvertently exposed to globalized forms of musical expression and related struggles through these new forms of forced migration. Globalization, and the mobility that accompanies it, translates into a broad desire for an infusion of international musical art forms among these aesthetic body-modified bohemians. These demands further unify racial and ethnic technical communities surrounding the demystification of evolving technologies used to advance the production of hybrid world music that expresses the camaraderie inherent in the nearly universal deprivation taking place among the downtrodden youth around the world.

> [Reggae] perhaps more than any other institution…was the site at which blackness could be most thoroughly explored, most clearly and uncompromisingly expressed. To a community hemmed in on all sides by discrimination, hostility, suspicion and blank comprehension, [it] came to represent, particularly for the young, a precious inner sanctum, uncontaminated by alien influences. There were ideological shifts inside reggae which threatened to exclude white youths. As the music became more openly committed to racial themes and Rastafarianism, the basic contradictions began to explode onto the surfaces of life, to burst into the arena of aesthetics and style. Dread, in particular, was an enviable commodity. It was the means by which to menace, and the elaborate free-masonry through which it was sustained and communicated on the street was awesome and forbidding, suggesting as it did an impregnable solidarity, an asceticism born of suffering.[10]

In response to industrial commodification thwarting music's liberating potential, coupled with the rise of computer technologies, artists from all musical genres, including genuinely defiant body modified punks and gutterpunks adhering to do-it-yourself worldviews, now have broad access to inexpensive three-track recorders that enable small-scale local music production to proliferate outside of the highly exploitative corporate music distribution systems. Punk and similar dependency-reversing worldviews espoused by producers of oppositional world music in all its hybrid genres of aesthetic resistance thus remain not only a viable mechanism to maximize the creative integrity and sabotaging potential of oppositional music for the imminent future, but also serve to expand the eclectic tastes of locally based, like-minded, body-modified bohemians committed to keeping the revolutionary aesthetic musical expressions alive through their support of the alternative music scene. Support of informal independent ("Indy") music production among body-modified bohemians has been so consistent and so substantial around the world, that there is now evidence of an evolution of a permanent, irreversible, Indy music industry indicative of profound self-sufficiency and self-exile among producers and consumers alike.

Authenticity through Music

In addition to its discursive potential to express outrage, and the way the processes of musical production and consumption unify distinct communities involved in its innovative independent sustainability, music also functions as authenticator of dissident culture and a grand arbiter of dissident style and adornment.

> Whether people form their interests or identities self consciously or unknowingly, in either case we can still ask whether they do so under ideal conditions, freely or under the influence of power. [T]his notion of free formation will provide a plausible interpretation of the authenticity of interests and a sounder basis for the project of emancipation. The dissident culture is a culture of emancipation. Dissident cultures attempt to combine an empowering virtue with an emancipatory authenticity. Alternative cultures flourish when they both emancipate and empower their followers. They emancipate if they offer a way of life which is more fulfilling and therefore more attractive. They empower if they propose forms of life which foster the collective strength and resolve of all those who belong to them. They need this strength in order to achieve the collective goals of their members in the face of the indifference or even hostility of the wider host society.[11]

Paradoxically, having dissident style both facilitates and hinders the bohemian project for genuine utopian living. To have musical capital is to exhibit an adherence to a particular combination of aesthetic adornment worn on, inscribed into, or impaled through the body. The extent to which aesthetic musical authenticity is considered a salient part of the bohemian identity is often determined by the depth (and thus irreversibility) to which these adornments permeate the body. Piercings and other forms of modification facilitate different degrees of musical identity construction, most often located in the musical genre of punk and its hybrids. Here, high-status aesthetic authenticity is directly correlated with *bodily invasion*. In other words, the extent to which fashion accoutrements of punk music exhibit invasiveness upon or within the body largely determines its translation potential into high-status musical aesthetic cultural capital. The superficial adornments utilizing clothing, chains, belts, and other fashion are considered suspect among genuine dissidents because they can be easily removed given the demands of conventional audiences. Cultural capital among these musically aesthetic body-modified bohemians is directly correlated with invasive tattoos, or even *more* invasive piercings, or even *more* invasive forms of scarification and branding, or the *most* invasive and expensive procedures, which have now evolved into surgically inserted cartilage, cutting, skin adhesions, and other specialized forms of body modification.

> "To have style" is, in other words, the result of goal-oriented actions directed toward a "cultural superelevation" of the everyday. It is a visible, unifying presentation, in which every individual action and every detail is included in

the goal of forming a...configuration or style and of presenting it. [In]ndi-
viduals can very strenuously try to appear unique or...authentic. Punk has
no message. Punk as a way of life and lived style is the message. The group
doesn't "proselytize" through teachings, appeals, or messages, but rather by
demonstrating a unified moral lifestyle. The group has no charismatic leader;
it lives on the self-charizmatization of the group and its lifestyle. Collective
presentation and orientation are secured through...deliberate public deployment of the style.[12]

Although reductivist analyses tend to oversimplify musical style as a binary
code wherein the subjects in question either have the desired dissident
forms or not; the notion of style, especially in regard to that which is rooted
in musical aesthetics, would be better served if viewed as a continuum of
authenticity that indicates different salient gradations of genuinely defiant dissident identities. Thus, highly aesthetic cultural capital displayed by
politically oppositional musicians who produce their cultural artifacts in
informal DIY distribution realms beyond the conventional music industry
often distinguishes itself with multiple body modifications.

The punk practice of multiple piercings and the diversity of commonplace and
offensive objects...were disturbing transformations of this form of adornment...a style of body art common in tribal cultures but relatively rare in
Western societies until recently. The piercing of the face with safety pins was
the most shocking aspect of punk style, communicating in a visceral manner
a complexity of...mutilation, masochism, suffering, self-destruction [that]
conveys further a sense of abuse and defilement by society. [S]imilations of
Mohican Indian hairstyles has connotations of youth on the "warpath" and
evoked stereotyped notions of the primitive, a designation that was used to
denigrate punk aesthetics and to label punk as a threat to western civilization.
[P]unk body adornment is a grassroots form of aesthetic behavior, largely
the creation of ordinary people who...developed the skills and mastered the
techniques necessary to produce forms of adornment that...reflected their
collective experiences and values [P]unks prided themselves on handmade
quality of their body art: they cut and colored their own hair, decorated
their own jackets, tattooed and pierced themselves, and created ensembles of
clothing and orientation from discarded [objects].[13]

Since safety pins were first used to adorn the ear by the British punk community, the oppositional body as blank canvas has been used as a veritable
road map of fluid, mobile temporality illustrating symbolic and experiential milestones authenticating defiant identity construction that unifies a
variety of defiant bohemians with a high degree of musical cultural capital
and related aesthetic style.

The early punk subculture was characterized by anti-commercialism, antiro-
manticism, and a lack of distinction between musicians and fans. [As] anarchists...punks offended as many people as they could. The punk subculture
flourished in England, because it captured the mood of the time and gave

expression to many of the frustrations and concerns of urban youth, such as high unemployment, dismal economic conditions, and a pervasive attitude of desperation and futility. [Their] participatory egalitarian ethos insist[ed] that every punk become actively creative as opposed to being a passive fan or consumer. Unlike British punk, American punk was not so much working-class and bohemian response to economic depression and authoritarian ideology as it was a middle-class alienation from and disgust with mainstream values. Like their British counterparts however, American punks embraced a sense of societal disintegration and futurelessness. The sentiment that society was collapsing and that there was no future pervaded American punk.[14]

As reiterated by Soeffner (1997), the do-it-yourself worldview and distinction-driven adornment remained a crucial aspect of decommodified punk culture.

> Anyone who has ever seen punks will remember the strange and characteristic composition of the "Iroquios look"...an allusion to the specific primitive people. "Punk" is the elaboration of a specific aesthetic of the ugly—and by implication, of poverty and shabbiness. The aims of this aesthetic are exactly the opposite of the usual efforts at make-up—they mean to demonstrate strict animosity to luxury, mass consumption and serial, reproducible beautification.[15]

There may be little consensus among outsiders with regard to how different musical genres function to advance the authentic self. Though there is no question regarding the genuine qualities of certain high status individuals involved with informal nonindustrial music production, punk as an authenticating mechanism of dissident expression among body modified bohemians might be problematic due to the music's rather inclusive communal nature and the deteriorating socioeconomic conditions facing most youth. Critics will argue that downwardly mobile young people have, in fact, little to lose when opting for participation in this musical genre to express their outrage. Other critics might argue that those seeking sanctity such as access to squatting or performance spaces offered by these aesthetic musical communities have little genuine adherence to political, consumption, or other relevant oppositional worldviews. Still others would suggest that some dissidents having the requisite musical and oppositional capital but lacking the fashion of dissident style properly displayed through highly contrived and excessive punk accoutrements risk exclusion from these superficial, visually oriented communities of style. These ethical dilemmas surrounding the judicious evaluation of genuine aesthetic musical oppositional capital are most frequently played out in the context of residential squats and performance spaces. In squats around the world, many gate-keeping mechanisms remain in place, which often overemphasize genuine capital of some, underestimate that of others. According to Miller (2003), so much effort is put into constructing and interpreting contestational style that these processes are anything *but* authentic. He argues, like Bourdieu

(1984), that it is the underlying *distinction* that we seek through immersion attempts in cultural networks. Miller suggests that authenticity is irrelevant. It is the *effort* of oppositional identity construction that brings such enjoyment.

> For purposes of faking it and our anxieties about our own fraudulence and authenticity, it makes little difference whether or not the self is there. The self, fictional or not, must measure up reasonably well as a legitimate self. [To fake it, use of a]ctual cosmetics, face-painting, have long been held to be a legitimate prerogative of women; men quite frequently have dabbled in it too, and not only in decadent Rome or Weimar Berlin. Like all practices it is subject to a thick array of rules, some articulated, most not. Make-up that calls and is meant to call aggressive attention to itself tends to indicate an aspiration for, or the fact of marginality: the whore or actor or superhip or gender-bending male or weirded-out teenager.[16]

Barnes (1994) argued that nonverbal communication through bodily discourse is a mechanism of disingenuousness. He suggests that the body is an important vehicle through which lies are corroborated. Without the body, the reliance on exclusively verbal mechanism to effectively disseminate lies is challenging.

> A spoken lie may form only one part of an act of deception; the liar may use, consciously or unconsciously, what has come to be known as body language as a means of enhancing the chances of success for deceit. Alternatively, the deception may be attempted by body language alone, without a supporting spoken lie.[17]

Gilsenan (1976) suggests that lying is a redistribution of knowledge and related power. From this perspective, disingenuousness would only be possible when aligning oneself falsely with groups who possess power. Walton (1998) concurs by suggesting that lies and other forms of disingenuousness are used in interactive dyads to express authority by the more powerful participant, who indulges in lies to establish rank and impose upon the weaker party a reconstructed reality. Wojcik (1995) deals with the question of authenticity by making the distinction between genuine punks and the commodified haute couture version he calls the *decontaminated*. Among experts on disingenuous cultures, lies appear to be a unidirectional phenomenon typically used to assert or align oneself with those in power. With few incentives and many sanctions associated with membership, the construction of false identity to align oneself with powerless punks and gutterpunks might therefore hold little appeal for those interested in advancing a fictive self.

Though there are certain excessive, occasionally erroneous evaluation activities that can be associated with aesthetic identity construction among style-centric members, and taking into consideration the worldwide popularity of body modification, a small minority of punks and gutterpunks presumably might be using body piercing or its musical hybrids for reasons other than those outlined, which may or may not advance their own constructions of authenticity. But given the invasive quality of many of these practices, as well as the difficulty in faking an appreciation for the loud raucous genre of hardcore punk, it remains unlikely that a significant number of individuals who have undergone intimate procedures such as multiple piercings upon their genitals or are longtime members of punk bands are genuinely *faking it*. There are significant costs associated with advancing a disingenuous self, and body-modified bohemians are not even remotely reluctant to exercise profound ostracism, isolation, eviction, and other severe subcultural sanctions that mirror the exclusionary mechanisms of normative social controls used by conventional society that inspired their rebellions in the first place.

> It is this alienation from the deceptive 'innocence' of appearances which gives the teds, the mods, the punks and no doubt future groups of yet unimaginable 'deviants' the impetus to move from man's second false nature to a genuinely expressive artifice. As a symbolic violation of the social order, such a movement attracts and will continue to attract attention, to provoke censure and to act...as the fundamental bearer of significance in subculture.[18]

Social ostracism both within body-modified punk subcultures and with society at large can be so severe that it makes provisional portrayals of fake punk and related inauthenticity for any consistent length of time highly problematic. West (1990) suggests that authenticity is a matter of *source*. Where identity constructions originate from within the individual, it is genuine. Where identity arises from exogenous societal pressures, it can only be construed as disingenuous. Dissident body-modified bohemians, therefore, with a high degree of aesthetic alternative cultural capital, are among the few truly authentic social actors in our world today. Those with membership among the obedient masses who do not express an orientation to alternative aesthetic expression, do not strive to demonstrate their individuality, and are instead highly dependent on exogenous elite to determine their aesthetic ways of life, are those actually living truly disingenuous lives—the conventional majority.

> A person's awareness of the merely provisional authenticity of her interests is, finally, reflected in the ability to undertake deliberately self-transformative action. [I]nterests which have been acquired freely, or which would survive the continuing test of free formation, can be regarded as authentic. In particular, interests which are imposed by society, which are the product by manipulation or indoctrination or ideology, are likely to be inauthentic. A political or social system can be legitimated only in terms of the authentic interests of its members. [T]he interpretations proposed by culture must be persuasive for the individuals themselves. They must have at least the appearance of authenticity. The struggle between universal demands of individual authenticity is manifested as conflict, both within the individual and within the culture.[19]

Punk Suppression and Nonrecognition

If punk is a true indication of *lived authenticity*, then which punks have been most effective? Far from faking it, the punks in the Soviet Union paid a high price for their individuality. Soviet punks were routinely exposed to imprisonment and other cruel forms of "resocialization" in retribution for the consumption and production of punk music prohibited under the totalitarian regime. The rise of punk music during communist times was generally attributed to either Western subversion or mental illness. Punk proliferated in nearly every communist country despite mental deviance labeling (Pilkington, 1994), criminalization (Ovchinskij, 1987), and policies of forced immersion of these "anomalous" youth within state-authorized resocialization programs they called "diversions" (Mitev, 1988). The official position of the apparatchiks was consistent with Miller's "faking it" paradigm. As a mental health deficiency they officially categorized as *imitation*, Soviet officials argued that any oppositional outrage among young punks must be suppressed, through institutionalized means if necessary, due to its disingenuous nature given societal abundance under Communism. Institutionalized means of resocialization of punks under the Soviet regime could be particularly cruel, and was widely used in an attempt to reverse these *imitators* of the rational outrage found among young people in the decadent material West.

> The imitation thesis claimed that youth subcultures were rooted in the specific conditions of capitalist countries where 'youth is poor, hungry, and unemployed' and hence there were no reasons for such deviant behavior under communism where such conditions did not apply. The analysts of the 'problem' of youth subcultures under communism and the different solutions…all reflect [s]trategies of repression, diversion, and incorporation [that] fear such forms of collective or individual expression. [S]ubcultures sprang more from a desire to escape than to confront and allowed a cultural space where alternative identities could be formed.[20]

Even during oppositional street protests or the bloody battles that have occurred during the wave of "eviction proceedings" of squats throughout Europe over the past half decade, punks in the EU and United States never experienced the level of persecution for their oppositional worldviews that the punks in the Soviet Union did. Now that archival data has been released, there is substantial evidence to indicate that Moscow was particularly fearful of the revolutionary potential of punks throughout the occupied territories composing the Soviet empire. The archival documents and undercover photographs released after the fall of Communism indicated that there were significant human, financial, and other resources devoted to the surveillance of a punk movement in Poland and throughout the empire (Lesiakowski et al., 2004). This long-awaited compendium of these newly released Soviet-era archival materials—complete with official commentary from NKVD[21] experts in punk resocialization—has become the new cult literary classic among contemporary body-modified bohemian anarchists throughout Poland. It may come as no surprise that during periods of Soviet repression, punk music and its fashion accoutrements proliferated even more, as everyone in society was well versed with the do-it-yourself punk paradigm thanks to routine conditions of artificial scarcity imposed by the coercive state to quell sporadic uprisings. To a certain extent, regime suppression in the Communist era brought out the disenfranchisement and smoldering rage against the state that elicited the punk spirit in nearly every demoralized citizen forced to spend half a day in line queued for a rationed roll of toilet paper that invariably was never delivered. Despite the threat of internment, hospitalization, or other mental "resocialization" programs under the regime, fomenting hostilities fueled the enthusiasm for punk among discontented youth throughout the Soviet empire.

Meanwhile, conventional social scientists in the West gravely underestimated the punk movement through profound nonrecognition that continues to this very day. This neglect is especially evident in their criticism of the apathetic disdain that allegedly accompanies punk music enthusiasts. These researchers, often collusive socialist leftists who engage in conspicuous consumption themselves, referred to the generation of punk music connoisseurs as *Generation X* in order to indicate an alleged adherence to nihilism. As evidence of these alleged nihilistic tendencies, outsider leftists highlight punks' anti-consumer orientation. In response, body-modified anarchist punks who are critical of the outsiders' consumption patterns and pseudorevolutionary image call these baby booming leftists *champagne socialists*. Body-modified punks defend their own disdain of consumption by calling themselves *transumers*, whose empowering tendencies merely *transcend* material culture, known as the turn toward postmaterial society. Punk music as lived activism does not subscribe to the values of consumer culture in conventional society. Punks believe such culture places too much primacy on the accumulation of identical mass-produced objects of conformist culture in order to demonstrate familiarity with tired conventions of planned obsolescence of the fickle design world through homogenized styles that bring fleeting status and conventional recognition from highly irrelevant audiences striving to display adherence to the accumulation of necessary goods and services required to display their neutralized, disindividualized, tasteless, obedient, unaesthetic, consumer lives.

> [We can] define power not as an intervention in someone's life which harms their real interests, but as whatever intrudes on their free praxis. Here 'praxis' refers to the full span of human activity from the formation of interests to the selection and achievement of particular goals. In other words, power either interferes with an autonomous action or the free formation of interests which informs that action. [I]t could be argued that it would be better, wants and desires more authentic, if they were formed without the pressures from advertising and consumer cultures. Beyond the realm of purely material

needs the affluent consume for a sense of power, for a sense of superiority, for status or sexual appeal, or simply for fun. The rituals of consumption convey a fantastical but nonetheless pleasurable feeling of power, a wish-fulfilling annihilation of the existential predicament of the individual. Social confidence, sexual potency, even a sanitised and secure death all are seemingly available at a price. The spiritualisation of consumption conceals the 'desire' of human beings for one another, their cultural, emotional, and sexual interdependence. The private acquisitiveness of western society is abundant evidence for its human impoverishment. Freed from these bonds, the individual is faced with the problem of making sense of a life which may include more suffering than pleasure, whose most cherished projects may be cut short or frustrated either by misfortune or the malicious interference of others. [A]s existentialist thinkers have made plain, an individual is responsible for her life. She may come to realize, when it is too late, that it has been built on errors and lies.[22]

To reiterate, West (1990) states above, "The private acquisitiveness of western society is abundant evidence for human impoverishment." Anarchist punks' reluctance to espouse hypocrisies inherent in the production and consumption ideologies of champagne socialism, and the ensuing backlash from the old new left that accompanies this break with the anachronistic, Marxist-obsessed, impotent past exposes the deep generational divisions that continue to fracture the industrialized left to the profound benefit of the hegemonic right. These conditions have left punks vulnerable to widespread misinformation campaigns of criticism involving delegitimating constructions of "X" from the demographic cohort of aging hippies dominating the same side of the political fence. Social scientists in advanced industrialized societies, most of whom are collusive materialist champagne socialist leftists, have produced an exorbitant volume of manipulative reductivist analyses to discredit the anarchist orientations of the new body-modified bohemians. They disseminate research that distracts audiences from their own hypocritical narcissistic excesses since the 1960s and 1970s (Lasch, 1978) and perpetuates false myths of nihilism among this powerful oppositional cohort, such as claims that nihilistic X'ers exhibit an unfounded mistrust of government (Black and Black, 1994), express high sentiments of cynicism (Strauss and Howe, 1991), prefer detachment from socioeconomic activity (Howe and Strauss, 1993), have exercised a decline in partisan politics (Craig and Bennett, 1997), and are apathetic toward forms of activism (Haynsworth, 2003). This body of literature should be characterized as both misrecognition and nonrecognition of the genuine qualities of body-modified punk anarchist activist culture.

The demand for recognition is a claim to humanity and the right to participate in shaping it and enjoying it. Potent forces released by one-sided globalizing process...conspire to neutralize it. The wars of recognition are here to stay. It is the joint task and responsibility of politics and social theory to release their potential as a powerful instrument of justice and humanity, dialogue and cooperation.[23]

The self-obsessed, self-referential myopic culture constructed by the huge demographic cohort composed of conspicuously consuming, baby booming, hypocritical "radical" leftists creates conditions that are extremely detrimental to the recognition of body-modified punk anarchists and their authentic revolutionary potential. Old new leftist culture dominating all aspects of non-right society prohibits any intergenerational discourse regarding the validity of new forms of resistance, consistently attempts to impose its own tired and failed tactics on youth and other resisters on the Left, and rushes, ex post facto, to the front of all successful political resistance activities engaged in by alterglobalizing body-modified anarchist activists, falsely claiming these sabotaging alterglobalizing achievements as their own. Unwilling to take any professional risks to render vulnerable their own highly material lifestyles, they make no effort to advocate on behalf of, or otherwise mentor young punk X'ers with any resistant pedagogy other than their own deflated and depleted myopic Marxist-centered vision for the future. In spite of the fact that there is not a single authentic labor union remaining in existence anywhere on the planet, vapid Marxists composing the intellectual left in the United States and the European Union continue to proselytize their fixation of this singular form of desired utopian revolution, while suppressing all other forms of revolutionary ideology and related aesthetic accoutrement. It is precisely due to the profound disingenuousness of these delusional, aging, overweight, materialist, high-consuming, hypocritical, champagne socialists composing the Western intellectual left that has paradoxically alienated authentic activists from conventional higher education and fostered the dynamic rise of a truly authentic, postmaterial, body-modified anarchist activist resistance effort of intellectual outsiders centered around punk and other powerful pedagogical genres of oppositional music and related resistance.

> Commercialized culture presents itself and is often accepted as the only alternative to control by such forces as those of the religious right, or of government. Though we have seen a remarkable freeing of culture from governmental control in what used to be the Soviet Union and in Eastern Europe, the spectre of governmental control of culture is still vivid and is intolerable to anyone who values free expression. The commercialized culture of the west often claims to be the only alternative, and it is only a failure of imagination and thought that keeps us from focusing on better arrangements for making and receiving culture than those which now prevail.[24]

Though the hegemonic core on the right may very well be amused by all the ideological squabbling around materialism and claims of nihilism between intergenerational factions on the left, the music produced and consumed by genuine body-modified anarchist activists tells a very different story of authentic oppositional culture. Exploring and contesting the role of institutions such as the state, education, and family that perpetuate oppressive gender stereotypes and related dependencies constraining both male and female emancipation is just one among many important themes of liberation articulated through contemporary punk and punk hybrid music.

[Girl power and its] attention on gender performance as a privileged site and source of political oppositionality...within alternative rock coincides with the appearance of the white male "loser" (e.g Beck, Billy Corgan of Smashing Pumpkins, and Kurt Cobain of Nirvana), whose performances of abject or disempowered masculinity [leads to] an ostensibly self-critical...political efficacy.[25]

The defiant nuances of these self-deprecating, hyper-obedient, critical messages contesting gender roles and other forms of punk opposition are often too subtle for the boisterous, bra-burning, baby-boomer mentality, and gets somehow lost in intergenerational translation during fleeting moments of body-modified interactions that threaten the sensibilities of the conventional materialist's pacified gaze. When 1960's resistance icon Joan Baez is replaced by modern-day 2000's androgynous resistance icon Marilyn Manson, the emaciated punk celebrity struts around stage with heavy eyeliner and ping-pong balls in his eye sockets to display his familiarity with artists producing similar visual conceptual criticisms while simultaneously expressing his defiant authentic aesthetically constructed self. Exposing his skinny buttocks to an otherwise obese allegedly social-justice–oriented American public and maintaining his masculine sexuality while prancing on stage wearing excessive make-up, long hair, and a woman's S/M latex bustier designed for private domination in heteronormative sexual interaction among monogamous couples in the suburbs provides the body-modified bohemian community not with evidence that he is faking it or even that he espouses nihilist ideologies as naïve audiences have suggested, but rather, with Manson's criticism of female subordination and the momentary artificial contexts of women's acceptable societal domination through his adherence to creative alternative consumption patterns through the DIY punk paradigm. Autonomous elements of his authenticity would eventually become diluted as he commercialized his hermaphroditic appeal and unique quasi-transvestite goth style by marketing his own brand of fishnet stockings and other naughty accoutrement to suburban boys and girls shopping for *ready-made rage* in franchised malls throughout North America. Yet even under the most commercial of circumstances, Marilyn Manson's particular musical and stylistic expressions of defiance remain highly authentic and can hardly be classified as nihilistic. For outsiders to get a better sense of the underlying oppositional spirit surrounding these increasingly excessive rituals, customs, and beliefs of punk rock musical dissidents, as well as their paradoxical appeal to the vicariously living conventional masses, social scientists must begin to seriously examine these complex processes of aesthetic opposition by looking beyond conventional analytic approaches that reduce civic engagement and social movements to mere periodic participation in anachronistic organizations and their tired placard-waving street protests, and take more of an interest in musical and lyrical content of genuine cultural artifacts. This way, researchers concerned with youth movements might be able to more accurately determine what genuine oppositional struggles, if any, are being articulated by iconoclastic, sexually exploratory, gender-bending, aesthetically oppositional, increasingly unconventional, body-modified bohemian punk connoisseurs that are unlikely to be found on any university campus.

Visual Cultural Capital

The visual impression left on naïve audiences by some of the more creative bohemian members of the body-modification community such as Marilyn Manson can indeed be an assaulting experience for the conventional senses. Many body-modified bohemians incorporate elaborate tattoos, piercings, skin stretchings, and epidermal implants that may or may not leave pleasant effects for the naïve gaze.

> The individual intuitively feels menaced, indeed overwhelmed. The money economy, bureaucracy, and the political state create rules that make citizens increasingly similar. To struggle against this standardization, the individual emphasizes the aesthetic details of the self.[26]

Regardless of the kind of outcome that manifests among observant others, body-modification plays an important role in the aesthetic construction of the oppositional body. Through these highly individualized expressions, bohemians are able to use the human body as a mobile conceptual canvas that presents opportunities for visual forms of aesthetic sabotage in any geographic context. Before proceeding further, it may be useful at this point to examine relevant aesthetic concepts that can help to demystify these emerging art forms on the body.

In tracing the contemporary use of body modification in the arts, any analysis must go back one decade earlier than the street spectacles created by British punks through their shocking preoccupation with the safety pin. Ten years earlier, since the 1970s, self-mortification had already been an important (albeit censored) element of Communist-era avant-garde theatrical live performance. Used by anarchist and feminist artists to communicate opposition to the body's victimization under totalitarianism, performance artists used the body to express the demoralizing consequences of life under socialism. This brought about the conceptualization of *negation*, a theme widely in use today among extreme piercing experts that renders the genital impotent (discussed elsewhere). Negation was first explored by these Communist-era performance artists as the ultimate conceptual obedience to the oppressive regime. Their cutting-edge oppositional visual discourses were outlawed by Communist authorities, but they proceeded undaunted to communicate, through live mortifying performances, their ambivalent obedience to the arts-supporting regime. This visual aesthetic discourse took the form of live impalements, stretching, and other symbolic forms of self-mutilation and self-negation. The most powerful of these discursive performances surrounding portrayals of the obedient Communist body were often conceptualized by women artists, who demonstrated the emotional toil of "political and biological claims" staked by authorities on their bodies.

> The purpose of avant-garde performance [under Communism] was to publicly expose the repressive conditions affecting all the people struggling under the structural social oppression presented by the regime. [Art] exposed the broader mechanism of women's functions in communist systems reflected the fallocentric and patriarchal culture, but also injected new expressions of political barriers prohibiting the social and cultural emancipation of women. Problems of the emancipation of women were identified as resting in the discourse surrounding visual culture, existentialism, and political and biological claims on female bodies and related identities.[27]

As documented in detail by Piotrowski (2006), female artists in the Eastern bloc begin to express an ambivalent relationship with their bodies in the early 1970s, arbitrarily crossing the borders of criticism and aestheticism to use visual culture to disclose their own sickness, disease, and death in light of political oppression. It is here that the themes of mutilation, amputation, surgical, and other forms of scientific elimination are first explored in the visual arts with any gravity or consistency. Through the leadership of women artists, the avant-garde visual arts community of communist East Central Europe captured the pathologized relationship between the totalitarian regime and the human body. The obedient citizen-worker is reduced to a mere economic and reproductive vessel, and once these functions have been fulfilled, it is preferred by the state that the body (and with it its consuming tendencies) cease to exist to prevent placing continued burdens on the matriarchal empire known as Mother Russia.

Soviet oppression of citizen bodies was not limited to women. The objectification of the female body as a sexual reproductive vessel for the state left the male body even more alienated from society as mere post-war reconstruction hard laborer. Reproductive heteronormativity under communism further marginalized the necessity for men in society, and prohibited possibilities for sexual pluralism to arise.[28] State homogenization of fashion, repression of eroticism, and prohibition of gender or other distinctions based on noncollectivized individuality together led to the criminalization of style, the denial of taste, and the crippling of visual culture under communist-authorized, monolithic, functionalist-driven, state aestheticism. As a result, opportunities for aesthetic discourse surrounding sexual and labor oppression of the body was made possible only through abstract explorations in avant-garde performance art that could bypass the excessive censorship by state authorities. Certain productions of the oppositional genre could not pass authorititarian censorship and went underground to become part of the larger opposition movement against the empire known as Samizdat (Hamersky, 2002). For purposes of the current treatment, the oppositional body and related oppositional consciousness was explored among avant-garde performance artists of the communist era through state-subsidized or underground spectacles that sought to criticize the eros-repressing, sensually negating, gender-neutralizing, vapid visual culture through abstract use of performative impalements and other body modification live on stage. One group that enjoyed particular notoriety based on their self-mortification performances originated in Dresden and was known as "Autoperforationsartistik."

> It is important to note that in the second half of the 1980's, a group of East German artists from Dresden affiliated with university and official government associations named "Autoperforationsartistik"… engaged in identity construction in art through creative impalements, mutilations, and other incapacitations of their own bodies that, according to the artists, expressed the kinds of defense mechanisms needed to combat routine everyday live [under communism]. In performances [Micha Brendel, Reiner Görß, Via Lewandowsky, and Else Gabriel] experimented publicly with the limits of the body's ability to physically tolerance excruciating levels of pain. By exposing audiences to such maltreatment and transgression of the body and their [inability] to observe these performances, they asked provocative questions regarding the ability of citizens to endure the torture of [life under totalitarianism].[29]

Western ethnocentrists are sure to question these documented assertions of the communist origins of avant-garde self-mortification theater, but as far as invasive body modification and the aesthetic conceptual performance arts are concerned, the evidence overwhelmingly supports the idea. Artists enduring life under the Soviet totalitarian regime were the first to pioneer the oppositional body to explore conceptual notions of self-mutilation and other forms of embodied negation with all its indignation via mortification through impalements, incisions, restrictions, suspensions, and other interactive exploratory devices on stage. These performances took place decades before oppositional avant-garde conceptual performance artists such as Karen Finley surfaced in the West.[30] The intention is not to diminish Finley's contributions to the genre, which are notable due to her efforts to popularize and legitimate self-mortification as a genuine art form in industrialized contexts. She was clearly a pioneer for having the courage to assume that self-deprecating, obedience-actualizing, defiance-denying avant-garde conceptual performances of this type could be grasped by conventional Western audiences given what by some accounts can be summarized as narcissistic, consumption-oriented, materialist, imperializing consciousness (Lasch, 1978). Although the conceptual self-mortifying feminist aesthetic movement in the United States is rooted in resistance efforts originally conceived decades earlier under communism, Western audiences were not the least bit naïve or incapable of grasping these abstract metaphors. Instead they thoroughly comprehended the conceptual diminution of the female body and related eros through their own personal familiarity with regime expectations in constructing the obedient politicized body necessary to sustain hegemonic capitalism. Regardless of state ideology that gave birth to the original concept, for our purposes it is interesting to note that conceptual esoteric abstract expressions of citizen resistance with their focus on the centrality of the state in thwarting embodied emancipation were understood ubiquitously by audiences in the East and the West surviving under oppressive systems of state hegemony whether socialist or capitalist.[31] To that end, Finley's object penetration and other genital self-manipulations live onstage were, not surprisingly, widely acclaimed by urbane avant-garde progressive audiences. Finley's calculation of broad embodied disenfranchisement among men and women paid off, and she became one of the most highly acclaimed conceptual visual artists in the history of western avant-garde for her resistance of exogenous bodily controls and her struggle for self-determination through her momentary on-stage portrayals of an indulgent, independent, self-determined, autonomous female and her exploratory interactions with the crevices composing her depoliticized, unmediated body.

Performance and the Conceptual Arts

Live genital self-explorations aside, performance remains one of the most universally oppositional art forms, because it represents an uncommodified existential approach to cultural production, leaving audiences with only the remnants of the experiential once the performance is complete. There is no object to buy, no framed piece to take home, and aesthetic "consuming" audiences leave these abstract venues with no object other than an experience of esoteric struggle for its meaning. Although usually highly challenging, the experiences associated with conceptual performing arts can be of great demand among discerning audiences with a proclivity for creative thinking. Seamon (2001) suggests that the turn toward abstract conceptual art with all its inherent challenges and ambiguities is part of a larger phenomenon of decommodification of the arts, as well as the world around us.

> What makes the work conceptual is that, in contrast to, for example, a nude sculpture, where we are not puzzled by the choice of object, it is not clear what the purpose of the work is, and our "natural" impulse at that point is to search for a conceptual meaning that will make sense of its very existence. Whereas there is considerable freedom to draw one's own moral from traditional [art], as long as one remains, so to speak, in the ballpark, gestures in conceptual art are much more enigmatic. [Some] interpreters dislike the conceptual dimension because they want to make their own contributions. The appeal of conceptual art and its theory is part of a major change in the world of art, and the world in general. The change I have in mind is preference for meaning over value, or the according of value to making meaning rather than artifacts.[32]

If we agree with Seamon's observations that the arts are beginning to place a higher aesthetic "value upon the making of meaning as opposed to arte-facts," does this indicate perhaps that we are finally ready to admit, at least in our aesthetic discursive cultures, that we are profoundly discontent with excesses surrounding materialist culture? The opening of a space conducive to a postmaterial dialogue in materialist culture is, in many ways, more important than the conclusion reached. When and where these decommodi-fied conceptual esoteric experiences involve the oppositional, aesthetic per-formances are constructing what we might call *aesthetic political culture*. Aesthetically oriented, body-modified bohemians can thus be construed as pioneers of this worldwide movement of postmaterial decommodifica-tion expressing creative embodied sensibilities toward the deconstruction of commercial visual (and later mass) culture through a multitude of sub-versive aesthetic methodologies including the experiential.

> One advantage of the political culture model is that it allows for a more subtle discussion of culture-making strategies, one that thus examines per-formative, rather than product-oriented, aspects of movements.[33]

The production of oppositional visual culture and the deconstruction of its commercial orientation is not limited to full-time avant-garde performance artists. On the contrary, many body-modified bohemians are inspired by the efficacy of the oppositional messages inherent in these aesthetic per-formances, and seek to emulate these expressive bodily devices to obtain the same oppositional expediency offstage in mundane life. Conceptual art, providing creative opportunities for the reanimation of experiential aesthetics, is increasingly used among body-modified aethetic bohemians to advance their particular resistant utopia by an innovative form of social movement that might be referred to as the *lived visual oppositional politi-cal culture* project.

Art and the Oppositional Body

But beyond its role in performances, can the pierced, branded, and stretched colonized body truly be considered both a work of living art and perpetual canvas of protest? According to Addison (2005), the value of art rests in the experiential both on the part of the artist-producer, as well as the audience-consumer.

> [One perspective] defines the work of art as a 'symbolically significant sensu-ous manifold where we have a concrete particular which is charged with…the conceptual and the sensual which enables art to express something of the depth and richness of the body-hold [embodiment].' The expressiveness of art and design is therefore manifest most trenchantly in the concept of self expression. [A]rtists are able to transcend the contexts in which they live to produce work that is both meaningful and autonomous. This unique individ-uality is revealed through a process of self-exploration, in which the novitiate

discovers and unfolds their true essence. Because the emphasis is on self-expression rather than communication, it does not matter, in a sense, that this process is merely one of transmission [through] a seamless and unmediated process.[34]

For our purposes, it is precisely the unmediated character of body art that bohemians seek to express through their modifications. Whether engaging in self-modification or through consultations with professionals for modification services, there are few interventions to mediate or otherwise complicate the relationship of the self to one's own body. For a fleeting moment, even the need for commodities marketed for purposes of neurosis-production and neuroses-appeasement associated with esteem-driven bodily consumption are temporarily suspended. The modification of the body must be instrumentalized by the individual *in situ*, and the final product, the modified body, is advanced as an original creation brought on by the unique experience inherent in the modification performed. This is one moment, one space, where state or other institutional authority is completely unable to intervene. Even under the most oppressive of circumstances, the Soviet Proletkult (apparatus for Proletarian Culture) could not possibly regulate the bodies of every performance artist on every stage throughout the crumbling empire. Nor are state regulations able to entirely eliminate access to body-piercing services today (though they have unsuccessfully tried). Thus, the relationship between body and the modifier remains unmediated. Nothing stands between the body-modifying artist and his or her canvas. Here begins the transformative potential of the body (and thus the self) through a variety of modifications involving pushing, pulling, tugging, and squeezing in a variety of dry, moist, or wet anatomical membranes. No matter what the modification obtained or where it is located, creative actors are seeking an autonomous, self-determinant, and highly sensual aesthetic experience from the creatively defiant transgression associated with body modification.

> The aesthetic experience…can denote both the object of the experience and the way the object is experienced. [It typically involves] transformation [through an experience of] pleasure, knowledge, perception, [and] intense feelings. Because aesthetics is considered a rather soft discipline that has trouble matching the scientific rigor and explanatory power of other academic fields, it is understandable that the contemporary aestheticians would be especially worried about the challenges to…rationality that [bodily functions such as] sex…seems to introduce. [The link inherent in the body-art experience] can inspire us to greater appreciation of our sexual experiences, and consequently, to more artistic and aesthetically rewarding performance in our erotic behavior, which surely forms one important dimension in the art of living.[35]

Can life really be an art form? Given that lived aesthetic activism is the goal of certain utopian bohemians, the aesthetic body similarly infuses politics and other spheres of life with the transformational aesthetic potential inherent in what we might call the *trangressive body project*. The entire experience of obtaining body modification, showing the body modification, and even addressing the criticism that comes with constructing the defiantly transgressive body all indicates profound transformation of the self and [dis]connectedness with others. This occurs through interpretations and translations that hope to provoke political and/or aesthetic repugnance, resistance, acceptance, status enhancement and attenuation, and related cognitive thought among relevant conventional and unconventional audiences. And herein lies the authentic autonomous aesthetic experience. The body is a unique autonomous site of iconoclastic rebellion. Historical use of the body as an aesthetic mechanism of rebellion has been an effective oppositional tactic in use among artist-activists for centuries, and is perhaps most effectively used by contemporary artists of the gay, lesbian, bisexual, transexual [GLBT] community such as Robert Mapplethorpe.

> The social organization of lesbians and gay men has centered around the shared experience of transgressive sexuality, which has been variously defined throughout the century. The stigma of perversion tainted the collective consciousness. Pervasive social attitudes that homosexuals were bizarre, criminal, or sick were reinforced by, and contributed to, a crushing isolation and invisibility. Secrecy was an institutional tyranny rather then an individual prerogative.[36]

Gay, straight, or bisexual, certain aesthetic forms of body modification, as well as the sensual experiences they provide, permanently render the conventional body with its conventional sexualities obsolete. The final bodily creations conceptualized by these rebellious aesthetic bohemians display self-imposed exile and a distinct and permanent alignment with aesthetic unconventional sexual iconoclasts on the margin. The intention here is to compel deeply discontent, non-exploratory, non-curious, sexually conformist audiences to think about the disingenuous passivity that goes against human nature and renders them so accepting of their obedient embodied missionary position conventionalities for procreative purposes. And the obedient masses are discontent. Even a superficial glance at the traffic jams winding their way through the "turn-abouts" and other public places where married, allegedly monogamous, staidly suburban males frequently cruise for anonymous homosexual group intercourse reveals they have become even more popular since the groundbreaking ethnography, *Tea Room Trade* was published in 1970.[37] The widespread popularity of visual arts portraying the grotesque and bloody increasingly produced by dilettante outsiders flying off exhibition spaces in the galleries of Paris and beyond may also be an indication of fomenting hostility, material disenchantment, and general decline of the aesthetically oriented, art-sponsoring, haute couture-consuming, vapid, desexualized, capitalist-connoisseur culture.[38] Nevertheless, when it comes to the arts, transgressive rebellion has, and will continue to be, a powerful force instigating social change both within the arts and throughout mass culture.

> For the last 200 years, and especially the late nineteenth century, the art-loving public has been fascinated by the artist as rebel. In this scheme of things, the great artists are those who see the world with new eyes. To realize their vision, they must do battle with the stifling forces of convention and cultural inertia, at the risk of ostracism, and, of course, poverty. History has vindicated these rebels so consistently that the story of modern art is a chronicle of rule-breaking. If we assume that all rule-breakers are ground-breakers, it follows that we should not just recognize them but reward them. [T]hey claim a privileged official standing because they are outside the system. Two centuries of romantic and modernist rebellion have raised the status of the outsider to the demigod. He or she is the great questioner, the agent of change, the person who, by making us think, prevents us from falling into complacency and stagnation. People do not always want to think.[39]

Given the powerful ambiguities that are unleashed at both ends of the production and consumption cycle of modification-constructed body art, the final creation that emerges from these esoteric and rebellious modification experiences forces audiences to be exposed both to the political and the aesthetic claims to raw authenticity and other hard truths that the artist seeks to convey through multiple modifications, the changing restrictive and decorative malleable devices they display, and the imagined sexual aesthetic community necessary to accomplish interactive episodic aspects of transgressive sexuality.[40]

> The artistic properties of the work invite the response, but that response is mediated by the form of engagement the audience has toward the work, and the form of engagement alters the response. Art has the power to encourage us to think about morality in terms that are not black and white, and works that do this deserve the greatest moral praise.[41]

The ambivalences that can arise in experiencing conceptual embodied visual arts on stage and in the bedroom are precisely the intention of these morally provocative forms of aesthetic expression. Body modification simply represents the beginning of the potential of aesthetic forms of conceptual sexual avant-garde expression of the lived visual political culture project.

In closing, it should be noted that critics will surely argue that the innovation and aesthetic expression that originally inspired body modification among bohemians from the original days has since lost much of its creative and oppositional potential, and this may indeed be true. But as Trilling (1997) points out, there are great discrepancies between art and repetitive craft.

> One issue, however, becomes intractable. This is originality vs. conventionality. To be original is to do something for the first time. The real issue

is responsibility. The more aspects the artist can claim responsibility for, the closer the artist comes to true originality. Craft implies [repetition and] control. The maker decides what to make and how to make it. The success of any project depends on strict adherence to the plan. Art, in contrast, may begin with a plan, but always goes further. The creative genius of art is such that something unintended, something bigger and more splendid than mere intention, finds its way into the finished work.[42]

Regardless of whether transgressive sexuality through body modification has maintained itself as art or redundant craft, the use of innovative or repetitive modification to advance all forms of the body art project is equally significant to the bearer of the unmediated body. There are many among the body modified who still place tremendous political and aesthetic importance in expressing reflexive creativity through their highly oppositional bodies. Some are Latino men facing long-term incarceration in prison, living in segregated Latino housing units, who seek elaborate tattooed tapestries of the Madonna and Child on their backs. This body modification is pure innovative art that functions as a powerful visual device for the devout that will physically prevent rape by other Latino males, usually devout Catholics, engaging in forced sodomy through the imposition of impotency brought on through the power of sacral art. Others use their piercings in suspension performance spectacles emulating ancient transcendental Malaysian rituals. Still others are simply pleased to replicate the tried and true devices already at their disposal at piercing franchises at the local mall to employ ready-made rage through the use of popular tattoo stencils and generic piercings with minimal invasiveness or originality. Whether modifications reflect genuinely innovative transgressive art or merely repetitive commodified craft, each is an equally important construction for the bearer to advance his or her particular authenticity through the oppositional body project. Inspired by mall-mediated franchised redundancy or a genuine work of innovative ritualized sacral art, body modification remains an important mechanism of aesthetic expression used by creative bohemians to transform and empower the self, thus authenticating their own unique utopian project for sensual and political sabotage of the established world order.

II

Organic Sabotage

Disobedience, in the eyes of anyone who has read history, is man's original virtue.
It is through disobedience that progress has been made.

Oscar Wilde, 1891

Humanity has reached a defining moment in history.
We can continue our present policies which serve to deepen economic divisions within and
between countries; which increase poverty, hunger, sickness and illiteracy worldwide; and
which are causing the continued degradation of the ecosystems on which we depend for
life on Earth.

Or we can change course.

Earth Summit: Agenda 21, 1992

In tracking the contemporary evolution of body modification, the analysis thus far has demystified the phenomena in light of a wide variety of socioeconomic, political, and cultural conditions. Yet one underlying theme unifies all the different people that seek these symbolic forms of expression. Body modification among diverse individuals has been used as a mechanism of emancipatory authenticity to facilitate liberating transformation. Given that there are so many regulatory processes that serve to *civilize* the body in society, it was only a matter of time before it emerged, *uncivilized*, as the site of ideological, socioeconomic, and political struggle. Any project of deregulatory emancipation, therefore, would have to begin with the liberation of the modern body. Those subscribing to the deregulation of society, such as anarchists, anarchosyndicalists, and libertarians, are therefore compelled to begin the process of usurping control of what Turner (1992) calls the "regimes of regulation" at the site of the body. Once the liberating potential of the body is harnessed, emancipation would eventually be achieved among the collective. According to Turner (1996),

> sociology of the body is a study of the problem of the social order and it can
> be organized around...the reproduction and regulation of populations in

time and space, and the restraint and representation of the body as a vehicle of the self. The control over the body is thus an 'elementary' 'primitive'
struggle.[1]

As a decivilizing mechanism of the transgressive, body modification is used
by all these diverse groups to advance the body as the primary site of the
utopian project for societal liberation. Be it the self, the community, or the
world around us, body modification is the discursive semiotic method of
primitivism that formalize the struggle for freedom, autonomy, and self-
determination for both the individual and the collective through identification with, and empathetic nostalgic alignment of, premodern organic
societies of the past. As reinforced through sexuality, digitized community-
building online, or social justice through political protest; individual liberation is connected to, rooted within, and impossible without, emancipation
of the collective situated throughout society. The body therefore, according
to the perspective of many embodied anarchists, is a primary site for the
struggle to maximize our potential for human emancipation.

> Indeed, the first step on the road to utopia began with the skin. [Dora]
> Russell believed that a radically reformed public world would be built on
> the emancipated body. A public utopia would arise from the private utopias
> between men and women. In this way, political desire was not only equated
> with sexual desire, but flowed from that desire. [T]he body [is] thus not mar-
> ginal to politics, but rather its centre.[2]

As the focus is on the emancipated body, modernity poses significant challenges to the project to liberate the embodied self from these regimes of
regulation. As part of an effort to reduce these obstacles to human liberation rooted in modernity, the nostalgic return to organic society begins
with the struggle for individual freedom offered through the philosophies
of Krishnamurti (1992),

> Freedom—to be free—is becoming more and more difficult. As society
> becomes more complex and as industrialization becomes wider and deeper
> and more organized, there is less and less freedom for man. [O]utwardly
> one becomes a slave to society, to the pressure of society; in this pressure
> of organized existence there is no tribal existence, but industrialized, orga-
> nized, centralized control. When there is more "progress" there is less and
> less freedom.[3]

As advanced industrialized nations provide the technology, the capital, and
the leisure time for the collusive servile masses to acquire unprecedented
scales of materialist accumulation, the yearning for freedom and emancipation from materiality has, paradoxically, never been greater. Many avenues
are explored in the quest to fill the void brought on by conspicuous consumption, all of them leaving their seekers more shallow and empty than
they were before. The intention of this book has been to document the

sensual, spiritual, and political means by which individuals are willing to deploy the body in service to their struggles to transcend an increasingly artificial, threatening, adversarial world. In all these various approaches deployed by genuine explorers of the authentic, the desire for human emancipation has led time and time again to the [re]assertion of human agency to combat the suffocating passivity and dependency brought on by a vicious combination of unregulated neoliberal market economics and the collusive state.

> In the past twenty years or so, large numbers of people have chosen various forms of body adornment, tattoos, piercings, and extreme hairstyles and colors as symbols that set them apart from society. By some estimates, almost one-third of US youth have some kind of tattoo or piercing. While extreme body modification may be considered "grotesque", it is a critique of domination and rejection of the dominant kinds of "modern" lifestyles and identities. The participants label themselves modern primitives, members of a premodern community of the imaginary, where status is ascribed (if not inscribed) in ways apart from materialist success and the standards of elites. Many report that their tats and piercings are initiation rites that signify passage away from dominant society into alternative cohesive communities of meaning; as simulations of the premodern, these communities provide a sense of belonging, in the face of general tendencies to attenuate ties. Moreover, insofar as extensive tattooing/piercing and modification is relatively permanent, it gives one a sense of stability and continuity in a rapidly changing world.[4]

Given so many varieties of human agency surrounding body modification deployed to resist these profound threats to human autonomy and self-determination, the different strategies of authenticity-advancing sabotage outlined thus far tend to exhibit a certain *rigidity* of response among body-modified individuals, regardless of their sensual, political, aesthetic, or other tactical orientation. Straw, Sandelands, and Dutton (1981) call this phenomenon the *threat-rigidity* paradigm.

> [O]ne of the most influential explanations of the effects of threat on group performance is the threat-rigidity hypothesis. This perspective suggests that a threat to the vital interests of an entity will result in various forms of rigidity, including centralization of structure, restriction, ... routinization, formalization, and repeated reliance of dominant or well-learned responses. According to this perspective, rigidity may have functional or dysfunctional consequences for the group. [Sometimes] the rigidity can be functional because it can motivate the production of well-learned responses that are appropriate for coping with the threat. [T]he group attempts to protect its collective identity ... under [these] conditions [through] a process ... undertaken to maintain and reinforce the positive image of a group [that is] questioned by a collective threat.[5]

This rigidity serves to combat an environment that is perceived as threatening the interests of the group, which deploys mass human agency to

[re]legitimate or otherwise reverse attempts to discredit the collective under attack by the hostile adversary. This rigidity is, of course, not limited to those using body modification as an element of resistance, and has been a tactic used by many marginalized groups in the history of social justice movements to advance the struggle for individual and collective authenticity (Eversley, 2005). Rigidity in the face of threatening adversaries serves to unify group members to resist attacks, while enabling them to gather momentum in the form of aggregated collective agency to reestablish credibility and validity in defense of continued threats.

The *social justice threat rigidity* phenomenon under examination first requires the clarification of participating parties, to define the "we" to whom attacks are directed and those being affected by the deleterious policies and practices of a given adversary. Given current conditions of the one-world economy, the clarification of the socioeconomic victims left in the wake of unregulated neoliberal markets are invariably unifying the people living in both first and third worlds, creating an *imagined community* of wounded combatants encompassing the globe. Most of these socioeconomic and cultural combatants are deprived of even the most minimal material conditions for survival, and are compelled to endure humiliating conditions of dependency to secure even the most rudimentary conditions for sustenance in a genuine Malthusian nightmare. The unification of victims of neoliberal economics beyond territoriality transcending nation-state boundaries in struggles linking the first and third world is a cognitive process that Bennett (2000) refers to as *cultural reterritorialization.*

> One way in which indigenous populations may seek to culturally relocate [or reterritorialize] themselves is by constructing idealized versions of national culture based upon an imagined past. One school of thought has maintained that globalisation can only have a pathological effect [based on] a one-direction flow of cultural commodities from the west.[6]

On guard from cultural threats brought on by globalization, individuals will rigidly defend themselves through the cognitive construction of a reterritorialized cohesive community to link protective strategies that, like circulating mobile capital, transcend nation-state boundaries. Such construction transcends immediate geopolitical boundaries and, based on an imagined or actual past, fosters a return to and reconstruction of organic solidarity inherent in underdeveloped cultural contexts. Like predatory capitalism and the coerced debt that accompanies it, this kind of organic reterritoriality goes far beyond modern political boundaries, forging camaraderies of resistance among victims located across core and periphery. The rigidity necessary to combat the threats of the one-world hegemonic predator has given rise to the identification with, and symbolic unification of, first- and third-world victims left devastated by the monolithic world system. Homeless, demoralized, and denigrated core inhabitants of the first world, through their own victimization by the same forces of imperialism and colonization that created centuries of suffering in the third world, have finally become cognizant of the genuine depth of deprivation brought on by coercive capitalism and the collusive state, this time in complex multinational forms associated with modern markets causing the third worldization of disposable people located at the core.

> It is this new pattern of uneven inclusion that generates anxiety and frustration. Globalization therefore invokes anger and anxiety in the South and tends to be experienced as yet another round of Northern hegemony, and another round of concentration of power and wealth. The common denominator . . . is imperialism, neocolonialism revisited. But analytically this is mistaken: imperialism was territorial, state-driven, centrally-orchestrated, and marked by a clear division between colonizer and colonized; none of these features apply to contemporary globalization. Contemporary accelerated globalization is multidimensional, non-territorial, polycentric, and the lines of inclusion/exclusion are blurred and run between the middle classes and the poor North and South.[7]

Although centuries too late, the knowledge and experiences linking complex struggles between core and periphery have finally resulted in an unprecedented level of empathetic global understanding among the oppressed worldwide needed to generate innovative discursive strategies necessary to rigidly combat these vehement forms of contemporary exploitation, or what Harvey (1999) calls "the distorted relationships that lie at the heart of civilized oppression." Coercive capital has now evolved into a metaphoric monster resembling a voracious octopus, wrapping its tentacles around the world's precious resources, and winning. Its venom is dependency. The host makes victims believe they are parasites, but in reality the system is incapable of operating without the failure-camouflaging dependencies it perpetuates such as debt and obedience. Construction of the cohesiveness and rigidity within communities of resistance that will be necessary to combat these forms of *civilized oppression* will take nothing less than a global revolution of dependency-dismantling egalitarian resistance around the planet. By many accounts, reversing these global forms of civilized oppression will require nothing short of a movement of decivilizing independence to create a truly self-sufficient, sustainable, egalitarian society in which control or authority of any kind is prohibited and all forms of power exercised by one human being over another are deemed unnatural, undesirable, and therefore prohibitive.

> Analyzing what is involved in civilized oppression includes analyzing the kinds of mechanisms used, the power relations at work, the systems controlling perceptions and information, the kinds of harm inflicted on the victims, and the reasons why this oppression is so hard to see even by contributing agents. Oppression obviously involves social structures and institutions, and it calls for political action. But oppression also reaches down into the lives of individuals, and some of the moral issues at this level are not readily seen. We

need some way of making relevant components of oppression more visible, and focusing on harm does not do the job. Oppression involves a systematic and inappropriate control of people by those with more power. The oppressed are treated with disrespect, moral rights are denied or blocked, their lives are deprived of proper fulfillment, and they experience series of frustrations and humiliations beyond all normal bounds. Except for explicit denial of rights, none of these need be intentional, and when no physical force is used, a lack of awareness on the part of contributing agents is more common than not. [Oppression is not limited to] a singular assault. The constant fear of attack, however, may be oppressive. This said, individual victims of oppression are typically recipients of cumulative harms, with compounding significance not grasped by the fortunate, especially when the oppression takes a civilized form. Civilized oppression will not be reduced if it is not approached as a mutual endeavor involving both the more powerful and more vulnerable. We need more adequate concepts of power, and an analysis of hidden power, in our own relationships and in social structures on the large scale. We need the perceptual skills to spot both patterns and specific incidents of power misuse, and we will need to work with rigorous honesty to curtail all the generally accepted slides into appropriate uses of power.[8]

Harvey's notion of *cumulative harms of hierarchy* is particularly insightful for advancing our concept of systems of egalitarianism that will be needed to transcend bureaucratic relations for the decivilizing organic emancipation project. Of primary importance is Harvey's conceptual link between applied equality in interpersonal relationships and its manifestation in collective governance. Here the body figures prominently. Many would highlight that this conceptual strategy for ethical life is impossible within the authoritative framework of a coercive (or any other) governing state. True egalitarian interpersonal and community relations could only be realized by preventing state interference in any aspect of social life. Is such reversal of civilized oppression and hierarchy-less living merely grandiose utopian thinking?

Roots of Global Emancipation

Looking back in history when egalitarian relations among humans were paramount and control over one human being was rarely attempted by another, one is nostalgically returned to simple agrarian life in rural villages. A return to organic simplicity with all its communal decision making is now one of the most powerful driving forces behind landless peoples movements, squatting, urban homesteading, and other sustainable ecological alterglobalization resistance efforts worldwide. In the third world, there are many examples of successful resistance against centuries of imperializing consciousness, where, until the recent proliferation and imposition of subsidized guns and amphetamines, strong communities have been able to successfully combat hegemonic attempts to oppress and colonize indigenous people in developing contexts. Despite the lure of diamonds, corrupt government officials, subsides to cease agrarian production, state-orchestrated famine, and other western material entrapments brought on by transnational economic agreements benefiting core nations; the third world has never provided dominating elite with the servility and obedience it demanded, usually at gunpoint. Inspired by the efficacy of these resistance efforts, alterglobalizing body-modified autonomous activists in advanced industrialized societies have now begun to formally and informally articulate, through embodied discourse, their dreams of underdevelopment. This has lead to the global resurgence of *village anarchy* as the viable alternative to the status quo.

> Of the two main kinds [of anarchy], one was usually associated with...theory and with terrorism at the level of practice. It was essentially violent, and engaged often in assassination—anarchist and terrorist were often used as interchangeable terms. The other kind is usually associated with Kropotkin and Tolstoy, and in the next generation with Ghandi. The theory of this kind of ethical anarchism, sometimes called village anarchism, recommends agriculture, small communities, distrust of state, and peace. Within ethical or village anarchism, one can distinguish again two main tendencies. Some anarchists invested their energies in peace, others in love, in erotic freedom. Pacifism was to be associated with Tolstoy, and he was one of those who most powerfully inspired [an] anarchism [which] was positively anti-erotic. On the whole, the erotic branch of ethical anarchism becomes the stronger of the two among intellectuals after Tolstoy dies in 1910. The political kinds of anarchism—obviously the violent but also the nonviolent forms thereof—lost their power with that constituency.[9]

As this summary of the popular evolution of anarchy indicates, we are now at a point where poignant visions of *ethical village anarchism* prevail, where peaceful and occasionally erotic self-sufficient living is desired in lieu of urban, fragmented, mechanistic, dependency-breeding violence or other hostilities. If we have the courage to indulge ourselves a bit further and move the body-modified anarchist activist utopian project from one of complacency resting on mere anarchist *theory* to one of construction working concretely toward ethical or village anarchist *praxis*, we find that the worldwide alterglobalization movement is already in the process of making this dream a reality. From landless people in Latin America, to land titling in the Middle East, there is a reversal of these civilized forms of oppression, with slow but significant resistance through the reinvigoration of organic forms of agrarian living, which may afford the individual fewer material comforts but much more immaterial abundance in terms of freedom, autonomy, and self-determination.

> The resurgence of interest in anarchism, which has been steadily percolating...over the past few decades, has now begun to form significant waves on a much wider scale, linking First and Third world struggles. This has resulted in the formation of a diversity of political alliances coalescing around the

politics of globalisation. What unites them is a fundamental questioning of the viability of existing mechanisms of decision-making, control, account-ability and justice throughout the world. Whilst it is clear that the diverse concerns of these countermovements are not reducible to single political pro-grams or monolithic analytical tools, the theoretical concepts most appar-ently to the fore appear to be those associated with anarchism. When we talk about global anarchism, we mean that it is impossible for anarchist theory and practice to be formulated in ways that do not acknowledge its relation-ship with global flows of people, ideas, technology, economics, and crucially, resistance. Indeed, it is significant that anarchism can no longer be said to be the preserve of white Westerners. If anything, an era of global anarchism calls for a repositioning of the individual within these global flows and the need to respond to complex ethical and strategic problems which involves new formulations of ... anarchism.[10]

We are, at the moment, in the process of witnessing historic resistance activities around the world that are actively advancing the utopian project for ethical global village anarchism. It is a peaceful, global, and emancipa-tory anarchism that seeks to reverse technological, neoliberal economic, and coercive state subjugation. This universal need for emancipation from technological, economic, and state subjugation is a strange and unprec-edented process in the evolution of historic social movements, in that it unifies diverse dissidents being subjugated around the world by the same documentable, oppressive, but *reversible* forces promulgated by lies, depen-dency, and material delusions associated with modernity.

> Dissident culture is a culture of emancipation. Dissident cultures attempt to combine an empowering virtue with an emancipatory authenticity. Alternative cultures flourish when they both emancipate and empower their followers. They emancipate if they offer a way of life which is more fulfill-ing and therefore more attractive. They empower if they propose forms of life which foster the collective strength and resolve of all those who belong to them. They need this strength in order to achieve the collective goals of their members in the face of the indifference or even hostility of the wider host society. How then can the dissident cultures of the 'advanced' industri-alized societies combine an emancipatory momentum with the values and commitments needed for a cohesive community? Fortunately, in its' initial phase of emergence the radical culture has several advantages, the surround-ing culture is, relative to the emerging alternatives, an oppressive culture. Consequently, the prospective members of the radical culture have good rea-son to become involved. The existing culture is a place of frustration and low self-esteem for them.[11]

The emancipation offered by the dissident utopian alterglobalization proj-ect through the framework of ethical village anarchism is one that seeks genuine living as opposed to thousands of years of deceit constructed to support the exploitative foundations of global capital. By now, these lies have become a well-known but mind-numbingly painful mantra: that unfettered mobility of capital around the world is beneficial to everyone, that the trickle down beneficence of markets will be universally experienced if patience is devoted to await its unregulated processes, that debt leads to a robust economy, that free trade distributes power more equitably, that labor unions are greedy and corrupt, that small-scale agrarian production is inefficient and therefore undesirable, that the ecology is resilient and global warming will not have deleterious consequences for the planet, that reductions in privacy and personal autonomy increase security and well-being and lead to technological progress, and that authority and abuses of power associated with evolving one world governance are necessary in order to prevent violent criminals from ruling the world. These delusions have resulted in such demoralizing deprivation in both first and third worlds, that victims now have little left to lose in their desire to return to systems of organic solidarity espoused through autonomous ecological living.

> The importance of peasant and agrarian ways of life to anarchism is sometimes overlooked. The critique of modern Western civilization...intersects with the strands often referred to as 'primitivist', 'anti-civilization', or 'anti-technological'. Agrarian peasant movements of the global South also form a significant component of the anti-globalisation movement, which recognizes the importance of helping defend traditional and indigenous ways of life from the onslaught of globalisation. The reality is that the worship of money, technology, consumer goods, modernization and development are not creating happiness. The domination of nature and of humans has left a gaping void in people that no amount of spectacular glitter, speed and technology can fill.[12]

Kuper (1988) describes the many illusions necessary for one people to legally and ethically justify the colonization of another. Many of the coercive and disingenuous processes of legally legitimated imperialism, normalcy of deprivation, and other fictitious constructions of authoritarian rule that took place in the nineteenth century are still in operation today.

> [C]riticism is not my main concern. I am more interested in accounting for the genesis of illusion, and more particularly for its persistence. [Colonizing elites] buried themselves for over a hundred years with the manipulation of a fantasy—a fantasy which had been constructed by speculative lawyers in the nineteenth century...whose primary concerns were with material culture and the development of religion. The first laws took the forms of judgments which were believed to derive from divine inspiration. In time aristocracy displaced the divinely-inspired leaders; in the west a political oligarchy, in the east a priestly caste. The new elite took over the judicial role of the king, but did not pretend to divine inspiration. Instead the elite claimed a monopoly of knowledge of custom. Under the cover of fictions the elite introduced reforms, while maintaining the illusion, so much cherished by the conservative majority, that nothing had really altered.[13]

Yet it has become increasingly difficult for hegemonic powers to convince the disobedient autonomous masses that human progress is still unfolding, when greed has resulted in such widespread misery and deprivation, that mere day-to-day survival is now what most families around the world aspire for, even those with two full-time working parents in advanced industrialized economies. The fact that two high-skilled full-time working parents, even in the West with primary tier employment under dual labor market conditions, are routinely incapable of achieving a level of subsistence living that exceeds the poverty line, is not viewed as an opportunity for indictments of exploitation inherent in the world system, but instead becomes evidence for power elites to suggest that economic failures of families are rooted within their own personal flaws inherent in their ethnicity, femininity, family size, consumption patterns, rebellious nature, or other pathology associated with individualisms beyond white male beneficiaries driving the alleged legitimacy of systemic entitlements to a chosen few in a collapsing global economy.

> [S]ettlers were prone to label as irredeemable savages the peoples resident in areas they wished to claim for themselves, thus justifying their cruel treatment of...unhappy victims of colonialism. The progress extension of colonial authority was correlated with declining degrees of accommodation to indigenous practices, although such accommodation could be essential to the very process of colonial conquest. The process of pacification of subject peoples proceeded unevenly.[14]

As a tactic in use for centuries to diminish the value of ethnically and racially diverse culture and peoples on the periphery, the pathologization of difference has always been quite familiar to communities of color in both the first and third worlds, and has its origins in the colonizing consciousness. What is new in the contemporary frameworks of the pathologization of difference driving contemporary civilized oppression, however, is that with such broad territories simultaneously under occupation by unregulated multinationals, and with so few collusive agents driven by diminishing rewards, hegemonic entities have gravely overestimated their ability to generate the pacification and obedience necessary to continue to expand their domination under existing socioeconomic and political arrangements. With so little at stake and such broad territories in question, multinational corporate-regimes have been unable to impose, even at gunpoint, the levels of dependency and collusion that would be necessary to secure control over the people, governments, and natural resources in the first and third worlds that is currently desired. As a result of the diminishing material rewards, these unregulated multinational corporate-regime structures are unable to generate the broad pacification and obedience necessary from superfluous populations to survive the oppressive forms of new civilized colonization. Resistance has never been as vehement as it is today. The righteousness driving these new forms of economic occupation has resulted in unprecedented levels of greed that does little to distribute rewards among collusive elites. Even the semblance of pluralism and indigenous accommodation that has always been superficially associated with early imperialism is no longer necessary, because corporate-regimes have no accountability to any ethical or moral publics whatsoever. With no material incentives and armed only with the threat of forced exile, the world's populations are becoming increasingly immune and disobedient to the colonizing consciousness. Where immunity to occupiers' demands is high, coercion and violence is generally too expensive to implement and sustain, so weapons and pharmaceuticals are simultaneously distributed in order to fuel tribal animosities to achieve normative mechanisms of social control. Facing threats of colonizing corporate-regime and festered chaos, hegemonic powers demanding the simultaneous assimilation, homogeneity, and dependency of the peripheral disposable populations of East Central Europe, Africa, and the Middle and Far East are finding collusion and occupation more difficult than ever. Legitimating hegemonic interests, social scientists have justified the elimination of all forms of individuality and cultural distinction for colonizing elites in the third world for centuries under the guise of technological progress. They continue to do so today through more sophisticated methods of modern criminology, psychology, political science, and business administration; using value-free, neutral, "scientific" methods to impose institutional and organizational isomorphism that seeks to eradicate cultural distinction and foist material dependency on the defiant masses.

> Within the ideology of progress, cultural diversity is regressive and must be "developed" into homogeneity or, failing that, simply locked up or snuffed out. The increasing exploration of these lost "primitive" practices and technique looks beyond the ideology of progress to a possible syncretic future. That this heresy is gaining momentum now, at the fin de millennium, signals a shift in terms from progress to survival.[15]

With the absence of material rewards, the new forms of civilized oppression, and the resurgence of organic living, it is strange that social scientists have failed to observe the authentic levels of community resistance to colonization by unfettered multinational corporate regimes that has been steadily taking place at both the core and periphery. This resistance involves a variety of creative forms of organic sabotage that, like colonization, is facilitated by media techniques that make dependency-breeding occupation increasingly problematic. The attempted corporate-regime colonization of Iraq and other occupied territories around the world has not been so easy in the current postmaterial cultural epoch. Instead, an unprecedented and concerted resistance endeavor to combat these social, cultural, and economic arrangements has been steadily taking place. Progress or development under the terms available is no longer desirable, and though miniscule numbers of political puppet elites with illusions of authority situated in largely irrelevant nation-states may be officially colluding with these failing hegemonic entities, a slow and steady revolution of resistance is taking place at the community grassroots level, which now involves individuated embodiment among disposable populations in the first and third worlds deleteriously affected by these systemic arrangements. Levi Strauss, (1958) refers to the phenomenon as mass *syncretic accommodation* that is unifying populations of struggle across racial, ethnic, gender, class, geographic, and developmental differences. These changes not only signal a shift from reassessing the cultural value of primitive practices and advantageous customs of the underdeveloped lifestyles around the world, but also indicate a wholesale resurgence and desire to adhere to these organic ways of life that can only be more superior to the unsustainable and devastating consequences of our own.

> [F]ragmentation, ethnic diversity, and internet savvy are central terms in popular discourse about...the definition of what it means to be part of transnational time. These three are...taken as signs of some democratic potential or of the loss of certain important forms of communal life. In this the working out of relations between local and global are partly a struggle between an imagined past and the reproduction of social relations tomorrow. Consequently, the young are a key site for the struggle between an imagined past and the reproduction of social relations tomorrow...the struggle of the meaning of the transnational circulation of culture and capital, in addition to the ongoing production of the new. The image of the young escapist cosmopolitan...so frequently appears...as the colonialized victim of globalization.[16]

Despite hegemonic core interventions in developing nations orchestrated by the West, that attempt to dismantle this organic solidarity, third world communities have exhibited tremendous fortitude in the face of adversities brought on by the first world. The hegemonic orchestration to dismantle organic solidarity in the third world includes simultaneous financing of oppositional warlord cultures, the proliferation of weapons, the distribution of aggression-enhancing pharmaceuticals, and the forced migration of malnourished, gang-raped, and HIV-infected women and children displaced as refugees by regime violence. Although genocidal tactics are often used to distract and destabilize territories in order for unregulated corporate-regime entities to secure control of precious resources such as diamonds and petroleum reserves, communal ways of life in underdeveloped contexts are still capable of sustaining enough social cohesion to unify tribal people in the face of these profound adversarial conditions threatening to destroy organic ways of life. It is precisely the success of these vehement forms of peripheral third-world strategic resistance and empowerment inherent in tribal community-building that has effectively resisted centuries of development and colonizing oppression that is currently inspiring the worldwide organic sabotage movement and related body modification that disenfranchised young people from the core and semi-periphery seek to emulate.

Modern Designers of Underdevelopment

The first social scientific treatment to document the phenomena under examination comes from Vale and Juno (1989), in which they specifically refer to body-modified political resistance as a community of *modern primitives* who participate in the resurgence of the customs, rituals, and community associated with premodern ways of life.

> The central pivotal change in the world of the 20 century—the wholesale de-individualization of man and society—has been accomplished by an inundation of millions of mass produced images, which, acting on humans, bypass any "logical" barriers of resistance. A primitivist is a person who prefers a way of life which, when judged by one or more of the standards prevailing in his own society, would be considered less "advanced" or less civilized.[17]

The first to document the return to organic cohesion was Turner (1984) through his notion of *retribalization* in society. Later, Wojcik (1995) was the first to specify the role of primitive forms of cohesion in punk music through piercing rituals. He noted that many punk enthusiasts engaged in self-impalement as a form of identification with primitive society, and referred to them as *neo-tribalists*.

> Unlike many neo-tribalists who now have their bodies modified by professionals in body piercing and tattoo studios, punks often did their own piercings and tattoos. Motivated in part by a sense of loss and disillusionment with the values and progress of western society.[18]

Later, Maffesoli (1996) made significant contributions by expanding the concept of modern tribalism beyond punk music cultures.

> [The tribe is] without the rigidity of the forms of organization with which we are familiar, it refers more to a certain ambience, a state of mind, and is preferably to be expressed through appearance and form.[19]

Through the notion of neotribalism, McDonald (2006) provided an even more thorough conceptualization of the tribal community cohesion being sought among these young body-modified resisters of modernity.

> [N]eotribes [are] temporary gatherings characterized by fluid boundaries and floating memberships. [These new] forms of sociality emerge out of networks...defined culturally rather than politically or socially. This means that these networks are defined not by social location, nor by political belief, but by forms of practice—forms of doing. This places sensuality at the center of the movement experience. [S]ocial life is increasingly made up of experiences of fusion, where...collective experiences become divine, transcending the artificial divisions created by civilization.[20]

Anderson (1991) discusses this neo-tribal fluidity as an embodied *imagined community* giving rise to new experiences of citizenships across and beyond borders.

> [G]lobalization consists of experiencing multiple places and multiple temporalities…confront[ing] us with the challenge of understanding new forms of partial connection, new experiences of border. The forms of action…cut across understandings of agency and experience. Within this framework, the relationship to the body is an instrumental one where the actor experiences himself or herself as being 'in' a body or being a self that 'has' a body. [By examining new borders] we constantly encounter embodiment and the senses:…from the embodiment of direct action in antiglobalization [to] opening out of individual autonomy that do not correspond to the rational, disembodied individual.[21]

As a staunch advocate of unregulated neoliberal market economics, Ayn Rand (1993 [1971]) was the first to warn of the threat to expansionist economic interests inherent in the rise of the anti-technological, anti-industrial social justice movement seeking to thwart the parasitic exploitation associated with technological "progress". In a similar vein, Beck (1997) calls participants of this social justice movement the *antimoderns*, but notes that the new counter-modernization tactics are highly syncretic, integrating and celebrating beneficial technologies while actively constructing creative resistance against more dangerous forms of science and technology to create optimal conditions of modernity.

> [The anti-moderns are] a community of opposition [which] is seen first in the pronounced aversion to all varieties of an automatic, action-free and thus, ultimately unpolitical modernization as in society and sociology. Theories of reflexive modernization try to capture the new savagery of reality. In that sense there is little in common with types of counter-modernization that attempt to turn back the wheel of modernity in theory and politics. Counter modernity is…internally ambivalent; it remains open to who does the construction as well as how and against whom it occurs.[22]

Body-modified anti-moderns are not struggling for a Luddite-like revolution or a reversal to primitive societies such as Rand suggests, but rather have become judicious outspoken critics of modern culture who, in their efforts to cease individual and market failure camouflage, are unwilling to allow social bonds to continue to attenuate to the levels necessary to maintain this exploitative world system. Anti-moderns such as the Unabomber Professor Theodore Kaczinski refuse to passively accept dependency and related coercive conditions of modernity in which communities are rendered fragmented with artificially induced, scarcity-fueled competition resulting in unprecedented levels of human alienation under socioeconomic and political hegemonic conditions that are now too powerful to be mediated by any government, least of all by collusive elites of the United States or the European Union.

> Technology organizes not only our relationship to nature but also our relationships to one another; moreover, it has transformed all forms of social organization. Yet technology is a major disorganizing force in society, for in its modern form it results in cultural disintegration (suppression of meaning) and personal alienation (suppression of subject). The proliferation of techniques for relating to others is unrelenting [and] assumes the form of the expert. If technique now mediates virtually all human relationships, then social institutions have lost their efficacy. Just as technology diminishes personal experience, it conspires against interpersonal or collective experiences. Human technique obviates the need for judgment, decisions, and responsibility. Technology colonizes our experiences, opinions, emotions, and consciousness. Communication too, has become vulgar.[23]

What makes the new counter-modernity particularly unique is the element of exile associated with alternative forms of capital and the related rise of Bohemianism. As described throughout the current treatment, these anti-moderns are what Allen (2006) calls the *new barbarians*, the new form of *global nomad*, who can be characterized as transient migrants in societally imposed and self-reinforced perpetual exile.

> Who are today's barbarians? The...transformative political power of the new global nomads should not be underestimated. Stateless and homeless, the new barbarians have no choice but to vote with their feet. [Artistic] collective...responds to this current fluid global situation, increasingly dominated by itinerancy, exodus, and desertion as people from around the world attempt to flee war zones, to escape oppressive regimes, and to follow the flows of newly-liberated capital. [Many] thinkers celebrate the barbarians as part of "the multitude" which gains its transformative political potential by remaining mobile and resisting territorialization.[24]

The new barbarians and others global nomads in exile within their own nation or banished to others find themselves particularly vulnerable to criticism and attack. It is precisely the pervasiveness of hegemonic assaults as well as the rigidity and social cohesion that accompanies it, that renders failure camouflage and other promulgated systemic delusions among these modern body-modified refugees impossible to address. As disposable victims of displacement brought on by contemporary socioeconomic conditions who usually find themselves in forced exile on their own soil in their own lands and by the policies of their own government, they are often characterized by yet another form of civilized oppression, the oversimplification, reductivization, and personal pathologization encapsulated by the now well-worn diagnostic aphorism known as homelessness.

> In their position of supplication and helplessness, homeless individuals do not stake a claim to the territory that has been taken away from them. They

are reduced to mere observers of the remaking of their neighborhood for others. Their homelessness appears as a natural condition, the cause is disassociated from its consequence, and the status of homeless as legitimate members of the urban community is unrecognized. A false notion of the homeless as individuals functioning in isolation from the urban community and from each other contributes to their current status as exiles in their own city. Although in our daily encounters with homeless people we are aware of their status as refugees, we generally fail to recognize that they are refugees from the transformation of the city itself. We are reluctant to discern the relationship between the physical transformation of the city—through real estate development and economic displacement—and the creation of homelessness. The fact that people are compelled to live on the streets is unacceptable. But failing to recognize the reality of these people's situation or holding up the fact of their living on the streets as proof of their universal insanity is a morally and factually untenable position.[25]

Hungry people on their own soil, in their own lands, displaced by their own people often use a variety of empowerment strategies to resist the adversity associated with their plight. Some of these barbarians momentarily sabotage society's olfactory senses through their inability to practice physiological hygiene and other acts of petty sabotage. Others create collectives, establish squats, and demand legal recognition as part of the worldwide landless people's movement. Homeless refugees are becoming so common even among the highly educated in industrialized nationstates, that technological or material needs are not denied, and are instead repackaged, de-pacified, reconstructed, and made empowering. Wi-fi networks, password cracking, and other forms of technological sabotage are a central part of the high-tech subtrefuge among these highly educated, body-modified, homeless, transient refugees unifying around the globe in the newly integrated landless exiled peoples movement. These body-modified, neotribal anti-moderns are now in worldwide solidarity with other third-world forced exiles displaced by economics, war, occupation, and increasingly more commonly, by ecological catastrophes associated with global warming. Tent cities and HUD trailers strewn throughout the city of New Orleans after Hurricane Katrina serve to further normalize the phenomenon.

Dangers and Pleasures of Forced Exile

Protest and other forms of public collective resistance among body-modified bohemians have been our focus, but there is also evidence to suggest that resistance is not limited to these public activities among the collective. Clandestine sabotage also occurs at the private individual level. Because there are many privileges that accompany the modern disposability associated with the new forms of exile, subtle technological subterfuge is among the favorite resistance tactics deployed by the new anti-modern body-modified bohemian barbarians. At Davos, for example, the anti-moderns penetrated the technological fortresses at the official five-star hotel conference venue, absconded with all G8 members' credit card information, waited patiently for the media to disseminate the embarrassing news that alterglobalizers were now in possession of all participants' financial sponsor information, and then proceeded never to use the potential billions they accessed in these stolen credit cards for any purpose whatsoever.[26] In one swift gesture, this powerful act of postmaterial technological sabotage by anarchist activists disclosed the susceptibility of G8 participants, the vulnerability of fortress-like security and other social distances assured to participants at these sanitizing hotel conference venues, as well as the technological specialization and anti-material orientation of members of the alterglobalizing project all at once. The identity of these transconsuming saboteur activists was of course never found, but similar acts of petty technological sabotage consistently take place around the world, though rarely reported through conventional media outlets. These subtle strategies to meticulously target the dangerous entities contributing to the hegemonic project that is causing such pain to the planet and its people have been used for years by alterglobalizing anarchists, who often act alone for this clandestine purpose. There are many of these unsung heroes of the violent and nonviolent anarchist consciousness, and although their highly skilled acts of sabotage are regularly conducted in order to disclose the vulnerabilities of the heinous elites that are demoralizing whole populations, these gestures are rarely publicized in the mainstream media. When these acts of subterfuge occur on a scale that cannot be denied, the public is deceived by either vilifying the entities involved or minimizing the sinister character of the activities of those targeted for attack, or minimize the expertise of sabotage deployed. The affiliation of those involved in isolated acts of sabotage such as the check disintegrating bandit (Slotter, 1996), or the hackers who penetrated the northeast power grid of the United States in the summer of 2005 may never be formally linked to organized anarchy, yet persistent use of nonviolent subterfuge that demonstrates the vulnerabilities of elites and inadvertently calls attention to economic and social inequalities that their domination causes, occurs often enough to make an ostensible link to independent anarchist resistance. Others, such as the math professor Ted Kaczynski known as the Unabomber, clearly articulate, through manifesto extracts published in the *New York Times*, their green, anti-modern, postmaterial anarchist orientation. Activists such as the Unabomber prefer violent means to sequentially disclose and eradicate, often with impressive levels of specificity, the morally odious scientists whose research causes irreversible damage to the planet and humanity. More often then not, these *resistance entrepreneurs* fade quietly back into exile, patiently awaiting another opportunity to engage in yet another episodic act of anarchist technological subterfuge, which may or may not become ideologically diluted and discredited in the evening news.

Exile and Anti-secularism

Even the most casual observer has to wonder what is making all this high and low tech subterfuge even possible. It is the privileged combination of transient mobility and clandestine obscurity associated with socially imposed and self-affirming bohemian exile making all these political indulgences, good and bad, possible. The resistance entrepreneurship is motivated, in part, by conceptual links of an imagined community of struggle between first and third worlds, forging empathetic ties among people who, by force or by choice, experience a permanent state of banishment or unwanted distance from their own land, nation, community, and/ or people.

> Exile is not a singular condition [but rather] a state of banishment, devastation, destruction 'one compelled to reside away from his native land' 'to banish to ravage'. The vocabulary articulating exile emphasizes the notion of force... but also of deliberate destruction, ravishment, and devastation. Exile is thus always the effect of force exerted upon a person or persons, resulting in a condition which is not freely chosen but inflicted. That state of permanent exile, of continued, forcible eviction, resulting in the objectification of the body into the abject, of a disassociation of body from mind in which the mind does continuous battle with the body in an effort to control it on behalf of hegemonic discourses of female decorativity, is the condition which fashions women's lives in western and many other cultures. [Oppositional cultures] are on one level a way of celebrating resistance, of suggesting opportunities of refusal in the interstices of regulatory regimes.[27]

Not only does modernity create the conditions that coerce reluctant but authentic individuals with a conscience to live under permanent conditions of forced exile, but it also results in a peculiar role for the body as it attempts to adjust to the unique circumstances of its own societally imposed marginality. Without territory, the nomadic exile has essentially nothing left to lose and forges social bonds among those experiencing these increasingly common forms of drifting disembodiment found in immediate proximity. Without conventional ties weighting the body to space, place, or other elements of material culture, the fortitude and resilience that is invariably needed to survive these demoralizing conditions of modernity lead not only to explorations of intense relationships with each other, but also to technology, science, and antithetical elements of rational modernity such as the *divine*. Forced exile creates conditions that solidify an postmaterial collective consciousness, which can only result in a search for cathartic emancipatory transformation via the *reclamation of indigenous spirituality*. Body modification is one element signifying the desire to explore ancient spiritualities that advance transcendental experiences of primitive anti-modern body-modified global nomads now fluidly moving around the world in a state of permanent exile without the need or desire for conspicuous consumption or failure camouflage.

The issue…is not that the human body is categorically material but rather that in certain communicative contexts its function is more…imagistic than linguistic. Whether sociocultural researchers limit their attention to the body as object of cultural inscription or expand their theoretical frame to include its spatializing effects on social practice, their empirical focus does not fully acknowledge the body's generative role in meaning making. [A]s primarily a material artifact, the human body embodies the inscription of culture in its' gestural, spatial, and imagistic presentation. As a semiotic tool in the spatial semiotic, however, the human body appears to be the site of signifying relations that integrate interior and exterior communication.[28]

By striving to participate in these ancient, immaterial, transcendental, spiritual experiences through interior and exterior communication, the body's attempt to forge extraordinary nondual communion with the divine facilitates resistance against conventional material forces unifying the experiences of socioeconomic victims of both first and third worlds. Rituals involving the ancient 'lost' practices are blended and reinvigorated with new scientific forms of out-of-body transcendental experiences that together enable body-modified bohemians in exile to witness (if not personally undergo) many esoteric, erotic, transformative rituals that further deepen their marginality from conventional rational industrialized society.

Sexuality, then, is the indelible mark of the sacred on our bodies, an endless evocative epigram written on the flesh, to delight and puzzle us so that we might know god/dess. The divine is not, as the phallic imaginary would have it, the absolute power to dominate all others while remaining curiously insensate; the divine is energetic, communicative and connective, desiring, sexual, and intelligent. By [sanctioning sex, patriarchal authority] seeks to discredit a complex sexual cosmology. That cosmology recognizes…quintessential female sovereignty; it respects sexuality and desire as emancipation of the sacred.[29]

Borrowing from worldwide practices documented as *savage* through centuries of colonial occupation, anti-modern participation in these non-Western spiritual practices are becoming widespread. Even a cursory glance at free weekly zines in urban environs throughout the United States in cities such as Miami and San Francisco provides evidence of weekend classes to discover Kundalini yoga, Tantric Sex, the Kama Sutra, and other eros-centric introductory spiritual pursuits to unlock the sensual mysteries of the ancient universe.

This has both positive and negative effects on spirituality in both first and third worlds. On the one hand, the distinctiveness of indigenous spiritual cultures suffers when material monolithic secular societies find themselves mesmerized by ancient practices and pursue the depths of their meaning in ways that both celebrate and inadvertently exploit those distinctions.

"Third World" and "indigenous [ritual and customs] have blossomed on the uneven playing field of today's global economy. Most Third World cultures are fundamentally hybrids—synthetic products of multiple global influences, including from the West. Despite the triumphs of synthetic culture, we should not ignore the costs of cross-cultural exchange. Coca-cola and Western tourists may succeed in doing what decades of coercive Communist intervention failed to achieve—weakening traditional Tibetan attachment to their rich brocade of history.[30]

Originating with the mysticism of voodoo of New Orleans, reduced barriers regarding the circulation of ritual spirituality have increased Western demands for world music, accoutrements of indigenous spiritual rituals, access to African drums and other instruments, domestic textiles from Indonesia, rugs from Persia, Pandit art of Indian Tabla, and the list goes on and on. All have commodified traditional societies and had a profound impact on child labor, theft of religious shrines, and other tragedies of cultural loss associated with the Western export and neutralization of artifacts and practices of everyday spiritual life. Yet there is evidence that the reclamation of indigenous spirituality can very well take place among body-modified bohemians without the imposition of the foreign and intrusive, particularly if these immaterial subcultures, like their aesthetic counterparts in music and the visual arts, remain independent, uncommodified, and underground.

> Yet, if we have lost touch with the shamanistic world view by which we have lived since paleolithic beginnings of human culture, there is one sense in which magic has not lost its power over us with the progress of civilization, [science]. Where the shaman looked to communal ritual to validate his vision of reality, scientific experts have had to look more and more to professional approval by self-selected authorities to validate their own esoteric knowledge. Mystery, as it was known in primordial rite and ritual, as it was experienced in the sacraments of the mystery cults, had stood as a boundary defining man's proper station in the world. It was that which was sacred and taught man wise limitations. The existence of mystery in this sense—as the non-human dimension of reality which was not to be tampered with but revered—served to enrich the lives of men by confronting them with a realm of inexhaustible wonder. With the appearance of scientific skepticism, however, the mysterious came to be seen as…an intolerable barrier to reason and justice. Yet science and technology, with their relentless insistence on specialization and expertise, were themselves to come full circle and be transformed into as closed a priesthood as any in history. All that remained to be done to turn such an authoritative professionalism into a new regime of bad magicians was for ruling political and economic elites to begin buying up the experts and using them for their own purposes. It is in this fashion that technocracy had been consolidated.[31]

To reverse these technocratic, anti-organic, science-worshipping, militantly secular trends of modernity, a variety of western rituals has emerged that are inspired by, and implemented through, the return to and familiarity with anti-rational, nondogmatic, nonhierarchical, unscientific, experientially oriented, genuinely transcendental, indigenous spirituality. These include the widespread popularity of transcendental suspensions known as Thiapusam, as well as Western and non-Western syncretic rituals which

> [represent an] effort to recover from this pathological culture the traces of our disintegrated psychic wholeness and to fashion of these remnants a reality principle based on the organic unity which predates the advent of repression. It was exactly [the] tendency of organized religion to indulge in self-seeking obscurantism and authoritarian manipulation which led to the series of great revolts against the churches of the West and culminated in the militant secularism of the Enlightenment.[32]

Despite vilifying claims of the media, suspension activities represent much more than mere masochistic meat hook inversion, and should be the focus of further social scientific inquiry.

Customizing Modern Mysticism

Discontent with paternalistic authority and the desire to reconnect, through ancient bodily practices, with the experiential divine has led to the rise of a variety of modern customs blending elements of old and new practices. One of the most popular of the western rituals that seeks to blend elements of ancient mysticism in light of modern culture is the mobile dance venue.

> Flying in the face of modernity's rigid individualism, this sense of unity [at the rave] resonates with the major goals of religion—namely the production of solidarity and community. Ravers, even as their egos melt, even as their bodies dissolve into a larger 'organism', still speak of something apart.[33]

According to Landau (2004), participants at these nomadic ritualistic dance venues are able to acquire the sense of community and spiritual exploration that is traditionally offered at conventional institutions of worship in a more egalitarian celebratory forum. Tramacchi (2004) acknowledges that many elements of these spiritual ceremonial pursuits at mobile techno parties are rooted, like their genuine non-Western counterparts, in the consumption of psychotropic substances in order to enhance the likelihood that participants can achieve the desired transcendental effect. Brown (1966) calls these new rituals blending secularism and transcendentalism the rise of a new *body mysticism*.

> Psychedelic parties, like their non-western counterparts...share many elements...that are functionally analogous; in all the instances social energy generated through ecstatic dance is harnessed and directed by ritual virtuosos in accord with the collective desires of the group to enhance the possibilities of producing a definite product: spontaneous communitas.[34]

In response to the ritually impoverished emptiness of the west, it may not really matter what elements the ritual has or what its meanings may entail.

With or without psychotropic stimulants, more and more anti-moderns in permanent exile are devoting significant interest to the blending of ancient rituals giving rise to alternative hybrids of modernity such as suspension. Many of these are so routine, that even Thiapusam is becoming a routine part of techno parties. Although there is little evidence that these pursuits are as cohesive as some would suggest, the popular Burning Man Festival is one example where the ritual itself does not attempt to impose any meaning or obligation on the participants, who are free to make fluid, autonomous interpretations for rules of spiritual engagement for themselves.

> Burning man attempts ideologically and ritually to distance itself from the mainstream market place, offering consumers a place where they can imagine they have suspended authoritarian market logistics. The result is the freedom from social distancing in which participants build community, and the freedom from passivity in which they express and transform themselves. [T]he sacred and the commercial exist in an uneasy cultural tension with one another throughout contemporary western society. Festivals provide ritual power for inverting, temporarily overturning, and denying currently dominant social order. The ritual fire, like the sacred dance floor, is a place to transport participants to a higher state of consciousness, a place that is particularly sacred, a place where self-transformation can occur. [T]hese are places where participants...gain an experience....and a bodily knowing of control and freedom. The dancers become less inhibited, more comfortable with their own bodies, with the dance, with others, with the idea of others watching them.[35]

The reclamation of indigenous spirituality is not limited to hybrid spiritual practices of the ancient world. Non-Western anti-Judeo–Christian spirituality is also gaining adherents among body modified anarchist activists, in the form of transgressive embodied spirituality through Islam (Bayat, 2005). Cultural resistance found throughout the Muslim world has enabled the indigenous people of Africa, the Middle East, and Far East to make their society highly inhospitable to the material dependency being imposed, often at gunpoint, by hegemonic forces of the West. Islamic religious revivalism, like other nonconventional spiritual paths, has appeal that is rooted in its "exclusion of the excluders by the excluded."[36] The empowerment brought on by an anti-Western, antifashion, *negated body* enveloped by traditional Islamic dress encourages small-scale local textile production similar to that originally begun by Gandhi. Muslim clothing discourages the use of synthetic fibers or ostentatious display of either the male or female body through restrictive design in order to provide an environment that does not objectify or otherwise divide members of society in order to give rise to *umma*, or cohesive Islamic community.

> Religious traditions provide another important space of opposition...have helped indigenous communities...resist assimilation. Whereas capitalist, state-based systems define ownership in terms of private property, many indigenous communities emphasize communal access to resources.[37]

These decommodified, deobjectified forms of body negation to reduce the likelihood for competition within the community through desensualization represents not only a defiant symbolism of this culture's ancient organic roots, but also expresses a refusal to accept the imposition of Western sexual objectification and related consumption and dependency patterns. Despite the continued hopes for pacifism brought on by American foreign policy in the Middle East by a Nobel Peace Prize award-winning President Obama, the Western activist romance with Nation of Islam and now conventional Islam seems rather short-lived. Just as fruitless as were bohemian attempts to immerse the self into traditional dogmatic principles inherent in traditional Jewish or Christian faiths, Islam provides similar institutional barriers that thwart the genuine seeker with a progressive political sentiment from subscribing to these teachings for long. In addition to Islamic, Jewish, or Christian faiths, Buddhism, Hinduism, Sufism, and all of the world's major religions are, to a certain extent, rendered problematic for the Western exploratory anarchist consciousness due to human interpretations that have evolved away from organic spirituality, in lieu of an often coercive imposition of modern bureaucracy, nonegalitarian gender role expectations, blind obedience to patriarchal religious authority, the diminution of feminine construction of the divine, and other manmade reductivist translations that have, by many accounts, diluted the beauty and authenticity of all these ancient divine organic pathways toward the Creator. The institutional turn away from many of the organic organizing principles among conventional dogmatic world religions has also been exacerbated by contemporary patriarchal tendencies to enhance the prestige of adherents reflecting nationalist fundamentalism, while simultaneously marginalizing the authority of religious leaders espousing pacifist, moderate, and progressively accommodating ideologies within Jewish, Christian, and Muslim faiths alike. This further impedes widespread participation by body-modified bohemians who might be genuinely seeking emancipatory paths toward spirituality through conventional communities of worship popular among the masses.

> [T]he strongest responses to modernity have been various forms of reactionary, antimodern resistance. One response has been widespread flourishing of fundamentalism; a resistance movement that not only rejects modernity but in its rejection attempts to restore an earlier moral order. As traditional communities have faced economic or political challenges, a variety of fundamentalisms have emerged that attempt to restore moral communities that are imagined to be lost, in which people lived in...more "authentic" lifestyles. The alienation of fundamentalist, resistance identities ensnares people in roles and lifestyles that, given the enormous range of options available in modern societies, thwart human potential, choice, and self-constitution.[38]

Spiritual pursuits through conventional dogmatic religious institutionalism often renders seekers obedient to just another form of economic, social, and cultural system of domination, rather than offering any real organic ancient transcendental emancipation. These conditions leave progressive body-modified bohemian spiritual seekers dissatisfied with any emancipatory potential that may have once been available through traditional mainstream religion. Furthermore, despite historic evidence that the adornment of the body has been extensively practiced since the earliest times of human civilization, contemporary piercing of the body is interpreted by older generations of patriarchal Muslim, Jewish, and Christian experts as a sin against the divine. Thus, despite persistent attempts at genuine immersion, body-modified bohemian activists are unable to find the spiritual liberation they are seeking through conventional hierarchical dogmatic religious institutions based on spiritual limitations inherent in prohibition of body piercing, obscurantist exclusionary practices, and relentless adherence to blind hierarchical obedience. The conventional choices left for the modern seeker have been reduced, by many accounts, to either worship of the rational experts of science or the irrational experts of dogma. Neither of these hierarchical institutional approaches to spirituality appeals to the progressive body-modified bohemian for obvious reasons.

> [I]n the case of technocracy, totalitarianism is perfected because its' techniques become progressively more subliminal. The distinctive feature of the regime of experts lies in the fact that, while possessing ample power to coerce, it prefers to charm conformity from us by exploiting our deep-seated commitment to the scientific world views and by manipulating the securities and creature comforts of the industrial affluence which science has given us. The research of experts can be popularized or vulgarized as a body of information—and inevitably distorted in the process. It cannot be democratized as a form of vital experience. Such is the price we pay for replacing the immediacy of the personal vision with the aloofness of objective knowledge. The old magic that could illuminate the sacramental presence in a tree, a pond, a rock, or totem is derided as a form of superstition unworthy of civilized men. Things, events, even the person of our fellow human beings have been deprived of the voice with which they once declared their mystery to men. They can be known now only through the mediation of experts. The New Left that rebels against technocratic manipulation...draws, often without realizing it, upon an anarchist tradition which has always championed the virtues of the primitive band, the tribe, the village. The spirit of Prince Kropotkin, who learned the anti-statist values of mutual aid from villagers and nomads little removed from the neolithic or even paleolithic levels, breathes through all the young have to say about community. Our beatniks and hippies press the critique even further. Their instinctive fascination with magic and ritual, tribal lore, and psychedelic experience attempts to resuscitate the defunct shaman of the distant past. As long as the spell of the objective consciousness grips our society; the regime of experts is not far off; the community is bound to remain beholden to the high priests of the citadel who control access to reality. It is participation of this order— experiential and not merely political—that alone can guarantee the dignity and autonomy of the individual citizen. The strange youngsters who don

cowbells and primitive talismans and who take to the public parks or wilderness to improve outlandish communal ceremonies are in reality seeking to ground democracy safely beyond the culture of expertise. They give us back the image of the paleolithic band. It is a strange brand of radicalism we have here that turns to prehistoric precedent for inspiration.[39]

The strange brand of prehistoric radicalism yearning to dismantle the passivity brought on by the masters of both scientific and spiritual knowledge results in highly creative responses among the disenchanted that drive empowerment through alternative mystical interpretation and ritual. Modern religion with its contemporary ready-to-wear translations by aging nationalist fundamentalist patriarchs of all the major spiritual traditions of the West has left authentic seekers longing for an emancipatory spirituality that they must design and create through hybrids using a combination of their own customized rituals through yet another arena in need of the do-it-yourself approach. DIY custom-made spirituality, like nearly every other aspect of body-modified bohemian existence, enables anti-modern nomadic seekers to build on their own transient experiences, to reject the prêt-a-porter options available through conventional paternalistic religious avenues, and to blend their own preferred elements of personalized exploratory spiritual paths in order to fulfill their own individualized haute couture mystical objectives.

Much like ancient spiritual practices, these custom-made DIY sacral circumstances provide new opportunities for spiritually oriented body-modified bohemians to incorporate piercing rituals into many of their religious practices and customs. As with the ancients, this may or may not include rituals that invoke both good and bad spiritual realms, and sometimes even culminates into practices known *as satan worshipping*. In ten years of interviews with body-modified Satanists on the streets of New Orleans, these self-proclaimed adherents to the supreme authority of the fallen angel have disclosed that they are consistently believers of God, articulated anger with God's apparent abandonment, and suggested that the pain inflicted through body piercing is an important ritualistic element in Satanism to transform the energy of the good in order to strengthen the forces of evil.

Among body-modified bohemians who do not believe in any presence of the divine, good or bad, as defined through organized religion, but who do claim to have a spiritual orientation, small numbers of exiles invoke their belief in the primacy of astronomy, the solar system, and the physical universe to articulate a worship of higher authorities that come in the form of interplanetary beings or UFOs, otherwise known as Unidentified Flying Objects. According to this small number of body-modified adherents, these superior life-forms are transported to us from other galaxies, and provide indications of the intergalactic presence of a supreme divine entity in the cosmos. The belief in UFOs and superior life-forms on other planets represents a form of imagined community dominated by observant paternalistic authority indicative of other life-forms beyond our own solar system, whose prognosis usually results in our eventual demise.

> [T]here is no boundary between what is artificial and what is real, since these boundaries, if they existed at all, are thoroughly dissolved. [This] notion contributes to cultural anxieties about nature. The narcissism inherent in consumer culture means people seek salvation, meaning and a sense of self through consumption activities that are increasingly associated with the cultivation of the body. Where the dominant culture emphasizes order, control, and restraint, dissident cultures emphasize openness. Practices such as scarification, tattooing and piercing mark the body in ways that overturn ideals of bodily representation in Western contexts. Modern Primitivism seeks affinity with non-Western cultures as a way of signaling discontent with the modern social order. Hence the marking represented in practices such as piercing, tattooing and scarification is perceived by Modern Primitivism as a 'radical gesture' against dominant norms.[40]

Regardless of which spiritual paths—New Age, Satanism, UFOs, or more conventional spiritual transcendental traditions—are explored, the turn away from material culture and the modern reclamation of indigenous spirituality consistently signifies the primacy of agency in the struggle to optimize the transformative potential of humanity through liberation beyond the increasingly brutal demoralizing contemporary conditions of the mundane physical world.

Emancipatory Limits of the Modified Body

Whether rocking at the Wailing Wall, circumnavigating for the Haj at Mecca, or prostrating before Michaelangelo's creations at St. Peter's Basilica, spiritual rituals and other deciviling transgressive practices are impossible without major involvement of the body. The body is, in fact, so central to spirituality and other forms of anti-modern transgression, that fringe groups seeking instant recognition and legitimation find themselves designing similar embodied rituals to attract adherents.

> Indeed the body has become an important site for rethinking such binary oppositions as masculinity and femininity, gender and sex, the public and the private, and the cultural and the natural. Contemporary attempts to expose these categories as ideological constructions buttressing Western and/or male supremacy and to disrupt them have focused on the body. Understanding the body not as simple materiality, but rather as constituted within language as in much contemporary thought, is intended to question traditional notions of the body as prior to, or outside of, culture. This move is, of course, just one of the latest attempts of the West to grapple with the relationship between the natural and the cultural and to put the body, and representations of it, in service to this struggle.[41]

At the center of all these different organic, often bizarre forms of spiritual sabotage, remains the exhausted, over-processed, pierced, stretched, and negated aging, anarchist activist body. There are some indications that, like the throbbing planet, the sabotaging project of body modification may have reached its limits of manipulation. Take, for example, the relevance of group sex mythologies that allegedly take place regularly on the devil-worshipping altars across America, or the focus on the prodding and poking in a variety of anatomical crevices on the bodies of reluctant females (often virgins) that has allegedly taken place in intergalactic exchanges on UFO vessels, or the promises of an afterlife filled with females (often virgins) that Islamic terrorists are allegedly assured awaits them upon completion of maximized carnage associated with their random dastardly deeds. According to Aaron (1999), there are tremendous costs associated with the now wildly misinterpreted unconventional pursuits of embodied transgression. Interplanetary travel, sadomasochistic group sex rituals, and many other vapid avenues forging emancipatory claims for liberation have left seekers' desires largely unfulfilled, and can even create much destruction to the self and others in the process of filling these voids.

> The 'marketability' of the body's perilous pleasures is of prime importance. The commercialism and exploitation of dangerous desires for the 'risk'-hungry Western audience delineates those desires that are sanctioned, to reveal how they implicate and yield those that are not. Rather than celebrating transgression for transgression's sake, a steady skepticism is necessary to evaluate the truly liberatory potential of these risky behaviors and images, to distinguish subversity from fashion or from a final restoration of hegemonic order.[42]

Though the preoccupation with virgins may represent opportunistic attempts to market fringe ideologies to eager spiritual seekers associated with the modern project against secular society, they remain overwhelmingly aimed at men, they sustain rather than dismantle power relations, and (unlike their more conventional religious dogmatic counterparts) openly deploy the male mystical body as yet another strategy of modern domination to bolster and solidify patriarchal systems of institutionalized oppression overpowering nature and one another, often through the sensual subordination of females.

> [T]he female body was interpreted increasingly in terms of its contrast to the male body, as a 'dark' continent to be explored by the developing profession of scien[ce]. Hence this new perception of the female body (as natural, weak, or troublesome) was a product of the social and political impulses that sought to exclude women from entry into the new public world of the bourgeoisie. [A]s political and social changes increasingly raised questions about women's place in the world, [elites] focused on body parts that differentiated the female body from the male body. In turn these body parts came to stand

for difference and to be used as the basis on which to make claims about female inferiority.[43]

As distances are bridged and exchanges between people struggling in both first and third worlds increasingly expose the limits of the potential of the worldwide emancipatory project rooted in body modification, they also serve to demonstrate the authentic truth of the vehemence with which individuals and institutions, even those claiming to espouse anarchist ideology, are often unable to break through the repressive hierarchical relativism and related bureaucratic domination that has characterized modernity. In exchange for adherence and loyalties to particular spiritual paths that typically offer vapid promises of customs and rituals that perpetuate male domination over nature and women, the faithful have few genuine obligations outside of cursory recreational interaction and financial support. The lack of asceticism, internal cathartic transformation, or other commitment to even minimal levels of nonfinancial obligations associated with these spiritual pursuits further exacerbates problems associated with any transcendental potential inherent in body-modified mystical liberation.

> At other times and in other civilizations, this path of spiritual transformation was confined to a relatively select number of people; now, however, a large proportion of the human race must seek the path of wisdom if the world is to be preserved from the internal and external dangers that threaten it. In this time of violence and disintegration, spiritual vision is not an elitist luxury but vital to our survival. So at the time of our most acute danger, when our very future is in doubt, we as human beings find ourselves at our most bewildered, and trapped in a nightmare of our own creation. The most important thing is not to get trapped in [searching] around from master to master, teaching to teaching, without any continuity or real, sustained dedication to any one discipline.[44]

Although the transgressive body is a signifier of the desire for transcendence *from* conventional culture, the socially constructed alternative brought about among body-modified bohemians has not been able to fully achieve the objectives of the utopian project originally envisioned. Though the bohemian community should be acknowledged for its continued dedication to construct a superior mystical alternative to the world we have now, the day-to-day utopia under construction sometimes represents little more than an unruly rearrangement of actors with competency in fashionable alternative cultural capital within the same predictable repressive structures of hierarchy indicative of dominating and submissive relations at intimate and group levels. The project of lived activism increasingly runs the risk of becoming usurped through a superficial movement of fashionable veneers, claiming its work is egalitarian but in reality seriously lacking any forms or processes that lead to such emancipation. Private egalitarianism at the local level is the crucial foundation necessary before attempting to construct public egalitarianism at the global level. Inimical bohemian

impostors often attempt these in reverse, limiting themselves to disingenuous style and fashion rather than a truly avant-garde lived autonomous
ideology. Among inimical impostors, the body is deployed merely as the
ends and not the means.

> [T]attooing and piercing arguably move the body further away from, rather
> than closer towards, the hegemonic Western ideal of the youthful, slim,
> and *unmarked* body which lies at the heart of Western (consumer) culture.
> Whereas in traditional or pre-modern societies identity was rather fixed and
> size, shape and appearance of the body accepted more or less as given,...iden-
> tity is [now] increasingly fluid and the body is mobilized as a...resource on
> to which a reflexive sense of self is projected in an attempt to lend solidarity
> to the narrative this envisaged.[45]

Rather than serving as the vehicle of genuine transcendental liberation,
the body instead becomes the sole marker of the superficial trangressive.
The popularity of protest activity surrounding *anti*globalization serving as
cultural adornment rather than genuine political utopianism to construct
an *alter*globalization is increasingly common, especially among unpierced,
unmodified, guilt-appeasing, affluent, highly materialistic, self-proclaimed
60s radicals. Their ex post facto participation in alterglobalization efforts
and demands to impose their anachronistic forms of leadership further
dilutes the authenticity of the body-modification project underway.

> Basically, the antisystemic movements intoxicated their members and their
> followers. They organized them, mobilized their energies, disciplined their
> lives, structured their thinking processes. It took twenty years for the revo-
> lution of 1968 to reach its climax in 1989 and for popular disillusionment
> with antisystemic forces to overcome the legacy of loyalty engendered by past
> indoctrination, but eventually it succeeded in breaking the umbilical cord.
> The process was aided and abetted by the reality of the fact that...the capi-
> talist world-economy could never offer a real prospect of universal prosperity
> that would ever overcome the ever-growing gap between core and periphery.
> The result of this disillusionment has been the turn against the state [and]
> neoliberalism. It is in reality a resurgence of collectivism.[46]

In view of the limits of these demographic bodies attempting to take credit
for the antiglobalization movement, younger activists on the left use body
piercing as a generational signal to distinguish them from what they consider to be aging, atheistic, overweight, highly material, hypocritical 1960s
radicals whose lifestyles and worldviews are antithetical to, and incapable
of, truly advancing the cathartic emancipatory utopian project at hand. As
these pseudoradicals rush to impose their failed bureaucratic hierarchies
and other tired agnostic tactics on the new alterglobalization movement,
the drive to use body modification as a generational signifier has, to a certain extent, diluted the phenomenon. Observers are therefore suggesting
that contemporary body modification has become little more than a form

of simple adornment (Curry, 1993), a communicative symbol of pain (Pitts, 2003), a sign of commercial wanderings (Parry, 1933), a way to develop intimate relationships with piercers and tattoo artists (Aaron, 1999), a mechanism to avoid social invisibility (Grossi, 2004), a method of creating alternate dominating cultures (Dyens, 2001), and has even evolved to become a nationalistic signifier of ascetic class and racial purity marking supremacy against poverty-stricken communities (Atkinson, 2003).

> [T]he body is simultaneously an environment (part of nature) and a medium of the self (part of culture). The body lies in the center of political struggles. [O]ur body maintenance creates social bonds, expresses social relations and reaffirms or denies them.[47]

As alterglobalization takes on serious momentum and as ideologically diverse individuals including skins and others who subscribe to racist nationalist fascism create their own body-modified movements to express sabotaging *style* as opposed to genuine anarchist bohemian egalitarian lived activism, intergenerational social bonds within resistance communities on the left have become clearly attenuated while the defiant potential of the transgressive organic body becomes significantly restricted by emulating postfascist movement members.

The elements of body-modified bohemian culture that have remained intact, that government, economics, science and technology, religion, and 1960s radicals have been unable to dismantle, are even under assault by business consultants eagerly working to decipher the last vestiges of authenticity among these genuine unconventional nomadic enclaves. Optimism-disseminating gurus such as Richard Florida are well compensated to dissect and deconstruct, using highly flawed methodological approaches, the essential elements of creativity and innovation that have given rise to these enclaves.[48] His dissection of bohemian communities is used by corporate strategic planners attempting to imitate the atmospheric conditions of faux-rebellion in suburban corporate industrial parks across America. These disingenuous corporate cultures hope to dilute, emulate, and repackage bohemian defiance for their obedient suburban employees, providing conventional masses with banal aesthetic distractions and other imitative illusions of autonomy and self-determination they require to fill the emptiness of their otherwise meaningless, material, corner cubicle-aspiring corporate lives. The imitation of creative culture by desperate decomposing business-sector elites during the economic decline of the new century capitalism is not merely an innocent scholarly attempt to reinvigorate innovation among the faltering uninspired overeducated paltry American professional classes, but represents a genuine predatory threat to the well-being of bohemian communities around the world. Analysis conducted by business gurus delivering vapid promises of this quick corporate cultural fix has been contracted primarily to drive corporate relocation decisions to the center of existing bohemian enclaves, in the hope that these moves will reinvigorate faltering businesses, eliminate the pervasive discontent associated with the cubicalized workforce, and reverse the new centers of innovation now located in China and India. These relocations attempting to salvage faltering American business by moving predatory business entities right to the heart of body-modified bohemia run the risk of destroying the world's authentic creative exiled enclaves by bringing with them urban gentrification, increased demand and costs for residential housing and commercial real estate, increased homelessness, and a parade of franchised businesses and services that imposes routinization and standardization to meet the consuming demands of conventional corporate actors. Fortunately, Florida's corporate formulaic equations attempting to define, emulate, and eradicate the essence of bohemia are so conceptually flawed and exorbitantly expensive, that little has really changed. It is therefore unlikely that predatory corporations will continue to dismantle genuine bohemian communities at any significant level for the future.[49]

The End of Sabotage?

Are these threats an indication of the end of body-modified bohemian resistance? Is it inevitable that, despite the best efforts by these authentic exiles striving to adhere to genuinely creative egalitarian aesthetic anarchist lifestyles, the disingenuousness of material cultures will continue to breed dependency enabling hegemonic entities to finally to rule the world? Are the spiritual components of these utopian resistance endeavors merely a superficial veneer perpetuating an illusion of third-world organic spiritual familiarity to drive conspicuous consumption of new globalized fashion style? If corporate imitators are eventually able to move into transgressive neighborhoods to emulate their transgressive inhabitants and in the process even resort to modifications to advance their constructions of a stylized inimical transgressive body, will future body-modified bohemians inevitably have to distinguish themselves by pulling out their piercings, skin grafting over their tattoos, and adhering to civilizing tendencies to give rise to yet another wave of rebellion, perhaps a retro obedience chic reminiscent of the 1950s?

Before offering a prognosis of the future we might have to take a cursory look at body modification's ancient past. Throughout history, nomadic people were the most difficult to conquer, and represented a threat to conventional cultures and economies built on foundations of an exploitative sedentary life. As Frank (1993) has outlined, nomadic lifestyles were always crippled by wars waged in order to assure sedentary peoples had a constant supply of submissive populations in order to extract surplus value from untapped labor coercively obtained from dangerously unencumbered meandering tribes harmoniously adapting to the constraints of nature. This same process can be observed in the destruction of indigenous American Indian culture in the United States, the Roma gypsy community throughout the Soviet and European empires, and more recently, in corporate threats to emulate and harness wild body-modified bohemian enclaves.

The destruction of migratory peoples is clearly not a new phenomenon. The very first modification ever created was, in fact, a functional manifestation of this very same principle.

In order to break the nonmaterial spirit of the wandering tribes of ancient peoples recorded only in vague hieroglyphic records as "the Sea People," an Egyptian ruler boasted of branding. We know only that they were migrating travelers around the Mediterranean, and were difficult to conquer based on strengths associated with flexible and adaptable migratory lifestyles. Ramses III [second ruler of the 20th dynasty, ruled between 1194–1163 BCE][50] put an end to their maritime vagabond lifestyle by capturing and branding their bodies in marks signifying enslavement, writing in official records, "I carried away those whom my sword spared, branded and made into slaves impressed with my name; their wives and children were made likewise."[51] Evidence also suggested that the enemies of Ramses III were sensual libertines who enjoyed physical sexual delights in their wanderings. Like many ruling elite he put an end to these sensual lifestyles and suggests that they threatened the safety and security of female citizens. In official records, Ramses III chronicled his accomplishments stating, "I enabled the women of Egypt to go her way, her journeys being extended to where she wanted, without any other person assaulting her on the road."[52] Was this pharaoh the first and last genuine feminist ruler of an empire? Or rather was he the first religious fundamentalist prohibiting libertine sensuality from proliferating during his administration? We may never know. No matter what the reason, Ramses III's use of body modification to distinguish captives from other citizens over three thousand years ago suggests that he was not only responsible for conceptualizing the first major invasive body modification in the history of human civilization, but that he also used body modification to distinguish dangerous wandering bohemian citizens from the ordinary.

Distinguishing non-sedentary unconventional citizens through branding may have been the first public policy to impede the libertine sexuality of women with outgroup males. Modifications in the form of body markings and piercing have a similar history of distinction for some and liberation for others in nearly every place in the world in nearly every civilization. Contemporary body modification serves the same purpose today as it did in Pharaonic times and throughout ancient history, as a marker of nomadic distinction and as a mechanism of liberation.[53]

What do these migrating bohemians of ancient times have in common with the contemporary body-modification project? Regardless of whether they are the wandering tribe of sea people with a penchant for Egyptian women, frolicking protesters at an alterglobalizing protest, Roma gypsies, goth punkrockers, motorcycle gang members, or gutterpunks, sedentary hegemonic oppressors have consistently attempted to dismantle, emulate, or otherwise weaken these materially unencumbered migratory bohemians throughout history. The threat that their nomadic lifestyles present to hegemonic oppressors is not necessarily rooted in their transience *per se*, but in the *fear* of the empowerment that comes from self-privileging of their exiled distinctiveness and autonomous adaptation to changing conditions no matter what the dominating forces of their prevailing circumstances. Utterly lacking in exogenous dependency-breeding validation and related normative manipulation, such cathartic transformation toward authenticity can only be attempted through the constructivist standpoint of creative independent self-exile.

> In their resistance, most of the [Bohemians] included in this book have embraced the position of marginality...viewed here as epistemically privileged, as an advantage. [The] resurgence of late...in the critical study of [bohemia] may be partially understood as part of a large-scale global response to the ever-increasing privatization of public spaces and community resources and near constant spectacle of dislocated populations fleeing the ravages of war, environmental disaster, and economic failure.[54]

Given the expectation that deteriorating socioeconomic and cultural conditions will surely continue, and the pervasive disingenuinousness of society that continues to accommodate or otherwise camouflage hegemonic oppressors under these barbaric conditions; the desire on the part of bohemians to maintain their authenticity no matter how high the costs will invariably result in continued attacks on these communities of resistance, in order to impose the conventional standards associated with dependent materialistic normativity benefiting fearful elites. Bohemians are not expected to succumb to these pressures, because to those with a conscience, the costs associated with inauthentic living are even higher. These costs are not only limited to hindrance of the self, but also of the global community, and of the planet.

> We have wandered down false paths for two hundred years. We have misled others, but most of all we have misled ourselves. We are in the process of writing ourselves outside the real game of struggle to achieve human freedom and collective welfare. We must turn ourselves around, if we are to have any hope of helping everyone else (or indeed anyone else) to turn the world around. We must most of all lower our arrogance decibels. We must do all these things because [activism] really does have something to offer the world. What it has to offer is the possibility of applying human intelligence to human problems, and thereby achieving human potential, which may be less then perfect but more than humans have achieved before.[55]

Will the embodied emancipatory project falter? On the contrary, with or without body modification, and in the face of constant disillusionment with the disingenuousness of modernity, it is unlikely that the struggle for embodied authenticity will end any time soon. Given persistent elite fears surrounding expanding numbers of unconventional, unencumbered, nomadic bohemians that will soon include mass populations of the newly displaced brought on by ecological catastrophes of rising tides associated with global warming, modern forms of sabotage are expected to enjoy even more creative, more aesthetic, more resilient, and more esoteric forms of embodied resistance among unprecedented numbers of exiles for the imminent future.

Notes

Chapter 2.   Verbal Communication

1. Lehtonen, p. 22.
2. Hester and Francis, p. 209.
3. Lehtonen, p. 33.
4. Briggs, p. 22.
5. Guy, p. 61.
6. Squatting is the occupation of unpopulated land and/or buildings, usually by the homeless and/or other people in need of shelter. In some jurisdictions the practice is illegal, whereas in others squatters are entitled to full or conditional ownership after a period of productive stewardship.
7. Widdicomb and Wooffitt, p. 126.
8. Langman and Cangemi, pp. 143, 146.
9. Ruddick, pp. 350, 354, 359.
10. Produced in New Orleans by Brent Sims and Ted Baldwin, distributed by Monarch Films. Documentary text provided in transcript form by Director Ted Baldwin and used by permission.
11. Data gathering and analysis all took place prior to Hurricane Katrina.
12. The drop-in center was a public health initiative directed by Tulane University to provide health interventions to low-income individuals living on the street, many of whom were gutterpunks.
13. Tuffin and Howard, p. 202.
14. West, p. 78.
15. Briggs, (1996), p. 22.
16. Kuipers, pp. 101, 104, 110.

Chapter 3.   Bohemian Network

1. Bennett, p. 146.
2. When examining specific individuals' interpersonal social networks in the socio-gram presented, *centrality* of highest status individuals [represented as black trian-gle (male) and diamond (female)] can be an important consideration as network ties exhibit increasing levels of complexity. The connections between two individuals (regardless if affective or not) are referred to as the *path*. The length of the path is the *social distance* between any points in a network. *Density*, as shown in the foci surrounding the pub, can also significantly impact network analysis. Furthermore, *egocentricity* [a particular high-status person's network location], *sociocentricity* [a particular social network's embeddedness within the larger social structure], or

global/local centrality [how well-connected points are within their local or global environments] are all very valuable theoretical constructs presented in the socio-gram but, due to manuscript constraints, not the focus of the current treatment.

3. As already developed elsewhere in the analysis, network ties, as well as status enhancement, develops along three foci of activity. One of the most prestigious social network clusters is based (predictably) around body piercing. Here, network members have different ascribed status based on many different criteria. For example, members have higher status the longer they have been committed to activities surrounding body piercing. This is often exhibited by multiple piercing adorned about the face, or by the width of impaled hole known as stretching signifying the duration of time since the piercing was acquired. Also, among lateral relations, status is ascribed based on salience of body-piercing identity as determined by loyalty exemplified by a lack of membership in other conventional networks. Finally, those with the highest status tend to be those who pierce people professionally, who are viewed as most thoroughly embodying desirable characteristics of piercing group networks. Professional piercers do not merely embody all the necessary qualities to be high-status members of this social network, but are also the most formidable gatekeepers determining admission among new members.

Chapter 4.   Ideological Apparatus

1. McAdam, McCarthy, and Zald, p. 5
2. Trotsky, p. 192
3. Luhmann, p. 85
4. Ricouer, p. 45
5. Spivak, in interview with Plotke, in Trend (ed.), p. 215
6. Haycock, p. 26
7. The Independent Sector, 1998
8. Rand, p. 93

Chapter 5.   Economic Contestation

1. Morris and Braine, pp. 29 and 31
2. Zizek, p. 193
3. Horowitz, p. 62
4. Langman, pp. 180, 187
5. Bhavnani, Foran, and Talcott, p. 323
6. Chase-Dunn and Hall, p. 6
7. Vail, p. 52
8. MacDonald, pp. 186, 191
9. Zielonka, p. 3
10. Nepstad, p. 133
11. Frank, p. 49
12. Podobnik and Reifer, p. 1
13. Wallerstein (2000), p. 255
14. Chirot and Hall, p. 90
15. Dawson, p. 97
16. Landmann, p. 126
17. Zundel, p. 122
18. Tsao, pp. 125, 127
19. Passerin d'Entreves, pp. 152, 161
20. Howarth and Stavrakis, p. 9

21. Pfeffer, p. 83
22. Belka, p. 31
23. Keller, p. 32
24. Gali, p. 28
25. Grossberg, p. 280
26. Kellner, p. 181
27. Simola, p. 340
28. Hall, p. 15
29. See for example, critical discussions of Jeffrey Sachs, Leszek Balcerowitz, FOZZ, and the Falzmann murder.
30. Boykoff, pp. 6, 11
31. Staniszkis, p. 14
32. Huddleston and Good, p. 384
33. Nee and Cao, p. 803
34. Macek et al., p. 551
35. Kilmann, p. 66

Chapter 6.   Digital Contestation

1. Aunger, pp. 67 and 75
2. Van Aelst and Walgrave, p. 469
3. Cantrill, p. 80
4. LaRose, Mastro, and Eastin, p. 406
5. Chalmers, pp. 395, 399
6. Ben-Rafael and Sternberg, p. 16
7. D'Arcus, p. 139
8. Nepstad, p. 133
9. McDonald, pp. 3, 5
10. Pinkett, p. 375
11. Parker, p. 46
12. Johnson and Kaye, pp. 305, 319
13. Dahlgren, pp. xv, xiii, 18
14. Mackie, p. 40
15. Featherstone, p. 12
16. Broedling, pp. 269, 271
17. Grossberg, p. 301
18. Dalh, pp. 48, 51
19. Entrena, pp. x, 196
20. Rosa Luxembourg was interred in the Wroclaw Municipal Detention Facility [prewar Breslau] by German authorities.
21. There are many notable episodes of hegemonic state attacks from German political and economic elites that drives radical anarchy in Wroclaw and Szczecin, but due to space constraints I include just a few. On October 10, 2008 the European Court of Human Rights in Strasbourg dismissed the lawsuit filed by German far-right nationalists known as the Prussian Trust (Preussische Treuhand) against the Republic of Poland seeking compensation for alleged human rights violations by Polish war survivors due to the forced displacement of surviving Nazi residents from Wroclaw and Szczecin brought on by Churchill-Stalin-Roosevelt's Yalta Agreement ending WWII. [Application no. 47550/06] The Bundestag (Germany's Parliament) recently blocked the development of a far-right extremist party-funded museum dedicated to commemorating Nazi survivors displaced by Yalta, but will continue development of a Nazi victimization memorial museum funded by multiple Bundestag parties and the EU nevertheless. On September 17, 2010, German historical revisionist

and Bundestag Member of Parliament Erika Steinback (previously of Preussische Treuhand) stated that the invasion of Poland by the Nazis and the subsequent outbreak of World War II was caused by Poland and its prewar defensive mobilization on Polish soil. See also Der Spiegel "World War II Revisited: Poles Angered by German Compensation Claims" 12/18/06; Rzeczpospolita "Powiernictwo Pruskie Bez Szans Na Wygrana" [Prussian Act No Chance of Winning] 12/22/06. One week after the decision, Der Speigel had not published any commentary online or in hard copy in German or English regarding the Strasbourg ruling [confirmed by the Goethe Institute of Wroclaw]. I have written an elaborate research article on deteriorating Polish-German relations from the Polish-Ukrainian perspective, but it has been rejected by every top ranked peer-reviewed sociological, public policy, and migration journal. Despite media portrayals to the contrary, the fact is that contemporary Austrian and German citizen voting patterns consistently have much higher support for their far-right extremist political parties than Poland. These aforementioned circumstances all have considerable influence upon the peculiar radically anarchist sentiment fomenting in Wroclaw and Szczecin.

22. This complacency has recently led to the state closure and sale of this squat property known as Rozbrat. Aside from a few concerts and street protests, resistance appears to be minimal and taking place very late in the eviction process.

Chapter 7.   Biker Contestation

1. Canadian authorities have even gone so far as to officially designate motorcyclists as one of 16 groups (including Hezbollah, Hamas, and al Qaida) considered to be terrorists (Humphreys, 2003).
2. American Motorcycle Association infamous statistical approximation of the composition of extremist biker outlaws, later embraced enthusiastically by biker club members throughout the world.
3. See the American Civil Rights movement, the Stonewall Riots among gays and the New York City police, Malcolm X and his earlier days with the Nation of Islam, as well as the eerily prophetic religious sect led by David Koresh whose members (including infants and children) were annihilated by ATF officials in Waco, Texas.
4. Successful lawsuits brought against police departments charging persistent systemic harassment against motorcycle clubs have already awarded gang members millions of dollars in damages.
5. After World War II, many veterans including patriotic fighter pilots returned from their successful battle against fascism and genocide to begin these motorcycle clubs in the United States. As such, it is highly ironic that white supremacists are found in clubs with such regularity, particularly in the Deep South.
6. To circumvent possible legal repercussions, "Big Four" gangs are now disseminating unscrupulous responsibilities to associates in peripheral "ghost" clubs, discreetly operating under their auspices.
7. Central Business District west of the French Quarter
8. These names are fictitious. "Property-owning" brothers usually have innovative nicknames demonstrated on their ol' lady's jacket.

Chapter 8.   Sexual Sabotage

1. For a full description of mechanisms to exercise erotic agency, see Linder, 2001. For full description of the history of state regulation of sexuality, see Weeks,

1981; 1999. For a full description of the history of sociology of sexuality, see Irvine, 2003. For a discussion of the pervasiveness of sexuality in popular culture, see Attwood, 2006.

2. Jackman, p. 262
3. Jackman, p. 270
4. In separate attempts to decriminalize sex work and child pornography, lobbying groups representing the widely distinct constituencies of prostitutes and pedophiles have recently received substantial attention in the media. As such, noncomforming members of subordinate sexual groups in America are reluctant to have any inadvertent associations.
5. Zafirovski, pp. 3–11
6. Rubin, p. 267, in Vance
7. Shorter, pp. 4, 80, 199, 218, 241
8. Despite legislation increasing the punitive severity of the category of "hate" crimes that encapsulates "gay bashing" activity, the FBI's Uniform Crime Reports and the NIJ's Bureau of Justice Statistics indicate that annual statistics regarding assault, battery, and murder of people *feared* to be homosexual are, in some areas of the United States, occurring with frightening regularity.
9. Jackman, p. 365
10. Some piercing requires restrictive devices whose performance is maximized through the interaction of several sex partners who assist in the preparation of these devices. Piercings are also obtained to be used with restrictive rings to maintain an erection longer than would normally be possible, with weights to stimulate tissue with forces of gravity, with hoops that deliver a subtle stimulation to nerve endings in particular areas of the body, or plugs that allow for multiple areas of erectile tissue to be stimulated simultaneously. Among these alternative sexual communities, courtship rituals require multiple partners as the precursors to sex, where consenting partners promote piercing's technical efficacy (expedition of male and/or female climax) through the intended consequence of modification (pursuit of particular sex practices) with related sexual expression (comfort with one's own sexual narcissism and the preferred role of dominance or submission through expeditious symbolic communication.
11. Rubin, p. 284, in Vance
12. One measure of professionalization involves certification, credentialing, and lengthy training. Body piercers often participate in lengthy apprenticeship periods over many years, have a professional membership association (APP), are required to obtain several safety certifications (OSHA certfication for recognition and prevention of transmission of Bloodborne Pathogens, Red Cross Safety and First Aid certifications), and are expected to obtain continuing clinical education training by attending association conferences (similar to ongoing CME training for medical professionals).

Chapter 9.   Political Sabotage

1. Farro and Vaillancourt, p. 212.
2. Mirowsky, p. 27.
3. Dahms, p. 37.
4. Touraine, p. 263.
5. Krishnamurti, pp. 33 65 100.
6. Berlin, p. 107.
7. Berlin (1998), pp. 91, 203.
8. Nehamas, p. xxxii .

9. Berman, pp. xvii, 32, 124, 129.
10. Rossinow, pp. 5, 345.
11. Widdicomb and Wooffitt, pp. 140, 144, 157.[In References, this is Widdicomb and Wooffitt (no Windance Twine) and the next entry, Kum-Kum and Kent DOES have Windance Twine]
12. Kum-Kum and Kent, p. 576.
13. Dahl, p. 14.
14. Ezrahi, p. 172.
15. Giroux, pp. 71–73.
16. Wolff, pp. 12, 18.
17. Zinn, p. xvii.
18. Miller, pp. 6–10.
19. See the case of Ward Churchill.
20. Pickvance, p. 127.
21. Wendt, p. 529.
22. Shannon, pp. 583–585.
23. Varela, p. 386.
24. Leeson and Stringham, p. 544.
25. Chomsky, p. 28.
26. For a German-centrist treatment of Wroclaw in and out of the fluctuating political boundaries of Bohemia since antiquity, see Davies and Moorhouse.
27. Humphrey, pp. 3, 6, 236, 253.
28. Kubik, pp. 142–151.
29. Soule and Earl, pp. 345–347.
30. Bookchin, p. 262.
31. Shorter, pp. 80, 121, 241.
32. For a full discussion of labor militancy and sexuality in the American civil rights movement, see Greene, 2006.
33. Berman, p. 29.
34. Ferrara, p. 89.
35. Shorter (1972), p. 348.
36. Maney, p. 41.
37. Miller, p. 109.
38. Della Porta and Rucht, p. 267.
39. Protests in large cities in both the US and the EU are public activities that are highly regulated by the state. requiring activists to pay rather exorbitant fees for police "protection," "parade" licenses, mobile toilets, and other accoutrements, making participatory democracy essentially impossible for organizations without access to substantial levels of financial capital.
40. Ferrara, p. 305.
41. Purkis and Bowen, p. 1.
42. I intentionally omit Polish-American anarchist-intellectual professor of mathematics Ted Kaczynski, also known as the Unabomber, due to his scrupulously meticulous methods of targeting the sinister scientists that he considered the planet's worst ecological and technological adversaries.

Chapter 10.   Aesthetic Sabotage

1. Frith, p. 14.
2. Longhurst, p.115
3. Bennett, pp. 146, 152, 158.
4. Hebdige, pp. 44, 34.

5. Mercer, pp. 420, 434.
6. Bennett, pp. 23, 49.
7. Hebdige, pp. 96, 98
8. Powers, p. 240.
9. Young. p. 141.
10. Hebdige, pp. 38, 58, 63
11. West, pp. 48, 71.
12. Soeffner, pp. 51, 65.
13. Wojcik, pp 12, 14, 54, 55.
14. Wojcik, p. 7.
15. Soeffner, p. 54.
16. Miller, pp. 128, 202.
17. Barnes, p. 18.
18. Hebdige, p. 19.
19. West, pp. 56, 69.
20. Wallace and Kovoatcheva, p. 176.
21. NKVD was the Polish KGB or secret police, known as Polski Narodnyi Komissariat Vnutrennikh or the Polish People's Commissariat for Interior Affairs, who were brutal in their methods of "resocialization" and reported to the Soviet oligarchy in Moscow.
22. West, pp. 58, 66, 68.
23. Bauman, p. 147.
24. Held, p. 99.
25. Wald, p. 590.
26. Stivers, p. 23.
27. Piotrowski, pp. 368, 399.
28. Heteronormativity is defined by Ingraham (1996, p. 169) as "the view that institutionalized heterosexuality constitutes the standard for legitimate and proscriptive sociosexual arrangements."
29. Piotrowski, p. 391.
30. See Piotrowski, 2005; Pejic and Elliot, 1999; Calinescu, 1987.
31. For a description of dissident theatre in China, see Xian, Zhang, 2004, Theatre and Repression, *American Theatre* 21(9): 32–104.
32. Seamon, pp. 143, 147.
33. Strom, p. 41.
34. Paul Crowther (1993) in Addison, pp. 21–23.
35. Shusterman, pp. 218–227.
36. Irvine, p. 222.
37. The author observed anonymous gay sexual interactions in public parks among allegedly heterosexual monogamous married men.
38. For a humorous criticism of this declining culture parodied in film, see Prêt-a-Porter.
39. Trilling, p. 583.
40. For an example of negotiation of hard truths and other conceptual aesthetic authenticities, consider when the acquisition of multiple genital piercings is disclosed at an S/M festival by a gay male. His commitment to gay dominant [dom] sexual positions is demonstrated by having the type of piercings that stimulates a male submissive's [sub's] prostate gland through rear penetration, and immediately sets in motion a variety of thoughts regarding potential sexual interactions.
41. Harold, pp. 263, 268.
42. Trilling, pp. 566, 571.

Chapter 11.   Organic Sabotage

1. Turner, p. 68.
2. Brooke, pp. 164–171.
3. Krishnamurti, p. 69.
4. Langman, p. 190.
5. Turner, pp. 449, 452.
6. Bennett, pp. 62, 138.
7. Hamel et al., p. 6.
8. Harvey, pp. 2, 20, 37, 53.
9. Green, pp. 73–75.
10. Bowen and Purkis, pp. 1, 5.
11. West, pp. 71, 73.
12. Goaman, p. 174.
13. Kuper, pp. 8, 29, 31.
14. Kuklick, p. 280.
15. Levi Strauss, p. 157.
16. Ackland, pp. 45, 49.
17. Vale and Juno, p. 5.
18. Wojcik, p. 35.
19. Maffesoli, p. 97.
20. McDonald, p. 93.
21. Anderson, pp. 10, 13, 17.
22. Beck, pp. 13, 14, 64.
23. Stivers, pp. 16–18.
24. Allen, p. 109.
25. Lurie, pp. 289, 291, 293.
26. See http://www.pushhamburger.com/hactivis.htm.
27. Griffin, pp. 111, 117.
28. Cheville, pp. 28, 34.
29. Caputi, p. 182.
30. Cowen, p. 7.
31. Roszak, pp. 258, 262.
32. Roszak, pp. 115, 258.
33. Landau, p. 120.
34. Tramacchi, p. 140.
35. Kozinets and Sherry, pp. 299–300.
36. Castells in Bayat, p. 894.
37. Hall and Fenelon, p. 99.
38. Langman, pp. 192–193.
39. Roszak, pp. 9, 264–265.
40. Howson, pp. 89, 96, 110, 112.
41. Mascia-Lees and Sharpe, p. 3.
42. Aaron, p. 4.
43. Howson, p. 45.
44. Rinpoche, pp. 127, 131.
45. Sweetman, p. 166.
46. Wallerstein, p. 152.
47. Turner, p. 66.
48. Richard Florida's definition of "bohemia" is problemmatic. Full-time employment in a formal occupation would never capture the necessary industrial impact of activity that bohemian artists and writers truly produce. He seems aware of this conceptual

flaw when he admitted that his bohemian research does not capture, "…the things we would have liked to measure—such as [data pertaining to] a city's music or art scene which were simply unavailable." (See "Technology and Tolerance: The Importance of Diversity to High Technology Growth" 2001.) The second major conceptual flaw is found in examining content validity in construction of his "Gay Index." Here he uses only data that indicate the presence of unmarried males sharing a household. For unknown reasons, he completely omits the category of unmarried females sharing a household. Let us indulge for a moment his assumption that all same-sex people sharing households throughout the United States are homosexual. In this logic, residuals of people residing in a city who do not co-habitate with another same-sex person are not included in his measure and thus must be considered heterosexual. Based on the mysterious extraction of females in this sample, coupled with the miscalculation of sexual orientation based on ambiguous living arrangements well known to be problematic in census files, his entire category of "Gay Index" must be completely disregarded. Because his "gay" data, coupled with his faulty 'bohemian' data, make up a majority of his constructed "Composite Diversity Index," I am of the opinion that any findings with regard to Bohemia are of little value. The analysis is even more reckless with regard to definitions of "talent," which he defines as residents having four years of college or more (New Orleans ranked 34th) and "coolness," which he defines as residents between the ages of 22 and 29 (New Orleans ranked 13th). He attempted to assert that "talent" is statistically associated with "bohemianism." Such models are so flawed that they cannot withstand even a preliminary test of construct validity (see "Geography of Bohemia" 2001). The most egregious error is found, however, in his highly creative definition of the cities in his rankings. In order for New York to rank in the top three places in his indeces, his definition of "New York City" includes census data from Newark and three counties in New Jersey, one of which is in rural southern New Jersey nearly 150 miles from NYC. He vacillates so much in his use of census data from city levels to metropolitan statistical areas [MSA] to portions of consolidated metropolitan statistical areas [CMSA] that the data are rendered completely irreconcilable.

49. Florida nationally ranked New Orleans as 40th, whereas Columbus was ranked as more bohemian at 33rd. See Florida, 2001 and Yerton, 2002.

50. Baines and Jaromir, p. 36.

51. Breasted, JH (Ancient Records of Egypt volume 1, paragraph 770) quoted in Hambly, p 305.

52. Baines and Jaromir, p. 204. Aside from the brandings Ramses III also had inexplicable interest in rings probably associated with body piercing of his captives. The 3000+ year old chronicle with visual evidence of heads inscribed in rings can still be viewed on the Medinet Habu adjacent to the Ramses III mortuary temple in Egypt known as Khnemt-neheh located south of the Valley of the Kings and west of Luxor where "his campaigns against the Libyans, Asiatics, and the 'Sea People' are shown on the North Wall [and] subjugated foreign lands and towns are represented by their names inscribed in rings that have human heads." Baines and Jaromir, p. 99.

53. For a full description of historic body modification in different cultures around the world, see Hambley.

54. Budney, p. 39.

55. Wallerstein, p. 155.

References

Chapter 1. Nonverbal Communication

Baumeister, Roy F. (ed.). 1986 *The Public Self and the Private Self* New York, New York: Springer-Verlag.

Berger, Peter.L. and Luckmann, Thomas. 1967 *The Social Construction of Reality: A Treatise in the Sociology of Knowledge* Garden City, New York: Anchor Books.

Blumer, H. 1969 *Symbolic Interactionism* Berkeley, CA: University of California Press.

Brame, G.G., Jacobs, J. and Brame, W. 1996 *The World of Sexual Dominance and Submission* Westminster, MD: Villard Books.

Callero, P. L. 1985 "Role Identity Salience" *Social Psychology Quarterly* 48(3):203–215.

Elkind, David 1994 *The Ties That Stress: The New Family Imbalance* Cambridge, Mass: Harvard University Press

Ferrell, Jeff and Sanders, Clinton R. (eds.). 1995 *Cultural Criminology* Boston: Northeastern University.

Goffman, Erving. 1959 *The Presentation of Self in Everyday Life* Garden City, New York: Anchor Books.

Hechter, Michael. 1987 *Principles of Group Solidarity* Berkeley, CA: University of California Press.

Heimer, Karen. and Matsueda, Ross L. 1994 "Role-Taking, Role-Commitment, and Delinquency: A Theory of Differential Social Control" *American Sociological Review* 59(6):365–390.

Hewitt, John P. 1976 *Self and Society: A Symbolic Interactionist Social Psychology* Boston, MA: Allyn and Bacon, Inc.

Hewitt, John P. 1989 *Dilemmas of the American Self* Philadelphia, PA: Temple University Press.

Knutagard, Hans. 1996 "New Trends in European Youth and Drug Cultures" *Youth Studies Australia* 15(2):37–43.

Levine, Harold. G. and Stumpf, Steven H. 1983 "Statements of Fear Through Cultural Symbols: Punk Rock as a Reflective Subculture" *Youth and Society* 14(4):417–435.

Mead, George Herbert. 1934 *Mind, Self, and Society* Chicago: University of Chicago Press.

Myers, James. 1992 "Nonmainstream Body Modification: Genital Piercing, Branding, Burning, and Cutting" *Journal of Contemporary Ethnography* 21(3):267–306.

Schement, Jorge R. and Lievrouw, Leah (eds.). 1987 *Competing Visions, Complex Realities: Social Aspects of the Information Society* Norwood, NJ: Alex Publishing Corporation.

Shlenker, Barry R. 1986 "Self-Identification: Toward an Integration of the Private and Public Self" in Baumeister, Roy F. (ed.) *Public Self and Private Self* New York: Springer-Verlag.

Shlenker, Barry R. 1985 "Identity and Self-Identification" in Shlenker, Barry R. (ed.) *The Self and Social Life* New York: McGraw-Hill.

Shibutani, Timotsu. 1994 "Reference Groups as Perspectives" *American Journal of Sociology* 60:552–569.

Smith, Emma. 2003 "Understanding Underachievement: an investigation into differential attainment of secondary school pupils" *British Journal of Sociology* 24(5):575–86.

Steffensmeier, Darrell, Schwartz, Jennifer, Zhong, Hua, Ackerman, Jeff. 2005 "An Assessment of Recent Trends in Girls' Violence Using Diverse Longitudinal Sources: Is the Gender Gap Closing?" *Criminology* 43(2)355–406.

Tedeschi, James T. 1985 "Private and Public Experiences and the Self" in Baumeister, Roy F. (ed.) *Public Self and Private Self* New York: Springer-Verlag.

Thrane, Lisa E., Hoyt, Danny R., Whitbeck, Les B., Yoder, Kevin A. 2006 "Impact of family abuse on running away, deviance, and street victimization among homeless, rural, and urban youth" *Child Abuse & Neglect* 30(10):1117–1128.

Turner, Ralph. H. 1980 in Stryker, Sheldon (ed.) *Symbolic Interactionism: A Social Structural Version* Menlo Park, CA: Benjamin Cummings Publishing.

Voloshinov, Valentin Nikolaevich. 1973 [1929] *Marxism and the Philosophy of Language* Cambridge, MA: Harvard University.

Wicklund, Robert A. and Gollwitzer, Peter. 1982 *Symbolic Self-Completion* Hillsdale, NJ: Lawrence Erlbaum.

Chapter 2.   Verbal Communication

Berger, Peter.L. and Luckmann, Thomas. 1967 *The Social Construction of Reality: A Treatise in the Sociology of Knowledge* Garden City, New York: Anchor Books.

Besnier, Niko. 1989. "Information withholding as a manipulative and collusive strategy in Nukulaelae gossip" *Language in Society* 18:315–41.

Bourdieu, Pierre. 1991. *Language and Symbolic Power* Cambridge, MA: Harvard University.

Bourdieu, Pierre. 1984. *Distinction: A Social Critique of the Judgment of Taste* Cambridge, MA: Harvard University.

Briggs, Charles L. and Bauman, Richard. 1992. "Genre, Intertextuality, and Social Power" *Journal of Linguistic Anthropology* 2:131–72.

Briggs, Charles L. 1996 "Introduction" in Briggs, Charles L. (ed.) *Disorderly Discourse: Narrative, Conflict, and Inequality* Oxford, UK: Oxford.

Denzin, N. K. and Lincoln, Y.S. (eds.). 1998 *Strategies of Qualitative Inquiry* Thousand Oaks, CA: Sage.

Dixon, John A., Mahoney, Berenice, and Cocks, Roger. 2002 "Accents of Guilt? Effects of regional Accent, Race, and Crime Type on Attributions of Guilt" *Journal of Language and Social Psychology* 21:162–170.

Drew, Paul. 1990. "Strategies in the Contest Between Lawyer and Witness in Cross-Examination" in Levi, Judith N. and Walker Anne G. (eds.) *Language in the Judicial Process* New York: Plenum.

Drew, Paul, and Heritage, John (eds.). 1992 *Talk at Work: Interaction in Institutional Settings* Cambridge, UK: Cambridge University Press.

Erickson, Frederick, and Rittenberg, William. 1987 "Topic Control and Person Control: A Thorny Problem for Foreign Physicians in Interaction with American Patients" *Discourse Processes* 10(4):401–16.

Gibbs, Graham R. 2002 *Qualitative Data Analysis: Explorations with NVivo* Philadelphia, PA: Open University.

Guy, Mike. 2003 "Gutterpunks" *Rolling Stone* May 15, 2003.

Hall, Robert A. 1975 "The Nature of Linguistic Norms" *Language Sciences* 34:11–12.

Hester, Stephen and Francis, David. 2001 "Is institutional talk a phenomenon? Reflections on ethnomethodology and applied conversation analysis" in McHoul, Alec and Rapley, Mark (eds.) *How to Analyse Talk in Institutional Settings A Casebook of Methods* London, UK: Continuum.

Hollway, Wendy. 1989 *Subjectivity and Method in Psychology: Gender, Meaning, and Science* London: Sage.

Howarth, David, Norval, Aletta J. and Stravrakakis, Yannis (eds.). 2000 *Discourse Theory and Political Analysis: Identities, Hegemonies, and Social Change* Manchester, UK: Manchester University Press.

Hutchby, Ian. 1996 *Confrontation Talk: Arguments, Asymmetries and Power on Talk Radio* Mahwah, NJ: Larence Erlbaum.

Jackman, Mary R. 1996 *The Velvet Glove: Paternalism and Conflict in Gender, Class, and Race Relations* CA: University of California Press.

Kuipers, Joel C. 1989 "'Medical Discourse' in Anthropological Context: Views of Language and Power" *Medical Anthropology Quarterly* 3(2):99–123.

Landweer, M. Lynn. 2000 "Endangered Languages: Indicators of Ethnolinguistic Vitality" *Notes on Sociolinguistics* 5(1):5–22.

Langman, Lauren and Cangemi, Katie. 2004. "Globalization and the Liminal: Transgression, Identity, and the Urban Primative" in Clark, Terry N. (ed.) *The City as Entertainment Machine* New York: JAI [working copy downloaded from Loyola University website].

Leander, Kevin M. 2002 "Silencing in Classroom Interaction: Producing and Relating Social Spaces" *Discourse Processes* 34(2):193–235.

Leblanc, Lauraine. 1999 *Pretty in Pink: Girls' gender Resistance in a Boys' Subculture* New Brunswick, NJ: Rutgers.

Lehtonen, Mikko. 2000 *The Cultural Analysis of Texts* Thousand Oaks, CA: Sage.

Lepper, Georgia. 2000 *Categories in Text and Talk: A Practical Introduction to Categorization Analysis* Thousand Oaks, CA: Sage.

Li, Yongyan. 2006 "Negotiating knowledge contribution to multiple discourse communities" *Journal of Second Language Writing* 15(3):159–78.

Markee, Numa. 2000. *Conversation Analysis* Mahwah, NJ: Lawrence Erlbaum.

McHoul, Alec and Rapley, Mark (eds.). 2001 *How to Analyse Talk in Institutional Settings* London: Continuum.

Palmer, Barbara. 2002 "Justice Ruth Bader Ginsburg and the Supreme Court's Reaction to its' Second Female Member" *Women and Politics* 24(1):1–22.

Rampton, Ben. 1999 "Sociolinguistics and Cultural Studies: New Ethnicities, Liminalities, and Interaction" *Social Semiotics* 9(3):355–74.

Ruddick, Susan. 1997 "Modernism and Resistance: How Homeless Youth Subcultures Make a Difference" in Skelton, Tracey and Valentine, Gill (eds.) *Cool Places: Geographies of Youth Culture* New York: Routledge.

Sacks, Harvey. 1992 *Lectures on Conversation* Oxford, UK: Blackwell.

Sangari, Kumkum. 1987. "The Politics of the Possible" *Cultural Critique* 7:157–86.

Schegloff, Emanual A. 1980 "Preliminaries to Preliminaries: 'Can I Ask You a Question?'" *Sociological Inquiry* 50(104–52.

Schenkein, Jim (ed.). 1977 *Studies In The Organization Of Conversational Interaction* New York: Academic Press.

Shotter, John. 1993 *Cultural Politics of Everyday Life: Social Constructionism, Rhetoric and Knowing of the Third Kind* Buckingham: Open University Press.

Skelton, Tracey and Valentine, Gill (eds.). 1997 *Cool Places: Geographies of Youth Culture* New York: Routledge.

Tuffin, Keith and Howard, Christina. 2001 "Demystifying Discourse Analysis" in McHoul, Alec and Rapley, Mark (eds.) *How to Analyse Talk in Institutional Settings A Casebook of Methods* London, UK: Continuum.

Watt, Paul. 2006 "Respectability, Roughness, and Race: Neighborhood Place Images and the Making of Working Class Distinctions in London" *International Journal of Urban and Regional Research* 30(4):776–797.

West, David. 1990 *Authenticity and Empowerment: A theory of Liberation* London, UK: Harvester Wheatsheaf.

Widdicombe, Sue and Wooffitt, Robin. 1995 *The Language of Youth Subcultures: Social Identity in Action* New York: Harvester-Wheatsheaf.

Wylie, Ruth C. 1979 *The Self-Concept* Lincoln, NB: University of Nebraska Press.

Yanay, Niza. 1996 "National hatred, Female Subjectivity, and the Boundaries of Cultural Discourse" *Symbolic Interaction* 19(1):21–36.

Chapter 3.   Bohemian Network

Allahar, Anton L. 2001 The Politics of Identity Construction *Identity* 1(3):197–208.

Bennett, Andy. 2000 *Popular Music and Youth Culture: Music, Identity, and Place* Hampshire: Palgrave.

Boissevain, J. 1974 *Friends of Friends* London: Basil Blackwell.

Coleman, J.C. 1961 *The Adolescent Society: The Social Life of the Teenager and its' Impact on Education* New York: Free Press.

Feld, S.L. 1981 "The Focused Organization of Social Ties" *American Journal of Sociology* 86:1015–35.

Festinger, L., Schachter, S., and Back, K. 1950 *Social Pressures in Informal Groups: A Study of Human Factors in Housing* Stanford: Stanford University Press.

Fischer, C.S. 1982 *To Dwell Among Friends: Personal Network in Town and City* Chicago: University of Chicago Press.

Grana, Cesar and Grana, Marigay. 1990 *On Bohemia: Code of the Self-Exiled* New Brunswick, NJ: Transaction.

Granovetter, M. 1973 "The Strength of Weak Ties" *The American Journal of Sociology* 78 (May):1360–80.

Greve, Arent and Salaff, Janet W. 2005 Social Network Approach to Understand the Ethnic Economy: A Theoretical Discourse *GeoJournal* 64(1):7–16.

Knoke, D. and Kuklinski, J.H. 1982 *Network Analysis* Thousand Oaks, CA: Sage Publications.

Sutherland, Edwin H. 1974 *Criminology* Philadelphia, PA: Lippincott.

White, Harrison. 1992 *Identity and Control: A Structural Theory of Social Interaction* Princeton: Oxford.

Chapter 4.   Ideological Apparatus

Aronowitz, Stanley. 1996 *The Death and Rebirth of American Radicalism* New York: Routledge.

Aronowitz, Stanley. 1992 *The Politics of Identity: Class, Culture, Social Movements* New York: Routledge.

Haycock, N. (pi) 1992 *The Non Profit Sector in New York City* New York: Nonprofit Coordinating Committee and the Fund for the City of New York.

Independent Sector. 1998 "Annual Report of Newly Incorporated Nonprofit Organizations" [http://www.independentsector.org/PDFs]

Luhmann, N. 1998 *Observations on Modernity* CA: Stanford University Press.

McAdam, D., McCarthy, J., and Zald, M. (eds.). 1996 *Comparative Perspectives on Social Movements: Political Opportunities, Mobilizing Structures, and Cultural Framings* New York: Cambridge University Press.

Rand, A. 1993 [1971] *The New Left: Anti-Industrial Revolution* New York: Penguin.

Ricoeur, P. 1994 "Althusser's Theory of Ideology" in Elliot, Gregory (ed.) *Althusser: A Critical Reader* Oxford: Blackwell.

Romanienko, Lisiunia. 2009 "Civil Society Economics" in Anheier, Helmut K. and Toepler, Stefan (eds.) *International Encyclopedia of Civil Society* New York: Springer

Spivak, Gayatri Chakravorty and Plotke, David. 1996 "Interview" in Trend, David. (ed.) 1996 *Radical Democracy: Identity, Citizenship, and the State* New York: Routledge.

Trotsky, L. 1957 [1924] *Literature and Revolution* New York: Russell & Russell.

Chapter 5.   Economic Contestation

Ahrne, Goran. 1990 *Agency and Organizations Theory of Society* London: Sage, pp. 132–33.

Altheide, David L. 2002 *Creating Fear: News and the Construction of Crisis* New York: Aldine Gruyter.

Anderson, Benedict. (1991) *Imagined Communities: Reflections on the Original and Spread of Nationalism* London: Verso.

Arendt, Hannah. 1958 *The Human Condition* Chicago, IL: University of Chicago.

Barley, Stephen R; Gordon W. Meyer; and Debra C. Gash. 1988. "Culture of Cultures: Academics, Practitioners and the Pragmatics of Normative Control." *Administrative Science Quarterly.* 33(1):24–60.

Belka, Marek (ed.). 1997 *The Polish Transformation from the Perspective of European Integration* Warsaw: Ebert Foundation.

Berger, Peter L. and Neuhaus, Richard J. 1996 *To Empower People: From State to Civil Society* Washington DC: American Enterprise Institute.

Berlew, David and Hali, Douglas T. 1966 "The Socialization of Managers: Reffects of Expectation on Performance" *Administrative Sciences Quarterly* 11:207–223.

Berger, Peter L. and Neuhaus, Richard J 1996 *To Empower People: From State to Civil Society* Washington DC: American Enterprise Institute

Beynon, Robert (ed.) 1988 *The Critical Dictionary of Global Economics* New York: Routledge

Bhavnani, Kum-Kum Foran, John and Talcott, Molly. 2005 "The Red, the Green, the Black, and the Purple: Reclaiming Development, Resisting Globalization" in Appelbaum, Richard P. and Robinson, William I. (eds.) *Critical Globalization Studies* New York: Routledge.

Blau. Peter M. 1964 *Exchange and Power in Social Life* New York: Wiley.

Bogardus, Emory S. 1926 *The New Social Research* Los Angeles, CA: JR Miller.

Boykoff, Jules. 2006 *The Suppression of Dissent: How the State and Mass Media Squelch American Social Movements* New York: Routledge.

Chase-Dunn, Christopher and Hall, Thomas D. 1991 "Conceptualizing Core/Periphery Hierarchies for Comparative Studies" in Chase-Dunn, Christopher and Hall, Thomas D. (eds.) *Core/Periphery Relations in Precapitalist Worlds* Boulder: Westview.

Chirot, Daniel and Hall, Thomas. 1982 "World Systems Theory" *Annual Review of Sociology* 1982:81–106.

Chomsky, Noam. 1999 *Profit Over People* Seven Stories.

Clarke, John, Cochrane, Allan, and Smart, Carol. 1987 *Ideologies of Welfare: From Dreams to Delusion* London: Hutchinson.

Cohen, Stanley. 1972 *Folk Devils and Moral Panics: The Creation of the Mods and the Rockers* London: MacGibbon and Kee.

Cohen, J. and Arato, A. 1992 *Civil Society and Political Theory* Cambridge, MA: MIT Press.

Coleman, James S. 1974 *Power and the Structure of Society* New York: Norton.

Cowen, Taylor (ed.). 1988 *The Theory of Market Failure: A Critical Examination* Fairfax, VA: George Mason University.

Dawson, Jane. 2002 "Egalitarian Responses in Postcommunist Russia" in Murphy, Craig N. (ed.) *Egalitarian Politics in the Age of Globalization* New York: Palgrave.

Ellis, Ralph D. and Ellis, Carol S. 1989 *Theories of Criminal Justice: A Critical Appraisal* Wolfeboro, NH: Longwood Academic.

European Federation of Journalists. 2003. *Eastern Empires-Foreign Ownership in Central and Eastern European Media: Ownership, Policy Issues, and Strategy.* Brussels, Belgium: EU.

Fowler, Roger. 1991 *Language in the News: Discourse and Ideology in the Press* London: Routledge.

Frank, Andre Gunder. 1994 "The Third Worldization of Russia and Eastern Europe" in Mesbahi, Mohiaddin (ed.) *Russia and the Third World in the Post Soviet Era* Gainsville, FL: University of Florida.

Frank, Andre Gunder. 1966 "The Development of Underdevelopment" *Monthly Review* 18(17):17–31.

Frank, Andre Gunder and Gills, Barry K. (eds.). 1993 *The World System: Five hundred years or five thousand?* London: Routledge.

Gali, Jordi. 1996 *Technology, Employment, and the business cycle: Do tech shocks explain aggregate fluctuations?* Cambridge, MA: Cambridge.

Giroux, Henry. 1983 Theories of reproduction and resistance in the new sociology of education. *Harvard Educational Review, 53*(3), 257–291.

Grossberg, Lawrence. 2005 *Caught in the Crossfire: Kids, Politics, and America's Future* Boulder: Paradigm.

Hall, Stuart. 1979 Culture, the Media and the 'Ideological Effect' in Curran, James, Gurevitch, Michael, and Woollecott, Jane (eds.) *Mass Communication and Society* London: Edward Arnold.

Handy, Charles. 1993 *Understanding Organizations* London: Penguin.

Handy, Charles. 1999 *Understanding Voluntary Organizations* London: Penguin.

Hofstede, Geert. 1984 *Cultures Consequences: International Differences in Work-Related Values* Beverly Hills, CA: Sage.

Horowitz, Irving Louis. 1966 *Three Worlds of Development: The Theory and Practice of International Stratification* New York: Oxford.

Howarth, David and Stavrakakis, Yannis. 2000 Introduction in Howarth, David, Norval, Aletta J., and Stavrakakis, Yannis (eds.) *Discourse Theory and Political Analysis: Identities, Hegemonies and Social Change* Manchester, UK: Manchester University Press.

Huang, Xu and Van de Vliert, Evert. 2003 "Where Intrinsic Job Satisfaction Fails to Work: National Moderators of Intrinsic Motivation" *Journal of Organizational Behavior* 24:159–79.

Huddleston, Patricia and Good, Linda K. 1999 Job Motivators in Russian and Polish Retail Firms *International Journal of Retail and Distribution Management* 9:383–392.

John Paul II, Pope. 1996 *Message to the Pontifical Academy of Sciences: On Evolution* [http://www.ewtn.com/library/PAPALDOC/JP961022.HTM] downloaded August 15, 2007.

Keller, Wolfgang. 1997 *Trade and the Transmission of Technology* Cambridge, MA: Cambridge National Bureau of Economic Research.

Kellner, Douglas. 2003 " Globalization, Technopolitics, and Revolution" in Foran, John (ed.) *The Future of Revolutions: Rethinking Radical Change in the Age of Globalization* London: Zed.

Kilmann, Ralph H. 1977 *Social Systems Design: Normative Theory and the MAPS Design Technology* Amsterdam: North Holland.

Kolinsky, Eva and Nickel, Hildegard M. (eds.). 2003 *Reinventing Gender: Women in Eastern Germany Since Unification* London, UK: Cass.

Kozol, Jonathan. 1991 *Savage Inequalities: Children in America's Schools* Crown: New York.

Kubicek, Paul. 2004 *Organized Labor in Postcommunist States: From Solidarity to Infirmity* Pittsburgh, PA: University of Pittsburgh.

Kuhn, Alfred and Beam, Robert D. 1982 *The Logic of Organization* London: Jossey Bass, pp. 26–157.

Landmann, Michael. 1984 "Critique of Reason From Weber to Habermas" in Marcus, Judith and Tar, Zoltan (eds.) *Foundations of the Frankfurt School of Social Research* New Brunswick: Transaction.

Langman, Lauren. 2006 "Globalization, Alienation, and Identity: A Critical Approach" in Langman, Lauren and Kalekin-Fishman, Devorah (eds.) 2006 *The Evolution of Alienation: Trauma, Promise, and the Millennium* Lanham, Maryland: Rowman and Littlefield.

Lewis, Robert A. 1971 Socialization into National Violence: Familial Correlates of Hawkish Attitudes Toward War *Journal of Marriage and Family* 33(4):699–708.

Luhman, Niklas. 1982 "The World Society as a Social System" *International Journal of General Systems* 8:131–138.

MacDonald, Robert. 1997 "Youth, social exclusion and the millennium" in MacDonald, Robert (ed.) 1997 *Youth, the 'underclass' and social exclusion* London: Routledge.

Macek, Petr, Flanagan, Constance, Gallay, Leslie, Kostron, Lubomir, Botcheva, Luba, and Csapo, Beno. 1998 Postcommunist Societies in Times of Transition: Prceptions of Change Among Adolescents in Central and Eastern Europe *Journal of Social Issues* 54(3):547–561.

Meister, Albert. 1984 *Participation, Associations, Development, and Change* New Brunswick, NJ: Transaction.

Mettler, Suzanne. 1998 *Dividing Citizens: Gender and Federalism in New Deal Public Policy* Ithaca, New York: Cornell University.

Millard, Francis. 2000 "Presidents and Democratization in Poland: The Roles of Lech Walesa and Alekander Kwiasnewski in Building a New Polity" *Journal of Communist Studies and Transition Politics* 16(3):39–62.

Munck, Ronaldo and O'Hearn Denis. 1999 *Critical Development Theory: Contributions to a New Paradigm* London: Zed Books.

Narozny, Michal. 2006 "High Unemployment in Poland Not only a Labour Problem" *ECFIN Economy Finance Country Focus* 3(6) [http://ec.europa.eu/economy_finance/publications/country_focus/2006/cf06_2006en.pdf]

Nee, Victor and Cao, Yang. 1999 Path Dependent Societal Transformation: Stratification in Hybrid Mixed Economies *Theory and Society* 28(6):799–834.

Nepstad, Sharon Erickson. 2002 "Creating Transnational Solidarity: The Use of Narrative in the US Central America Peace Movement" in Smith, Jackie and Johnston, Hank (eds.) *Globalization and Resistance: Transnational Dimensions of Social Movements* Lanham, MD: Rowman & Littlefield.

Nurmi, J.E. 1991 How Do Adolescents See Their Future: A Review of the Development of Future Orientation and Planning *Development Review* 11:1–59.

Ost, David. 2005 *The Defeat of Solidarity: Anger and Politics in Postcommunist Europe* Ithaca, New York: Cornell University.

Passerin d'Entreves, Maurizio. 1992 "Hannah Arendt and the Idea of Citizenship" in Mouffe, Chantel (ed.) *Dimensions of Radical Democracy: Pluralism, Citizenship, Community* London: Verso.

Patten, Monica. 2002 Democracy, Civil Society, and the State in Brock, Kathy L. (ed.) *Improving Connections Between Governments and Nonprofit and Voluntary Organizations* Montreal: McGill University.

Pfeffer, Jeffrey. 1982 *Organizations and Organization Theory* Boston:Pitman.

Piven, Francis Fox and Cloward, Richard A. 1971 *Regulating the Poor: The Functions of Public Welfare* New York: Pantheon.

Podobnik, Bruce and Reifer, Thomas. 2005 "The Effort to Transform Globalization: Historical and Contemporary Struggles" in Podobnik, Thomas and Reifer, Thomas (eds.) *Transforming Globalization: Historic and Contemporary Struggles* Leiden: Brill.

Romanienko, Lisiunia. 2007 "Antagonism, Absurdity, and the Avant-Garde" *International Review of Social History* 52:133–151.

Romanienko, Lisiunia. 2002 "The Role of Western Media in the Construction and Maintenance of Religious Antagonism in Poland" in Gunitskiy, Vsevolod (ed.) *New Currents: East European Arts, Politics, and Humanities* Ann Arbor, MI: University of Michigan.

Romanienko, Lisiunia. 2001 "Dual Labor Market Theory and the Institutionalization of Farmers Markets: Marginalized Workers Adapting to Inhospitable Conditions" *Journal of Interdisciplinary Economics* 12(4):359–73.

Salamon, Lester M. and Anheier, Helmut K. 1997 *Defining the Nonprofit Sector: A Cross National Analysis* Manchester, UK: Manchester University Press.

Scott, Hilda. 1984 *Working Your Way to the Bottom: The Feminization of Poverty* Pandora Books

Simola, Hannu. 1998. Constructing a School-Free Pedagogy: Decontextualization of Finnish State Educational Discourse *Journal of Curriculum Studies* 30(3):339–56.

Staniszkis, Jadwiga. 1991 *The Dynamics of the Breakthrough in Eastern Europe: The Polish Experience* Berkeley, CA: University of California.

Staniszkis, Jadwiga. 1995 "In Search of a Paradigm of Transformation" in Wnuk-Lipinski, Edmund (ed.) *After Communism: A Multidisciplinary Approach to Radical Social Change* Warsaw: Polish Academy of Sciences Press.

Tunick, Mark. 1992 *Punishment: Theory and Practice* Berkeley, CA: University of California.

Tsao, Roy T. 2004 Arendt and the Modern State: Variations On Hegel in The Origins of Totalitarianism *The Review of Politics* 66 (2):207–231.

Vail, John. 1999 "States of Insecurity The political foundations of insecurity in Vail, John, Wheelock, Jane and Hill, Michael (eds.) *Insecure Times: Living with Insecurity in Contemporary Society* London: Routledge.

Van Til, Jon. 2000 *Growing Civil Society: From Nonprofit Sector to Third Space* Bloomington, IN: Indiana University.

Wallerstein, Immanuel. 2000 *The Essential Wallerstein* New York: New Press.

Ware, Alan. 1989 *Between Profit and State Intermediate Organizations in Britain and the United States* Princeton, NJ: Princeton.

Wilensky, Harold. 1975 *The Welfare State and Equality: Structural and Ideological Roots of Public Expenditures* Berkeley, CA: University of California.

Wright, Erik O. 1997 *Class Counts: Comparative Studies in Class Analysis* Cambridge: Cambridge University Press.

Zielonka, Jan 2000 *Enlargement and the Finality of European Integration* Harvard Jean Monnet Working Paper Symposium Cambridge, MA: Harvard.

Zizek, Slavoj. 1992 "Eastern Europe's Republics of Gilead" in Moufee, Chantal (ed.) *Dimensions of Radical Democracy: Pluralism, Citizenship, Community* London: Verso.

Zundel, Alan F. 2000 *Declarations of Dependency: The Civic Republican Tradition in US Poverty Policy* Albany: SUNY.

Chapter 6.   Digital Contestation

Appold, S, Siengthai, S. and Kasarda, J. 1998 "The Employment of Women Managers and Professionals in an Emerging Economy: Gender Inequality as Organizational Practice" *Administrative Sciences Quarterly* 43(1998):538–565.

Bansler, Jorgen P. and Havn, Erling. 2006 Sensemaking in Technology-Use Mediation: Adapting Groupware Technology *Organizations Computer Supported Cooperative Work* 1:55–91.

Ben-Rafael, Eliezer and Sternberg, Yitzhak. 2001 "Analyzing our Time: A Sociological Problematique" in Ben-Rafael, Eliezer and Sternberg, Yitzhak (eds.) *Identity, Culture and Globalization* Leiden: Brill.

Bennhold, Katrin. 2005 Amid Tears and Protest French Evict Squatters *International Herald Tribune* September 3.

Bodker, Susanne and Christiansen, Ellen. 2006 "Computer Support for Social Awareness in Flexible Work" *Computer Supported Cooperative Work* 15:1–28,

Broedling, Laurie A. 1977 The Uses of the Intrinsic-Extrinsic Distinction in Explaining Motivation and Organizational Behavior *Academy of Management Review* 2(2):267–276.

Cantrill, James G. 1993 Communication and our Environment: Categorizing Research in Environmental Advocacy *Journal of Applied Communication* 2:66–95.

Chalmers, Matthew. 2002 Awareness, Representation, and Interpretation *Computer Supported Cooperative Work* 11:389–409.

D'Arcus, Bruce. 2006 *Boundaries of Dissent: Protest and State Power in the Media Age* New York: Routledge.

Dahl, Robert. 1971 *Polyarchy, Participation, and Opposition.* New Haven, CT: Yale.

Dahlgren, Peter. 2005 "Forward" in Van de Donk, Wim, Loader, Brian D. Nixon, Paul G. Rucht, Dieter (eds.) *Cyberprotest: New Media, citizens, and Social Movements* London: Routledge.

Dobbin, Frank R. 1994. "Cultural Models of Organization: The Social Construction of Rational Organizing Principles." in Diana Crane (ed.) *The Sociology of Culture.* Cambridge, MA: Blackwell.

Earl, Jennifer. 2006 Pursuing Change Online: The Use of Four Protest Tactics on the Internet *Social Science Computer Review* 24(3):362–377.

Eisenberger, Robert and Cameron, Judy. 1998 Reward, Intrinsic Interest, and Creativity: New Findings *American Psychologist* 53(6):676–679.

Entrena, Francisco. 2003 "Introduction: Facing Globalization from the Local" in Entrena, Francisco (ed.) *Local Reactions to Globalization Processes: Competitive Adaptation or Socioeconomic Erosion* New York: Nova.

Entrena, Francisco. 2003 "A Systemic Approach to the Present Social Structure" in Entrena, Francisco (ed.) *Local Reactions to Globalization Processes: Competitive Adaptation or Socioeconomic Erosion* New York: Nova.

Featherstone, Mike and Burrows, Rogers. 1995 "Introduction" in Featherstone, Mike and Burrows, Rogers (eds.) *Cyberspace, Cyberbodies, Cyberpunk: Cultures of Technological Embodiment* Thousand Oaks, CA: Sage.

Gillett, James. 2003 Media Activism and Internet use by people with HIV/AIDS *Sociology of Health and Illness* 25(6):608–624.

Grossberg, Lawrence. 2005 *Caught in the Crossfire: Kids, Politics, and America's Future* Boulder, CO: Paradigm.

Huang, Xu and Van de Vliert, Evert. 2003 "Where Intrinsic Job Satisfaction Fails to Work: National Moderators of Intrinsic Motivation" *Journal of Organizational Behavior* 24:159–79.

Isherwood, Julian. 2007 Danish Anger Smoulders Over Squat *BBC News* March 6.

Johnson, Steven. 1997 *Interface Culture: How new technology transforms the way we create and communicate* San Francisco, CA: Harper/

Johnson, Thomas J. and Kaye, Barbara K. 2003 Around the World Wide Web in 80 Ways: How Motives for Going Online are Linked to Internet Activities Among Politically Interested Internet Users *Social Science Computer Review* 21:304–325.

Jones, Steve/ 1999 *Doing Internet Research: Critical Issues and Methods for Examining the Internet* Thousand Oaks, CA: Sage/

Jordan, Tim and Taylor, Paul A. 2004 *Hacktivism and Cyberwars: Rebels with a Cause?* London: Routledge.

LaRose, Robert, Mastro, Dana, and Eastin, Matthew S. 2001 Understanding Internet Usage: A Social-Cognitive Approach to Uses and Gratifications *Social Science Computer Review* 19:395–413.

Leinonen, Piritta, Jarvela, Sanna, and Kakkinen, Paivi. 2005 "Conceptualizing the Awareness of Collaboration: A Qualitative Study of a Global Virtual Team" *Computer Supported Cooperative Work* 14:301–322.

Lutomski, Pawel. 2004 The Debate About A Center Against Expulsions: An Unexpected Crisis in German Polish Relations? *German Studies Review* 27(3):449–468.

Mackie, Fiona. "The Ethnic Self" in Kellehear, Allan (ed.) 1996 *Social Self, Global Culture* Melbourne: Oxford.

Markham, Annette N. 1998 *Life Online: Researching Real Experiences in Virtual Space* Walnut Creek, CA: AltaMira.

McDonald, Kevin. 2006 *Global Movements: Action and Culture* Oxford: Blackwell.

Nakamura, Lisa. 2002 *Cybertypes: Race, Ethnicity, and Identity on the Internet* London: Routledge.

Nepstad, Sharon Erickson. 2002 "Creating Transnational Solidarity: The Use of Narrative in the US Central America Peace Movement" in Smith, Jackie and Johnston, Hank (eds.) *Globalization and Resistance: Transnational Dimensions of Social Movements* Lanham, MD: Rowman & Littlefield.

Parker, Noel. 2003 "Parallaxes: Revolutions and 'Revolution' in a Globalized Imaginary" in Foran, John (ed.) *The Future of Revolutions: Rethinking Radical Change in the Age of Globalization* London: Zed.

Pinder, Craig C. 1977 Concerning the Application of Human Motivation *Academy of Management Review* 2(3):384–397.

Pinkett, Randal. 2003 "Community Technology and Community Building: Early Results from the Creating Community Connections Project" *The Information Society* 19:365–379.

Robertson, Toni. 2002 "The Public Availability of Actions and Artifacts" *Computer Supported Cooperative Work* 11:299–316.

Sanchez-Franco, Manuel and Roldan, Jose L. 2005 Web Acceptance and Usage Model: A Comparison between Goal-Directed and Experiential Web Users *Internet Research* 15(1):21–48.

Squatters Practical Network. 2005 *Why the Sudden Attacks on Europe's Squatters?* [http://squattercity.blogspot.com/2005/11] downloaded August 15, 2007.

Stivers, Richard. 2004 *Shades of Loneliness Pathologies of a Technological Society* Boulder: Rowman & Littlefield.

Szelenyi, Ivan. 1988 *Socialist Entrepreneurs: Embourgeoisement in Rural Hungary* Madison: University of Wisconsin.

Terranova, Tiziana. 2004 *Network Culture: Politics for a Global Age* London: Pluto.

Tolbert, Pamela S. and Lynne G. Zucker. 1983. "Institutional Sources of Change in the Formal Structure of Organizations: The Diffusion of Civil Service Reform, 1880–1935," *Administrative Science Quarterly.* 28(1):22–39.

Van Aelst, Peter and Walgrave, Stefaan. 2002 New Media, New Movements? The Role of the Internet in Shaping the 'Anti-Globalization' Movement *Information, Communication, and Society* 5(4):464–493.

Chapter 7. Biker Contestation

Broach, D. 1993 "Sulpher Man Held in Bar Shooting, 11 Charges Filed in St. Charles" *Times-Picayune of New Orleans* July 10.

Burrell, I. 1998 "Police Brace for Mayhem as Bikers Fallout" *The Independent* July 8.

Davis, R.E. 1996 *Inventing the Public Enemy: The Gangster in American Culture* Chicago: Chicago University Press.

Davis, R.H. 1984 *Outlaw Motorcyclists: A Problem for Police* Washington, DC: US Department of Justice.

Gibson, L. 1995 "Biker Gang is Called an International Racket, But Members Claim Entrapment" *National Law Journal* 17(37):10.

Hardy, D. 2002 "Police Put Damper on Bikers' Toy Ride" *Philadelphia Inquirer* November 11.

Hernandez, M. 1990 "Hawthorne Settles Vagos Police Suit for $2M" *Los Angeles Times* May 18.

Hopper C.B. and Moore, J. 1990 "Women in Outlaw Motorcycle Gangs" *Journal of Contemporary Ethnography* 18(4):365–90.

Kelly, R.J. 2000 *Encyclopedia of Organized Crime in the United States* Westport, CT: Greenwood Press.

McGuire, P. 1987 *Outlaw Motorcycle Gangs: Organized Crime on Two Wheels* Washington, DC: Bureau of Alcohol, Tobacco, and Firearms.

Murphy, D.E. 1996 "Bikers Feud in the Land of the Vikings Playing Out a Rivalry Between Hell's Angels and Texas-Based Banditos" *Los Angeles Times* June 10.

Newman, M. 2000 "Motorcycle Gang Members Held in Sex Assault on Nude Dancers" *New York Times* January 28.

Perlstein, M. 1999 "Lengthy Probe Unravels Drug Network, New Orleans Area Bikers' Ties to Meth Operation Found" *Times-Picayune of New Orleans* June 20.

Rowe, J. 1989 "Hells Angels Claim Movie Makers Used Gang's Trademarks, Bikers Allege 'Nam Angels' Falsely Depicts Members as Disloyal and Remorseless" *Wall Street Journal* October 30.

Thomas-Lester, A. 1991 "Outlaw Biker Gangs Larger, More Violent: Officials Say Rivalries Escalating" *The Washington Post* November 6.

Werner, L.M. 1985 "Federal Agents Arrest 82 in 8-State Drive Against Motorcycle Gang" *New York Times* February 22.

Wolf, B.W. 1991 *The Rebels: A Brotherhood of Outlaw Bikers* Toronto: University of Toronto Press.

Chapter 8. Sexual Sabotage

Attwood, Feona. 2006 Sexed Up: Theorizing the Sexualization of Culture *Sexualties* 9(1):99–116. [proof shared by author].

Irvine, Janice M. 2003 'The Sociologist as Voyeur': Social Theory and Sexuality Research 1910–1978 *Qualitative Sociology* 26(4):429–456.

Jackman, M.R. (1996) *The velvet glove: Paternalism and conflict in gender, class, and race relations.* Berkeley, CA: University of California Press.

Linder, Fletcher. 2001 Speaking of Bodies, Pleasures, and Paradise Lost: Erotic Agency and the Situationist Ethnography *Cultural Studies* 15(2):352–374.

Pareto, Vilfredo. 1963 *The Mind and Society* New York: Dover.

Pareto, Vilfredo. 2000 *The Rise and Fall of Elites* New Brunswick, NJ: Transaction.

Reynolds, S. and Press, J. (1995) *The sex revolts: Gender, rebellion, and rock and roll.* London: Serpent's Tail Press.

Romanienko, Lisiunia. 2008 "Aesthetic and Legal Communities in the Struggle for Sexual Human Rights in Poland" *UNESCO Observatory on Multi-disciplinary Research on the Arts* 1(2):1–16.

Rubin, G. (1992) "Thinking sex: Notes for a radical theory of the politics of sexuality" in Vance, C. S. (ed.) *Pleasure and danger: Exploring female sexuality* London: Pandora Publishing.

Shorter, Edward. 2005 *Written in the Flesh: A History of Desire* Toronto: University of Toronto.

Snyder, C.R. and Fromkin, H. L. (1980) *Uniqueness: The human pursuit of difference.* New York: Plenum Press.

Weeks, Jeffrey. 1999 *The Sexual Citizen Theory, Culture, and Society* 15(3/4):35–52.

Weeks, Jeffrey. 1981 *Sex, Politics, and Society The Regulation of Sexuality since 1800* Longman: London.

Zafirovski, Milan. 2003 The Pareto Theorem Restated and Examined: Democracy and Conservative Imposition of Morality by Law *Critical Sociology* 30(3)1–31.

Chapter 9.   Political Sabotage

Baldwin, Debbie, Coles, Bob, and Mitchell, Wendy. 1997 "Disparate processes of social exclusion" in MacDonald, Robert (ed.) *Youth, the 'underclass' and social exclusion* London: Routledge.

Bell, Duncan. 2002 Anarchy, power and death: contemporary political realism as ideology *Journal of Political Ideologies* 7(2):221–239.

Berlin, Isaiah. 1948 *Russian Thinkers* New York: Penguin

Berlin, Isaiah. 1998 *The Proper Study of Mankind: An Anthology of Essays* London: Pimlico.

Berman, Marshall. 1971 *The Politics of Authenticity: Radical Individualism and the Emergence of Modern Society* London: George Allen & Unwin.

Bookchin, Murray. 1979 "Post-Scarcity Anarchism" in Perlin, Terry M. (ed.) *Contemporary Anarchism* New Brunswick, NJ: Transaction.

Boykoff, Jules/ 2006 *The Suppression of Dissent: How the State and Mass Media Squelch AS American Social Movements* New York: Routledge.

Branch, Taylor. 1998 *Pillar of Fire: America in the King Years* New York: Simon and Schuster.

Chesters, Graeme and Welsh, Ian. 2006. *Complexity and Social Movements Multitudes at the Edge of Chaos.* London: Routledge.

Chomsky, Noam. 2000 Talking 'Anarchy' with Chomsky *The Nation* April 24.

Dahl, Robert. 1971 *Polyarchy, Participation, and Opposition.* New Haven, CT: Yale.

Dahms, Harry F. 2006 "Does Alienation Have a Future? Recapturing the Core of Critical Theory" in Langman, Lauren and Kalekin-Fishman, Devorah (eds.) *The Evolution of Alienation: Trauma, Promise, and the Millennium* Lanham, MD: Rowman and Littlefield.

Davies, Norman and Moorhouse, Roger 2003 *Microcosm: A Portrait of a Central European City* London: Pimlico

Della Porta, Donatella and Rucht, Dieter. 1995 "Left Libertarian Movements in Context" in Jenkins, J. Craig and Klandersmans, Bert (eds.) *The Politics of Social Protest: Comparative Perspectives on States and Social Movements* London: University College London.

Edelman, Murray. 1971 *Politics as Symbolic Action: Mass Arousal and Quiescence* Chicago: Markham.

Ezrahi, Yaron. 1990 *The Descent of Icarus: Science and Transformation of Contemporary Democracy* Cambridge, MA: Harvard.

Ferrara, Alessandro. 1993 *Modernity and Authenticity: A Study of the Social and Ethical Thought of Jean Jacques Rousseau* Albany: SUNY.

Farro, Antimo and Vaillancourt, Jean-Guy. 2001 "Collective Movements and Globalization" in Hamel, Pierre, Lustiger-Thaler, Henri, Nederveen Pieterse, Jan and Roseneil, Sasha (eds.) *Globalization and Social Movements* New York: Palgrave.

Giele, Janet Zollinger. 2002 "Life Careers and the Theory of Action" in Setterstein, Richard A. Owens, Timothy (eds.) *New Frontiers in Socialization* Oxford, Elsevier.

Giroux, Henry A. 2004 "Disposable Youth/Disposable Futures: The Crisis of Politics and Public Life" in Campbell, Neil (ed.) *American Youth* New York: Routledge.

Greene, Christina. 2006 What's Sex Got to do With It: Gender and the New Black Freedom Movement Scholarship *Feminist Studies* 32(1):163–183.

Hozic, Aida. 1990 "The Inverted World of Spectacle: Social and Political Responses to Terrorism" in Orr, John and Klaic, Dragan (eds.) *Terrorism and Modern Drama* Edinburgh, Scotland: Edinburgh University.

Humphrey, Robert E. 1978 *Children of Fantasy: The First Rebels of Greenwich Village* New York: John Wiley and Sons.

Krishnamurti. 1992 *On Freedom* London: Victor Gollancz Ltd.

Kubik, Jan. 2001 "Rebelliousness and Civility: Strategies of Coping with Systemic Change in Poland" in Buchowski, Michal, Conte, Edward, Nagengast, Carole (eds.) *Poland Beyond Communism: Transition in Critical Perspective* Fribourg, Switzerland: University of Fribourg.

Kum-Kum, Bhavnami, Kent, Kathryn R., and Windance Twine France. 1998 Editorial *Signs* 23(3):575–583.

Leeson, Peter T. and Stringham, Edward P. 2005 Is Government Inevitable? Comment on Holcombe's Analysis *The Independent Review* IX(4): Spring.

Maney, Gregory M. 2002 Transnational Structures and Protest: Lin king Theories and Evidence in Smith, Jackie and Johnston, Hank (eds.) *Globalization and Resistance: Transnational Dimensions of Social Movements* Lanham, MD: Rowman and Littlefield.

Meyer, David S. and Tarrow, Sidney. 1998 "A Movement Society: Contentious Politics for a New Century" in Meyer, David S. and Tarrow, Sidney (eds.) *The Social Movement Society: Contentious Politics for a New Century* Lanham, MD: Rowman and Littlefield.

Miller, David. 1984 *Anarchism* London: Dent.

Milosz, Czeslaw. 1990 *The Captive Mind* New York: Vintage International.

Mirowsky, John and Ross, Catherine E. 1986 Social Patterns of Distress *Annual Review of Sociology* 12:23–45.

Nehamas, Alexander. 1999 *Virtues of Authenticity: Essays on Plato and Socrates* Princeton: Princeton University Press.

Pelling, Rowan (ed.). 2006 *The Decadent Handbook: For the Modern Libertine* London: Dedalus.

Perry, Brea L. 2006 "Understanding Social Networks: The Case of Youth in Foster Care" *Social Problems* 53(3):371–391.

Pickvance, Chris. 1995 Social Movements in the Transition from State Socialism: Convergence or Divergence? in Maheu, Louis (ed.) *Social Movements and Social Classes: The Future of Collective Action* London: Sage.

Purkis, Jon and Bowen, James. 1997 "Introduction" in Purkis, Jon and Bowen, James (eds.) *Twenty-First Century Anarchism: Unorthodox Ideas for a New Millennium* London: Casell.

Rossinow, Doug. 1998 *The politics of Authenticity: Liberalism, Christianity, and the New Left in America* New York: Columbia.

Schwartz, Pepper. 2000 Creating Sexual Pleasure and Sexual Justice in the Twenty First Century *Contemporary Sociology* 29(1):213–219.

Shannon, Vaughn P. 2005 Wendt's Violation of the Constructivist Project: Agency and Why a World State is Not Inevitable *European Journal of International Relations* 11(4):581–587.

Shorter, Edward. 2005 *Written in the Flesh: A History of Desire* Toronto: University of Toronto.

Shorter, Edward. 1972 Capitalism, Culture, and Sexuality: Some Competing Models *Social Science Quarterly* 53(2):338–356.

Soule, Sarah A. and Earl, Jennifer. 2005 A Movement Society Evaluated: Collective Protest in the United States, 1960–1989 *Mobilization: An International Journal* 10(3):345–364.

Touraine, Alain. 1995 "Democracy: From a Politics of Citizenship to a Politics of Recognition" in Maheu, Louis (ed.) *Social Movements and Social Classes: The Future of Collective Action* London: Sage.

Varela, Charles R. 1999 Determinism and the Recovery of Human Agency: The Embodying of Persons *Journal for the Theory of Social Behavior* 29(4):385–402.

Wendt, Alexander. 2003 Why a World State is Inevitable *European Journal of International Relations* 9(4):491–542.

West, David. 1990 *Authenticity and Empowerment: A Theory of Liberation* London: Harvester Wheatsheaf.

Widdicomb, Sue and Wooffitt, Robin. 1995 *The Language of Youth Subcultures Social Identity in Action* London: Harvester Wheatsheaf.

Wolff, Robert Paul. 1970 *In Defense of Anarchy* London: Harper.

Zinn, Howard. 1971 "The Art of Revolution" in Read, Herbert (ed.) *Anarchy and Order: Essays in Politics* Boston: Bacon.

Chapter 10.   Aesthetic Sabotage

Addison, Nicholas. 2005 Expressing the Not Said: Art and Design and the Formation of Sexual identities *International Journal of Art and Design Education* 24(1): 20–30.

Barnes, John Arundel. 1994 *A Pack of Lies: Towards a Sociology of Lying* Cambridge, MA: Cambridge University.

Bauman, Zygmunt. 2002 "The Great War of Recognition" in Lash, Scott and Featherstone, Mike (eds.) *Recognition and Difference: Politics, Identity, Multiculture* Sage: Thousand Oaks.

Bennett, Andy. 2000 *Popular Music and Youth Culture: Music, Identity, and Place* Hampshire: Palgrave.

Black, Gordon S. and Black, Benjamin D. 1994 *The Politics of American Discontent* New York: Wiley.

Bourdieu, Pierre. 1984 *Distinction: A Social Critique of the Judgment of Taste* Cambridge, MA: Harvard.

Craig, Stephen C. and Bennett, Stephen Earl (eds.). 1997 *After the Boom: The Politics of Generation X* Lanham, MD: Rowman & Littlefield.

Frith, Simon. 1978 *Sociology of Rock* London: Constable.

Gilsenan, Michael. 1976 "Lying, honor and contradiction" in Kapferer, Bruce (ed.) *Transaction and Meaning: direction in the anthropology of exchange and symbolic behavior* Philidelphia, PA Institute for the Study of Human Issues.

Hamersky, Heidrun (ed.). 2002 *Samizdat: Alternative Culture in Central and Eastern Europe* Bremen, Germany: University of Bremen.

Harold, James. 2006 On Judging the Moral Value of Narrative Artworks *Journal of Aesthetic and Art Criticism* 64(2):259–270.

Haynsworth, Leslie. 2003 "Alternative" Music and the Oppositional Potential of Generation X Culture" in Ulrich, John M. and Harris, Andrea L. (eds.) *Gen X-egesis: Essays on "Alternative Youth (Sub)Culture* Madison, WI: University of Wisconsin.

Hebdige, Dick. 1979 *Subculture: The Meaning of Style* London: Routledge.

Held, Virginia. 1993 *Feminist Morality: Transforming Culture, Society, and Politics* Chicago: University of Chicago Press.

Howe, Neil and Strauss, William. 1993 *13th Gen: Abort, Retry, Ignore Fail?* New York: Vintage.

Humphreys, L. (1970). *Tearoom Trade: Impersonal Sex in Public Places.* Chicago: Aldine.

Irvine, Janice M. 1996 "A Place in the Rainbow: Theorizing Lesbian and Gay Culture" in Seidman, Steven (ed.) *Queer Theory/Sociology* Cambridge, MA: Blackwell.

Lasch, Christopher. 1978 *The Culture of Narcissism: American Life in an Age of Declining Expectation* New York: Norton.

Lesiakowski, Krzysztof, Perzyna, Paweł and Toborek, Tomasz (eds.). 2004 *Jarocin w obiektywie bezpieki [Jarocin in light of public safety]* Warsaw: Instytut Pamię ci Narodowej.

Longhurst, B. 1995 *Popular Music and Society* Cambridge: Polity.

Mercer, Kobena. 1987 "Black Hairstyle Politics" in Gelder, Ken and Thornton, Sarah (eds.) *The Subcultures Reader* London: Routledge.

Miller, William Ian. 2003 *Faking It* Cambridge, UK: Cambridge University Press.

Mitev, PE 1988 *Youth and Social Change* Sofia, Bulgaria: Moscow People's Youth Press.

Ovchinskij, V. 1987 Criminal Behavior in Youth Settings *Sociological Studies* 4:85–8.

Pilkington, H. 1994 *Russia's Youth and its Culture: A Nation's Constructors and Constructed* London: Routledge.

Piotrowski, Piotr. 2006 Awangarda w Cienu Jalty [Avante-garde in the Shadow of Yalta: Art in Eastern Central Europe 1945–1989] Poznan, PL: Rebis.

Romanienko, Lisiunia A. 2001 "Disputing Marxian Alienation and Hegelian Dialectics through the Elective Affinities of Techno Music" in *No Walls* Leicester, UK: De Montfort University.

Rose, Tricia. 1994 *Black Noise: Rap Music and Black Culture in Contemporary America* Hanover: Wesleyan University.

Seamon, Roger. 2001 The Conceptual Dimension in Art and the Modern Theory of Artistic Value *Journal of Aesthetic and Art Criticism* 59(2):139–151.

Shusterman, Richard. 2006 Aesthetic Experience: From Analysis to Eros *Journal of Aesthetics and Art Criticism* 64(2):217–229.

Soeffner, Hans-Georg. 1997 *The order of rituals: the interpretation of everyday life* New Brunswick, NJ Transaction.

Stivers, Richard. 2004 *Shades of Loneliness Pathologies of a Technological Society* Boulder: Rowman & Littlefield.

Strom, Kirsten. 2004 Avant-Garde of What? Surrealism Reconceived as Political Culture *Journal of Aesthetics and Art Criticism* 62(1):37–49.

Trilling, James. 1997 Freedom and Convention: Old Art for a New Century International *Journal of Politics,Culture, and Society* 10(4):563–589.

Wald, Gayle. 1998 Just a Girl? Rock Music, Feminism, and the Cultural Construction of Female Youth *Signs* 23(3):585–610.

Wallace, Claire and Kovoatcheva, Sijka. 1998 *Youth in Society: The Construction and Deconstruction of Youth in East and West Europe* London: MacMillan.

Walton, Marsha D. 1998 Ostensible Lies and the Negotiation of their Shared Meanings *Discourse Processes* 26(1):27–41.

West, David. 1990 *Authenticity and Empowerment: A Theory of Liberation* London, UK: Harvester Wheatsheaf.

Wojcik, Daniel. 1995 *Punk and Neotribal Body Art* Jackson, MS.

Young, James O. 2005 Profound Offense and Cultural Appropriation *Journal of Aesthetics and Art Criticism* 63(2):135–147.

Chapter II.   Organic Sabotage

Aaron, Michele. 1999 Introduction in Aaron, Michele (ed.) *The Body's Perilous Pleasures: Dangerous Desires and Contemporary Culture* Edinburgh: Edinburgh University.

Ackland, Charles R. 2004 "Fresh Contacts: Global Culture and the Concept of Generation" in Campbell, Neil (ed.) *American Youth* New York: Routledge.

Allen, Jennifer. 2006 "The New Barbarians" in Scardi, Gabi (ed.) *Less: Alternative Living Strategies* Milan, Italy: Continents.

Anderson, Benedict. 1991 *Imagined Communities: Reflections on the Original and Spread of Nationalism* London: Verso.

Atkinson, Michael. 2003 The Civilizing of Resistance: Straightedge Tattooing *Deviant Behavior* 24:197–220.

Baines, John and Jaromir, Malek. 1980 *Atlas of Ancient Egypt* Oxford: Phaidon.

Bayat, Asef. 2005 Islamism and Social Movement Theory *Third World Quarterly* 26(6):891–908.

Beck, Ulrich. 1997 *The Reinvention of Politics Rethinking: Modernity in the Global social Order* Oxford: Polity.

Bennett, Andy. 2000 *Popular Music and Youth Culture: Music, Identity, and Place* Hampshire: Palgrave.

Bowen, James and Purkis, Jonathan. 2004 "Introduction" in Bowen, James and Purkis, Jonathan (eds.) *Changing Anarchism: Anarchist Theory and Practice in a Global Age* Manchester, UK: Manchester University.

Brooke, Stephen. 2005 The Body and Socialism: Dora Russell in the 1920s *Past and Present* 189:147–177.

Brown, Norman O. 1966 *Love's Body* Berkeley, CA: University of California.

Budney, Jen. 2006 "Seeking Structures and Opportunities" in Scardi, Gabi (ed.) *Less: Alternative Living Strategies* Milan, Italy: Continents Editions.

Caputi, Jane. 2003 The Naked Goddess: Pornography and the Sacred *Theology and Sexuality* 9(2):180–200.

Castells, Manuel. 1997 *The Power of Identity* Oxford, UK: Blackwell.

Cheville, Julie. 2006 The Bias of Materiality in Sociocultural Research: Reconceiving Embodiment *Mind, Culture, and Activity* 13(1):25–37.

Cowen, Tyler. 2002 *Creative Destruction: How Globalization is changing the World's Cultures* Princeton: Princeton.

Curry, D. Decorating the Body Politic *New Formations* 19 1993 69–82.

Dyens, Ollivier. 2001 *Metal and Flesh: The Evolution of Man: Technology Takes Over* MIT Cambridge.

Eversley, Shelly. 2005 *The Real Negro: The Question of Authenticity in Twentieth Century African American Literature* New York: Routledge.

Florida, Richard. 2002 The Geography of Bohemia *Journal of Economic Geography* 2:55–71.

Florida, Richard. 2001 The Geography of Bohemia *Heinz Endowment Working Papers*.

Florida R. and Gates G. 2001 Technology and Tolerance: The Importance of Diversity to High Technology Growth in *Brookings Institute Survey Series*.

Frank, Andre Gunder and Gills, Barry K. (eds.). 1993 *The World System: Five hundred years or five thousand?* London: Routledge.

Goaman, Karen. 2004 "The anarchist traveling circus: reflections on contemporary anarchism, anti-capistalism and the international scene" in Bowen, James and Purkis, Jonathan (eds.) *Changing Anarchism: Anarchist Theory and Practice in a Global Age* Manchester, UK: Manchester University.

Green, Martin. 1999 "Weber and Lawrence and Anarchism" in Whimster, Sam (ed.) *Max Weber and the Culture of Anarchy* London, UK: Macmillan.

Griffin, Gabriele. 2004 Exile and the Body" in Everett, Wendy and Wagstaff, Peter (eds.) *Cultures of Exile: Images of Displacement* New York: Berghahn.

Grossi, Anna Maria. 2004 "Piercing, Tattoos, and Branding: Latent and Profound Reasons for Body Manipulations" in Katz, James E. (ed.) *Machines that Become US Social Context of Personal Communications Technology* New Brunswick: Transaction.

Hall, Thomas and Fenelon, James. "Trajectories of Indigenous Resistance Before and After 9/11" in Podobnik and Reifer.

Hambly, W.D. 1925 *The History of Tattooing and Its Significance* London: Witherby.

Hamel, Pierre, Lustiger-Thaler, Henri, Pieterse, Jan Nederveen and Roseneil, Sasha. 2001 "Introduction: The Shifting Global Frames of Collective Action" in Hamel, Pierre, Lustiger-Thaler, Henri, Pieterse, Jan Nederveen and Roseneil, Sasha (eds.) *Globalization and Social Movements* New York: Palgrave.

Harvey, Jean. (1999) *Civilized Oppression* Lanham, MD: Rowman and Littlefield.

Howson, Alexandra. 2004 *The Body in Society: An Introduction* Cambridge: Polity.

Kozinets, Robert V and Sherry, John F. 2004 "Exploring the Sacred in Burning Man" in St. John, Graham (ed.) *Rave Culture and Religion* London: Routledge.

Krishnamurti. 1992 *On Freedom* London: Victor Gollancz Ltd.

Kuklick, Henrika. 1991 *The Savage Within: The Social history of British Anthropology 1885–1945* Cambridge: Cambridge University Press.

Kuper, Adam. 1988 *The Invention of Primitive Society: Transformations of an Illusion* London: Routledge.

Landau, James. 2004 "The Flesh of Raving" in St. John, Graham (ed.) *Rave Culture and Religion* London: Routledge.

Langman, Lauren. 2006 "Globalization, Alienation, and Identity: A Critical Approach" in Langman, Lauren and Kalekin-Fishman, Devorah (eds.) *The Evolution of Alienation: Trauma, Promise, and the Millennium* Lanham, MD: Rowman and Littlefield.

Levi Strauss, David. 1958 *Structural Anthropology* [http://www.marxists.org/reference/subject/philosophy/works/fr/levistra.htm]

Lurie, David. 2006 "Homeless Vehicle Project" in Scardi, Gabi (ed.) *Less: Alternative Living Strategies* Milan, Italy: Continents Editions.

Maffesoli, Michael. 1996 *The Time of the Tribes The Decline of Individualism in Mass Society* London Sage.

Mascia-Lees, Francis E. and Sharpe, Patricia. 1992 "Introduction" in Mascia-Lees, Francis E. and Sharpe, Patricia (eds.) *Tattoo, Torture, Mutilation, and Adornment: The Denaturalization of the Body in Culture and Text* Albany, New York: SUNY.

McDonald, Kevin. 2006 *Global Movements, Action, and Culture* Oxford: Blackwell.

Parry, Albert. 1933 *Tattoo: Secrets of a Strange Art as Practiced among the Natives in the United States* New York: Simon and Schuster.

Pitts, Victoria L. 2003 *In the Flesh: The Cultural Politics of Body Modification* New York: Palgrave.

Rand, Ayn. 1993 [1971] *The New Left: Anti-Industrial Revolution* New York: Penguin.

Rinpoche, Sogyal. 1992 *The Tibetan Book of Living and Dying* London: Random House.

Roszak, Theodore. 1968 *The Making of a Counter Culture: Reflections on the Technocratic Society and Its Youthful Opposition* Berkeley: University of California.

Slotter, Keith. 1996 Check Fraud: A Sophisticated Criminal Enterprise *FBI Bulletin*.

Stivers, Richard. 2004 *Shades of Loneliness Pathologies of a Technological Society* Boulder: Rowman & Littlefield.

Straw, B.M., Sandelands, L.E., Dutton, J.E. 1981 "Threat-rigidity effects in organizational behaviour: a multilevel analysis" *Administrative Science Quarterly* 26:501–24/

Sweetman, Paul. 1999 "Only Skin Deep? Tattooing, Piercing, and the Transgressive Body" in Aaron, Michele (ed.) *The Body's Perilous Pleasures: Dangerous Desires and Contemporary Culture* Edinburgh: Edinburgh University.

Tramacchi, Des. 2004 "Des Entheogenic Dance Eastasis: Cross cultural contexts" in St. John, Graham (ed.) *Rave Culture and Religion* London: Routledge.

Turner, Bryan S. 1996 *The Body and Society* London: Sage.

Turner, Bryan S. 1992 *Regulating Bodies: Essays in Medical Sociology* London: Routledge.

Turner, Victor. 1984 "Liminality and the performative genres" in John T. MacAloon (ed.) *Rite, Drama, Festival, Spectacle: Rehearsals toward a theory of Cultural Performance* Philadelphia, PA: Institutue for the Study of Human Issues

Vale, V. and Juno, A. 1989 *Modern Primitives: An investigation of Contemporary Adornment and Ritual* San Francisco: Re/Search.

Wallerstein, Immanuel M. 1999 *The end of the World as we know it: a social science for the twenty-first century* Minneapolis, MN: University of Minnesota.

West, David. 1990 *Authenticity and Empowerment: A Theory of Liberation* London, UK: Harvester Wheatsheaf.

Wojcik, Daniel. 1995 *Punk and Neotribal Body Art* Jackson, MS.

Yerton, Stewart. 2002 The Last of the Bohemians *Times Picayune* July 14.

Index